The

LOGIC

of

SUBJECTIVITY

The

LOGIC

of

SUBJECTIVITY

Kierkegaard's Philosophy
of Religion

Louis P. Pojman

The University of Alabama Press

The following published articles have been used in this work with the
permission of the publishers: "Christianity and Philosophy in
Kierkegaard's Early *Papers*," in *Journal of the History of Ideas* (January
1983); "Kierkegaard on Faith and History," in *International Journal for
Philosophy of Religion* (Summer 1982); and "The Logic of Subjectivity,"
in *Southern Journal of Philosophy* (Fall 1981), vol. XIX, number 1.

Library of Congress Cataloging in Publication Data

Pojman, Louis P.
    The logic of subjectivity.

    Bibliography: p.
    Includes index.
    1. Kierkegaard, Søren, 1813–1855—Religion.
    2. Christianity—Philosophy—History—19th century.
    I. Title.
    B4378.C5P64   1983   230'.044'0924   83-1053
    ISBN 0-8173-0166-6

to
Trudy, Ruth, and Paul

Contents

PREFACE

My thesis is simple but controversial: Kierkegaard is a philosopher, a thinker who uses arguments, develops concepts, and employs 'thought projects' to establish conclusions. He is a rationalist, who makes use of reason even if it is to show reason's limits. He does not offer systematic, orderly syllogisms whose premises wear their meaning on their sleeve. The main lines of his arguments are often diffuse, devious, and difficult to state precisely, let alone follow. He purposely uses poetic devices, indirect communication, parables, pseudonymns, anecdotes, and metaphors to make his points. All this has led many scholars either to deny that he is a philosopher or to undermine that aspect of his work, seeing him primarily as a "kind of poet," religious thinker, or existentialist antiphilosopher "with no opinion of his own."

Furthermore, Kierkegaard has been known as an antirationalist, even as an irrationalist, who eschews the use of reason in coming to religious faith.

There is some truth in the charges of such scholars. It is probably not too much of an exaggeration to say, as one of the foremost Kierkegaard scholars of our day does, "Whatever philosophy or theology there is in Kierkegaard is sacramentally transmitted in, with, and under poetry"; but it is, I think, more than an exaggeration to go on to say, as this scholar does, that, for Kierkegaard, "subjectivity is all the truth there is" and his work is a piece of "anti-philosophy," "a piece of rhetorical exhortation masquerading as discursive presentation. It is not an attempt to describe subjective truth in objective terms."[1]

In this work I will challenge this thesis. I will try to show that although Kierkegaard often uses indirect forms of communication and *does* exhort as much as argue, he has a message to communicate which is founded in a belief in objective truth. He claims that the goal of his work is to reach what he calls the "highest truth," objectively and eternally true, though not accessible by normal objective processes—not directly, at least. I will try to show that there is more reasoning in Kierkegaard than is usually realized and that his work is an exercise in giving "reasons why there are no reasons," so that there are grounds for pursuing the truth *through* subjectivity, a very specific kind of subjectivity, chastened by reason and experience.

Until recently, analytic philosophers have not taken Kierkegaard seriously as a thinker. He has been left to the poets, Existentialists, theologians, and psychologists. After an introduction to Kierkegaard's work as a philosopher by James Collins (*The Mind of Kierkegaard*) and Heywood Thomas (*Subjectivity and Paradox*) in the mid 1950s and Herbert Garelick's provocative monograph, *The Anti-Christianity of Kierkegaard* in 1964, little was done in this area until the late 1970s. The leading Kierkegaard scholars were theologians (Dupre, Hirsch, Holmer, Sløk, Sponheim, and Thulstrup) and literati (Auden, Grimsley, and Henriksen). If they were philosophers, they were not in the analytic tradition (Elrod, Malantschuk, Mackey, Swenson, and Taylor).

In the last few years, articles have begun to appear by analytic philosophers concerned with the arguments used by Kierkegaard in his works. Philosophers such as Robert Adams, J. Donnelly, Stephen Evans, Paul Edwards, Alaister Hannay, Earl McLane, and Gregory Schufreider have published articles dealing with specifically analytic concerns: conceptual analysis, the use of argument, and the structure of theory. My book, which reflects the concerns of these writers, is in the same tradition, and has profited from these writers far more than I have been able to show in the text.

This work is offered as a comprehensive examination of Kierkegaard's ingenious attempt to construct a Christian philosophy—or, as he put it, a "Christian epistemology." In this regard there are two interesting features to his thought. First, he develops self-consciously Christian ideas out of the rudiments of secular concepts. His treatment of 'dread' and 'despair' in *The Concept of Anxiety* and *Sickness unto Death* are good examples of this strategy. With this in mind, we shall examine the concept of 'faith' in chapters 4 and 5. The process of Christologizing secular concepts, infusing them with a potency they didn't appear to have at first glance, is interrelated with the second important feature of Kierkegaard's philosophy: the strategy of constructing a framework in which the move into Christian faith is shown (albeit indirectly) to be eminently reasonable. In many ways what he does is similar to what Paul Tillich in our own day has called the 'correlation method' of theological inquiry, where Christian faith is seen as the answer to questions which arise within the deepest moments of human existence.

I have no objection to calling this study an exercise in philosophical theology; however, the emphasis is on the philosophical structure of Kierkegaard's thought, especially the arguments inherent in the Climacus writings. Hence it would be more accurate to describe this work as a philosophical analysis of Kierkegaard's philosophy of the Christian religion.

I claim that Kierkegaard was, among other things, a philosopher, a Christian philosopher, concerned with explicating and defending the Christian faith at the same time he sought to win his fellow Danes for the faith. Why should these two purposes be separate? His published works may be seen as an endeavor to construct a reasonable case for Christianity. Indeed, I shall argue that if his analysis is correct, it follows that Christianity is the only reasonable world view for a rational person to accept and integrate into his existence.

With regard to this apologetic strategy, Kierkegaard has both a positive and a negative thrust: Positively, he develops a theory of the stages of existence which consummate in a leap of faith into the Christian form of life. He works out a phenomenology of human consciousness wherein the quest for authentic selfhood leads inevitably to the Incarnation. Negatively, he offers an ingenious, quasiskeptical argument that denies reason in the name of reason and opens the way for an acceptance of subjectivity whose logic leads to Christian faith as the only way left.

The positive strategy seems an appropriation of Hegel's thought in the *Phenomenology of Mind*, but for a diametrically opposed purpose (as Mark Taylor has shown in his *Journeys to Selfhood: Hegel & Kierkegaard*). The negative strategy is reminiscent of and, I believe, derives from Kant's work, where he denies reason in order to make room for faith. Kierkegaard advances Kant's thought in a way that Kant would never have dreamed. My study will concentrate on this second feature of Kierkegaard's work, though I shall say something about the stages at the end of the first chapter and again in chapter 4. I have written on this in another place.[2]

The plan of this study is founded on a hypothesis that there is an overall argument in the Climacus writings (and reflected and supported in Kierkegaard's private papers and other writings) that may be formulated in the following form:

1. There are two opposing ways to approach the truth: the objective and the subjective ways.
2. The objective way fails.
3. Hence the only appropriate way is the subjective way.
4. Christianity is the subjective way of life that meets all conditions for the highest subjectivity.
5. Hence Christianity is the appropriate way to teach the truth.

These are the bare bones of the argument that underlies the plan of this book. The concepts 'truth', 'subjectivity', 'objectivity', and their cognates will be examined in the following chapters, and the argument will be developed chapter by chapter and brought to a climax in the final chapter ("A Justification of Christian Faith").

This present work is critical—not always favorable to Kierkegaard. I have tried to treat his work sympathetically but with a sharp eye for underlying assumptions, entailments, missing premises, and logical form. While recognizing the polemical stance of the "melancholy Dane" in the face of a spiritless Christendom, which no doubt caused him to exaggerate his claims at various points, in the last analysis I have wanted to know what Kierkegaard has to say to us today with regard to faith. Extricated from his historical situation, does he have a message for us? How valid is his argument for the reasonableness of the leap of faith? If I have dealt too harshly with Kierkegaard at places, it is because I take these questions and Kierkegaard's work with utmost seriousness. I offer my critique with no sense of having said the last word on the subject, but rather to raise the discussion to a higher plane. Let those who believe that Kierkegaard can be defended take this study as a challenge to do just that.

Although most of this book is directed to the Climacus writings, I have used material from the *Papers* and other writings where the context warrants their use in providing further support or illustrative material for the issue at hand. This work is necessarily selective, and giving the full picture of Kierkegaard's thought is still far from accomplished. Nevertheless, I believe common threads run through his works, and that what I have outlined is based on weighty evidence.[3]

A synopsis of this work is in order. In chapter 1 I orient the reader to some of the fundamental, background ideas in Kierkegaard's thought. I point out the Christian presuppositions that motivated his thought; show how these concerns arose in his university days, when he wrestled with the relationship of Christianity to philosophy; and give an overview of his anthropology, suggesting that it outlines an argument for the existence of God and showing how the theory of the stages of existence fits into his teleological view of man.

In chapter 2 ("Attack on Objectivity") I begin an analysis of Kierkegaard's use and critique of reason. I analyze several of his attacks on the use of reason and try to show how he approaches the subject. The second main section deals with one of his attempts to give reasons why *there are no reasons* for religious knowledge: his analysis of the relationship between faith and history in the Climacus writings. I also offer a brief discussion of his criticisms of the apologetics of his contemporaries, and point out Kierkegaard's 'cognitive disjunct principle', which I claim is central to his work and has largely gone unnoticed in the literature.

In chapter 3 ("Subjectivity and Epistemology," which might well be labeled "The Way of Subjectivity") I analyze—more closely than anyone has done heretofore—Kierkegaard's epistemological foundations and show how his theory of subjectivity fits into this broader framework. In the second main section of the chapter I argue that there are at least three versions of the doctrine in his works: what I call the Socratic, Platonic, and necessary-condition versions. Most commentators have noticed only the Socratic version, but the Platonic version may be more prominent on closer scrutiny.

In chapter 4 ("Faith in the Stages of Existence") I show that the concept 'faith' is polymorphous in Kierkegaard's works, and I trace some strands of its development in the theory of the stages of existence. I critique his analysis of Abraham's "absurd" leap of faith in *Fear and Trembling*, arguing that his analysis is incorrect and that Abraham was entirely rational in hearkening to the voice that commanded him to sacrifice Isaac.

In chapter 5 ("Faith in *Philosophical Fragments*") I continue to treat faith, this "happy passion," the highest form of subjectivity, as it appears in the *Philosophical Fragments*, distinguishing it from 'opinion' or ordinary believing, and showing its role in interpreting historical data. In the second main section I offer a comprehensive critique of Kierkegaard's volitionalism, showing his inaccurate notion of believing as involving the will.

In chapter 6 ("Faith in *Concluding Unscientific Postscript* and Later *Papers*") I describe how the concept continues to develop in Kierkegaard's most important philosophical work and offer three criticisms of these developments. Finally, I show an interesting development of the notion of faith which converges with hope, an interpretation to be found in the later *Papers*.

In chapter 7 ("A Justification of Christian Faith") I bring the strands of my argument together in a formal argument, to the effect that Christianity, on certain of Kierkegaard's premises, is rationally justified in its claim to truth. That is, I show an argument in Kierkegaard's work which, if sound, would make choosing Christianity imperative for every rational person. This of course is counter to most interpretations of Kierkegaard, which view him as an irrationalist.

I conclude the book with a brief assessment of Kierkegaard's thought with regard to philosophical inquiry.

A personal word regarding the author's relationship to his subject is appropriate in works like this. In my case, no thinker has more deeply influenced my life and thought than Kierkegaard. His works, especially *Fear and Trembling*, brought me out of undergraduate complacency and gave my life and thought focus. My thinking has developed in ways far different from Kierkegaard's, especially in the evaluation of objectivity, but many of his emphases are very much part of my philosophy of life. His wit and humor, his ability to get to the heart of the matter—even if, once there, he may spin about, indulging his caprice—his ability to make philosophy personal, all are virtually without peer. The effect is often devastating. As my former teacher, Roger Shinn, puts it: "Like a literary boxer, Kierkegaard jabs, feints, catches his reader off balance. He drives you (for his writings are always directed at *you*) into a corner, pummels you, offers you a way out, and dares you to take it. He makes you laugh as he turns his whiplike wit on someone, then agonize as the backlash catches you. He pours out sarcasm and invective, then instantaneously shifts to humble and reverent prayer" (*The Existentialist Posture*, p. 50).

Several persons have been influential in the writing of this book. I have profited from the criticisms and suggestions of Anton Hugli, Paul Holmer, Louis Mackey, Basil Mitchell, Heywood Thomas, and Merold Westphal.

My prime debt is to two persons: first, my teacher at the University of Copenhagen, Dr. Gregor Malantschuk, who may be the most important Kierkegaard scholar of our generation. Our discussions in his apartment constitute one of the most important experiences of my life as a scholar. One cannot help but feel keenly the loss of this great man.

Of equal importance is my debt to Professor John Macquarrie of Christ Church, Oxford University, whose patience and wisdom were vital to my doctor's dissertation at Oxford (*Faith and Reason in the Thought of Kierkegaard*, Oxford, 1977). It is from my dissertation research during my stay at Oxford, under the supervision of John Macquarrie, that this present work arises.

I also express my appreciation to several organizations for their support in the research for this work: the U.S. State Department, in making me a recipient of a Fulbright Fellowship to Denmark; the Danforth Foundation, in awarding me a Kent Fellowship; the Rockefeller Foundation, for a generous grant; and the University of Oxford, for a scholarship and support while I studied in England.

Most of all, I am indebted to my wife, Trudy—for an enormous debt which can only be stated. To her and our children this work is dedicated.

LOUIS P. POJMAN

BIBLIOGRAPHICAL NOTE
and
ABBREVIATIONS

I have used *Søren Kierkegaards Samlede Vaerker,* edited by A. B. Drachmann, J. L. Heiberg, and H. O. Lange (14 vols.; Copenhagen: Gyldendals, 1901), and *Søren Kierkegaards Papirer,* edited by P. A. Heiberg and Victor Kuhr (20 vols.; Copenhagen: Gyldendals, 1909).

All translations from the published works of Kierkegaard are given in the standard English translations unless otherwise noted. All translations from the unpublished works and private *Papers* are mine, unless otherwise stated.

The system of abbreviations in the citations is as follows:

CA   *The Concept of Anxiety,* tr. Reider Thomte (Princeton: Princeton University Press, 1980).

CE   *Kierkegaard: A Collection of Critical Essays,* ed. Josiah Thompson (Garden City, N.Y.: Doubleday, 1972).

CUP *Concluding Unscientific Postscript to the Philosophical Fragments,* tr. David F. Swenson and Walter Lowrie (Princeton, N.J.: Princeton University Press, 1944).

E/O *Either/Or,* tr. David F. Swenson and Walter Lowrie (2 vols.; Princeton: Princeton University Press, 1944).

Fragments *Philosophical Fragments or a Fragment of Philosophy,* tr. David F. Swenson and rev. by Howard V. Hong (Princeton: Princeton University Press, 1962).

FT   *Fear and Trembling,* tr. Walter Lowrie (Princeton: Princeton University Press, 1954).

H   *Søren Kierkegaard's Journals and Papers,* ed. and tr. Howard and Edna Hong and assisted by Gregor Malantschuk (Bloomington: Indiana University Press, 1967–70).

JC   *Johannes Climacus or De Omnibus Dubitandum Est,* tr. T. H. Croxall (Stanford, Calif.: Stanford University Press, 1958).

Mackey Louis Mackey, *Kierkegaard: A Kind of Poet* (Philadelphia: University of Pennsylvania Press, 1971).

Papers *Søren Kierkegaards Papirer,* ed. P. A. Heiberg and Victor Kuhr (20 vols.; Copenhagen: Gyldendals, 1909).

PV   *The Point of View for My Work as an Author and My Activity as an Author,* tr. Walter Lowrie (New York: Harper & Row, 1962).

SL   *Stages on Life's Way,* tr. Walter Lowrie (Princeton: Princeton University Press, 1945).

SuD *Sickness unto Death,* tr. Howard and Edna Hong (Princeton: Princeton University Press, 1981).

SV   *Søren Kierkegaards Samlede Vaerker,* ed. A. B. Drachman, J. L. Heiberg, and H. O. Lange (14 vols.; Copenhagen: Gyldendals, 1901).

TC   *Training in Christianity,* tr. Walter Lowrie (Princeton: Princeton University Press, 1957).

The

LOGIC

of

SUBJECTIVITY

1

INTRODUCTION

and

ORIENTATION

An exercise in critical thinking about Kierkegaard's philosophy of religion, this book is an attempt to analyze the arguments, explicit and implicit in his works, which support his radical views on the nature of faith and reason. However, before I begin my analysis of Kierkegaard's reflections on reason, subjectivity, and faith, I want to provide a brief orientation to his thought. Because some parts of the analysis depend on understanding these wider aspects of his philosophy, such orientation should help the reader appreciate Kierkegaard's overall aim, which sets his work on faith and reason in proper perspective.

First, a short section on the decidedly Christian purpose of Kierkegaard's authorship maintains that we must view our subject within a classical tradition of faith-seeking understanding if one is to understand what he tried to do. Next, I illustrate this motif by examining his earliest journal entries, written while he was a university student going through a crisis of faith. To close this chapter, I give an overview of Kierkegaard's concept of man, diagramming his theory of the developmental nature of human existence, which he refers to as 'stages of existence'.

The Christian Purpose of Kierkegaard's Authorship

Kierkegaard, who is often referred to as the Father of Existentialism,[1] is sometimes treated as a poet or ironist, someone with "no opinions of his own."[2] Some writers view him as an ontologist[3] while others see him as a weak imitation of Hegel.[4] Without denying that all such interpretations contain some truth (some more than others) and that the Existential motif, the poetic and ironic motifs, and an ontological and Hegelian aspect are present to some degree in Kierkegaard's work, I maintain that they are subordinate to one overriding theme—understanding *what is involved in being a Christian.* Unless this is seen as the dominant motif, which gives unity and perspective to all other themes, Kierkegaard will not be correctly understood.

In *The Point of View for My Work as an Author* (written in 1848 but left unpublished until after his death), Kierkegaard writes: "The content of this little book affirms, then, what I truly am as an author, that I am and was a religious author, that the whole of my work as an author is related to Christianity, to the problem of becoming a Christian, with a direct or indirect polemic against the monstrous illusion we call Christendom, or against the illusion that in such a land as ours all are Christians of a sort."[5]

Together with the pamphlet "My Activity as a Writer" (1851), this "little book" provides a comprehensive interpretation by Kierkegaard of the purpose of his entire authorship: the pseudonymous, the semipseudonymous, and the acknowledged writings. These writings, individually and corporately, served but one major purpose, Kierkegaard tells us: to depict, as clearly and accurately as possible, what is involved in becoming a Christian. All other considerations of form and content, of dialectics and poetic expression, are to be seen as subservient to that overriding aim.

This announcement surprised Kierkegaard's contemporaries. Copenhagen society tended to divide Kierkegaard's writings into two classes: aesthetic and religious. The pseudonymous writings belonged to the first class and the edifying discourses and devotional writings belonged to the second. On the face of it, it is difficult to see what is specifically or even indirectly Christian about *Either/Or,* "The Diary of a Seducer," *Repetition,* or the *Stages on Life's Way.* Even the *Edifying Discourses* and *Fear and Trembling* cannot be classified as distinctly Christian but simply as religious homilies. The first work in which Christian concepts appear is *Philosophical Fragments* (1844), a thought experiment, presenting Christianity—without naming it—as an alternative to Idealism. This experiment is carried further in the postscript to *Fragments*: Kierkegaard's *magnum opus,* the 550-page *Concluding Unscientific Postscript* (1846).[6] But even here the pseudonymous author, Johannes Climacus, represents himself not as a Christian but as a humorist.

How, then, does Kierkegaard reconcile the strands of aesthetic, ethical, religious, and Christian writings into a single, unified body serving the Gospel? The answer is found in Kierkegaard's conception of indirect communication:

1. All successful communication involves beginning at the place and predicament of the audience.

2. The educated public in Denmark exist primarily in the aesthetic realm.

3. Therefore, if we would begin to proclaim the Gospel to these aesthetes (whose minds are insensitive to Christianity; having become accustomed to the sound of its doctrines, they cannot appreciate its force), we must begin by clothing our message in aesthetic garb—not mentioning the Gospel at all but simply showing the auditor—or rather by helping the auditor to see— the inadequacy of the aesthetic way of life.

Hence the pseudonymous writings serve the Gospel negatively, by destroying any possibility of finding happiness in the aesthetic domain and by showing the dead end of even the higher stages of existence: the ethical and religious.[7] By the man who has thought carefully and consistently with the writer, the Gospel will once more be seen in all its power and decisiveness. This is not to say that the auditor will become a Christian automatically, if he has followed Kierkegaard, for the Gospel is double edged: it offends and blesses. But the air will be cleared. No longer will people take the name of Christ in vain; no longer will people confuse Christianity with an eclectic salad of aestheticism, culture, and primitive piety. Those who become Christians will do so in full knowledge of what they are doing, and those who do not become Christians will refrain because the leap is too great.

Kierkegaard seems to have thought that Christianity would, or could, be shown—by negative reasoning, by dissolving all other hopes and options— to be the only coherent world view; but he never explicitly says this. Part of my task is to show that this strategy is a vital part of Kierkegaard's "doctrine," but it is not clear how aware he was of the implications of this idea.

It may be questioned whether Kierkegaard was not idealizing the unity of his work in *Point of View*. It is clear that he was, and he admits as much. It is not that he was absolutely clear of his task from the beginning or that everything in the pseudonymous works is consciously set forth as specifically propaedeutic to Christianity. Closer to the truth is that Kierkegaard began with his personal problems: What shall I do with my life? Shall I marry Regina, and if not, why not? What is the purpose of my life? When he began to think and write about these questions as a poet, it became clearer that the answer to all his questions lay in Christianity, and furthermore, that a Providential hand was guiding the enterprise and enabling him to produce a literature which was serving to illuminate Christianity.[8]

Perhaps the best summary of how Kierkegaard saw his writing is in his words at the end of *Point of View,* which constitute a fitting epitaph on Kierkegaard's life:

He found here on earth what he sought. He himself was "that individual," if no one else was, and he became that more and more. It was the cause of Christianity he served, his life from childhood on being marvellously fitted for such a service. Thus he carried to completion the work of reflection, the task of translating completely into terms of reflection what Christianity is, what it means to become a Christian. His purity of heart was to will only one thing. What his contemporaries complained of during his lifetime, that he would not abate the price, would not give in, this very thing is the eulogy pronounced upon him by after ages, that he did not abate the price, did not give in. But the grand enterprise he undertook did not infatuate him. Whereas as author he had dialectically a survey of the whole, he understood Christianly that the whole signified his own education in Christianity. The dialectical structure he brought to completion, of which the several parts are whole works, he could not ascribe to any man, least of all would he ascribe it to himself; if he were to ascribe it to anyone, it would be to Providence, to whom it was in fact ascribed, day after day and year after year, by the author, who historically died of a mortal disease, but poetically died of longing for eternity, where uninterruptedly he would have nothing else to do but to thank God. [*Point of View*, p. 103]

Sometimes Kierkegaard is interpreted as a poet, sometimes as the Father of Existentialism, sometimes as the scourge of Idealism. The important thing is to see that Kierkegaard's fundamental purpose was to make eminently clear what Christianity is all about. It would not be too much to say that what we call his "philosophy," his "existentialism," is little more than an attempt at a faithful exposition of the New Testament. It is in the tradition of Augustine, Aquinas, and Anselm—*fides quaerens intellectum*.

Let us turn to Kierkegaard's earliest journals to see the sort of concerns and struggles which led him to develop an existential Christian philosophy.

Christianity and Philosophy in Kierkegaard's Early *Papers*

During the period 1835 to 1840, the young Kierkegaard struggled with the relationship of Christianity to philosophy. His private papers set forth a series of preliminary formulations on the subject which are of interest in that they exhibit the kinds of concerns which motivated his later theories.

During the years 1834–35 Kierkegaard was severely tempted to forsake Christianity. He was offended by his father's religion, deeming it a "monstrous inhumanity" and its followers a narrow-minded folk possessed by the idea that they alone had the truth and, therefore, no other human beings were capable of judging them, since no other humans had the criterion for judgment, namely, the truth.[9] Kierkegaard saw this circular reasoning as an escape from facing the need to find a suitable criterion for assessing religious claims. In a letter to his relative, Peter Wilhelm Lund, he wrote:

In Christianity . . . the contradictions are so great that, to say the least, they prevent one from a clear view. . . . I grew up . . . in orthodoxy; but as soon as I began to think for myself, the tremendous colossus began to totter. I refer to it as a colossus on purpose, for taken as a whole it is very consistent and in the course of centuries the different parts have fused so tightly together that it is difficult to quarrel with it. Although I could agree with some parts of the doctrine, these would have to be treated like shoots, found in the cracks of a rock. On the other hand, I also saw what was wrong with it at many points, but I felt bound to suspend judgment on the fundamentals for a time. [*Papers,* I A 72, June 1, 1835]

Not only did Kierkegaard have trouble with the doctrine, he was contemptuous of the dehumanizing effect of Christianity on its adherents. It emasculated humanity. Instead of giving its followers strength, Christianity robbed them of their manhood: "When I look at the large number of particular phenomena in the Christian life, I feel that Christianity instead of giving individuals strength—especially in comparison with heathen—actually deprives them of their manhood and causes them to compare to heathen as gelding to stallions" (*Papers,* I A 96). The whole phenomenon was as ridiculous as "Don Quixote mistaking windmills for giants and seeing demons chasing him."[10]

A short time later, his position softened. He contemplated Christianity as a possibility. "It is the same with Christianity or with becoming a Christian, as it is with all radical cures. One postpones it as long as possible."[11] The journals show that it became increasingly difficult for him to postpone the decision. However, three years were to elapse before the postponement came to an end and Kierkegaard experienced a religious conversion. We know from his journals and from the testimony of his contemporaries that he lived an intensely aesthetic existence during this period, alternating between a high emotional pitch and despair, to the point of considering suicide.

Between his first steps toward Christianity and his conversion in 1838, a number of entries record his struggle with the significance of Christianity vis-à-vis the intellectual world of his day, dominated by Hegelian speculation. His initial negative judgment of 1835 gradually changed to appreciation of Christianity as a type of anthropomorphic speculativism, not altogether unlike Hegel's characterization of it. Christianity contains philosophical truth which must be discovered beneath the myth and parable. "Every doctrine is nothing other than a more concrete extension of the universal human consciousness."[12] It is the consciousness of the "mediate relation, through which men must always approach the divine." Even prayer in Christ's name is interpreted as a symbolic act which acknowledges the universal consciousness of man:

> To pray in Christ's name is to pray in such a way that involves the conscious-
> ness that we are a link in the development which lies within the race. Only in
> this way can man place himself in relation to God, whether he acts or prays.
> Therefore almost every nation had had one or more deity in whose name it
> prayed, but it was confined to them, because the whole world-consciousness
> was not involved in these deities, but merely the national consciousness and
> the local consciousness. [*Papers,* I A 172, June 12, 1836]

The whole scheme of Hegelian mediation plays a central role in Kierkegaard's philosophical theology, or what he refers to as "my dogmatic point of view": "The three great ideas (Don Juan, Faust, and the eternal Jew) represent . . . life outside of the religious consciousness in its threefold direction. Only when these ideas in life are translated into the individual person and become mediate, only then does the moral and the religious aspect come forth. Such is my view of these ideas in relation to my dogmatic point of view" (*Papers,* I A 150, March 1836).

At this point in Kierkegaard's life, "speculation" is not the bad word it will become. He finds a place for it within a personalistic view of theology, and even speaks of "Christian speculation."[13] He does, however, draw back from the implications of his speculative endeavors and concludes that while there may be a Christian philosophy, it must be on Christianity's terms, not philosophy's.

> Philosophy and Christianity will never allow themselves to be united, for if I
> hold to the most essential element in Christianity, namely, the redemption, so
> that this element must, if it really is to be something, be extended over the
> whole person. Or must I consider his moral ability as impaired while viewing
> his cognitive faculties as unimpaired? I certainly could consider the possibility
> of a philosophy according to Christianity, but it would be a Christian philoso-
> phy. The relation would not be philosophy's relation to Christianity but
> Christianity's relation to Christian cognition. [*Papers,* I A 94, October 17, 1835]

We see, then, two poles in the young Kierkegaard's thought during this period. One is speculative and metaphysical, emphasizing philosophical speculation and mediation: only by being conscious of his relation to the race as a whole can man come to the truth. The other pole is subjective and personalistic, emphasizing the superlative importance of one's personal existence and moving in the direction of a leap in faith. For all his attraction to logical consistency and the comprehensiveness of speculative philosophy, the second pole seems to pull him more strongly than the first. He cannot follow philosophy uncritically. He must ask personal and existential questions.

> The thing is to find a truth which is true for me, to find *the idea for which I can
> live and die.* What would be the use of discovering so-called objective truth, of

working through all the systems of philosophy and [being able] to review them all and show up the inconsistencies within each system? What good would it do me to be able to develop a theory of the state and combine all the details into a single whole, and so construct a world in which I did not live? . . . what good would it do me to be able to explain the meaning of Christianity if it had no deeper significance for me and for my life? What good would it do me if truth stood before me, cold and naked, not caring whether I recognized her or not, and producing in me a shudder of fear rather than a trusting devotion? I certainly do not deny . . . an imperative of understanding and that through it one can work upon men, but it must be taken up into my life. [*Papers,* I A 75; Dru's translation, #22]

We begin to see the existential motif dominate Kierkegaard's thought. Knowledge is good, but action is the goal. "What I really lack is to be clear in my mind what I am to do, not what I am to know."[14] This emphasis on the good over the true, on personal action as the *conditio sine qua non* of meaningful living, is applied to theology: "Christian dogmatics . . . must grow out of Christ's activity, and all the more so because Christ did not establish any doctrine; he acted. He did not teach that there was redemption for men, but he redeemed men" (*Papers,* I A 27, 1835).

The decisive moment of turning toward Christianity as essentially antispeculative, as that which does justice to the subjective aspect of man's nature, appears to come through Kierkegaard's reading of Hamann in the fall of 1836. The young theology student is first struck by Hamann's comparison of speculative reason to the Mosaic law, which must be superseded by the Gospel: "Our reason is therefore exactly what Paul calls the Law—and the Command of Reason is holy, righteous, and good; but is it given to make us wise? Even so little as the Law of the Jews made them righteous, but it is given to lead us from the opposite, to show us how irrational our reason is, and that our errors through it should increase, as sin increased through the Law" (*Papers,* I A 237, 1836; quoted by Kierkegaard in German).

Reason is as inadequate for solving the ultimate problems of human life as the law is inadequate for solving the problem of sin. Knowledge is abrogated by grace through the Gospel, whose truth cannot be understood through reason. It is, continues Hamann, *"incredible sed verum"* (incredible but true): "Is it not an old idea which you often have heard from me: 'incredible but true.' Lies and novels, hypotheses and fables must be deemed probable; but not the truth and fundamental teachings of our faith" (*Papers,* I A 237; a quotation from Hamann).

Through Hamann, Kierkegaard discovered the category of humor which comes to replace the category of irony as the deepest attitude toward existence. Irony is necessity's iron law of negation, which cancels all human strivings and aspiration, causing them to add up to zero. Irony is the grim fate which inevitably wins out over man's finitude, causing all his projects to end in death. Humor, on the other hand, is seen as divine freedom, which is disjunctive with irony's grim necessity. It is positive and affirms that there is hope even though there is no reason for hope. Humor is the insight that God is wholly other, and so if his truth is ever to break into the sphere of human endeavor, it will surely appear very different than our finite comprehension of what it ought to look like. That is, divine reason is fundamentally disjunctive with human reason; consequently it is bound to appear to man as absurd. Humor in man is the appropriate attitude toward Divine Folly. Only in the absurd does the possibility of seeing God arise.

The Hamannian theme continued to dominate Kierkegaard's thought through the fall of 1836. Reasoning, when brought to its ultimate conclusion, always ends in an absurdity, a *reductio ad absurdum*. In an entry which adumbrates a discussion in the third chapter of *Philosophical Fragments,* Kierkegaard says that reason's goal is paradoxicality: "Just how much the Understanding can achieve in a speculative sense can best be seen in the fact that when it is carried out to its highest potential in explaining the Highest, it must be expressed as a contradictory statement" (*Papers,* I A 243, September 19, 1836; cf. II A 239, III A 108).

The significance of humor, then, is to show just how impoverished finite reason is, to laugh at all man's attempts by his understanding to scale the heavens. Secondly, it has a positive function of opening a person to accept the reality of paradoxical truth, and ultimately to acceptance of the highest paradox of all, the paradox of the Incarnation. Thus humor is the road to salvation.

At this point, Kierkegaard was struck by a paragraph in Hamann on the absurd nature of the Christian message. Apparently, Kierkegaard believed the quote to be Hamann's, but it came from the heart of British skepticism. It is a prolepsis of what will appear in fully developed form in the *Postscript*: "The Christian religion not only was at first attended with miracles, but even at this day cannot be believed by any reasonable person without one. Mere reason is insufficient to convince us of its veracity. And whoever is moved by *faith* to assent to it is conscious of a continued miracle in his own person which subverts all the principles of his understanding and gives him a determination to believe what is most contrary to custom and experience" (*Papers,* I A 100).

The quotation comes from the famous section 10 of Hume's *Inquiry Concerning Human Understanding*. What Hume stated with tongue in cheek, Kierkegaard took to be an instance of the humorous and profound insight of Hamann. Miracle or "wonder" stands in disjunctive relationship with human reason, and unexpectedly breaks into the affairs and lives of men. The proper response to the wonderful is wonder, not reason. Wonder, in the sense of being awed by the supernatural, is the appropriate response to the miracles in life, even as humor is the appropriate preparation for it. At this point Kierkegaard returned to the writings of Schleiermacher, the theologian of wonder.

> Schleiermacher is essentially the basis for a proper orthodox theology (and he will therefore play an important role), however heterodox he is in many regards, and this will naturally be modified significantly since the dogmatic content will receive an entirely other objective determination and definiteness. But his position is correct in many parts as he has taken the concept of 'wonder' in its inwardness into the system instead of as something preliminary remaining outside. His whole position is wonder, and his whole self-consciousness is a pure new Christian self-consciousness. [*Papers,* II A 199, December 7, 1837]

In Schleiermacher the two poles, abstract systematizing and the personal subjective tendency, meet for Kierkegaard. Whereas Hamann is too one sided and lacking in systematic comprehensiveness, Schleiermacher seems to have balanced both tendencies, creating a personal philosophical theology. On closer investigation, however, Schleiermacher turns out to be deficient regarding the paradoxical, even though his response to wonder is correct. "What Schleiermacher calls 'Religion' and the Hegelians 'Faith' is at bottom nothing but the first immediate condition for everything—the vital fluid— the spiritual atmosphere we breathe in—and which cannot therefore with justice be designated by those words."[15] Kierkegaard developed this criticism by charging that Schleiermacher is to be identified with the subjective Idealists, Fichte and Schelling, in his dependence on the theory of reciprocity (*Wechselwirkung*). This theory states that the infinite One is moving within the infinite many, always becoming yet always complete in itself. It is pure immanence. Although Kierkegaard seems to have adhered to this idea in 1836, he never did so uncritically, and now he rejected it as philosophical Calvinism, in which both the individual and the system become predestined.

> This system does not really acquire in time the Christian doctrine of time . . . nor does it acquire the doctrine about the devil's fall from eternity, nor man's fall in time . . . nor does it acquire the atonement in time, nor faith (only the immediate consciousness). The first creation gives the immediate consciousness . . . but beyond this one cannot come. Christianity is the second creation (therefore Christ is born of a pure virgin, which again is a creation from nothing. Therefore God's Spirit overshadowed Mary just as it previously hovered over the waters at creation), a new moment, the hearing of the word: —faith, which is the immediate consciousness of the second stage. [*Papers,* II A 31, February 1837]

Thus Kierkegaard leads us to the conclusion that philosophy suffers the same devastating criticism as predestination. It is ultimately fatalistic, not being able to leap out of immanent necessity onto a place where man can be liberated or redeemed. Since without liberation, or the possibility of it, life becomes meaningless, there is something essentially meaningless about speculative philosophy. Even if freedom were an illusion, it would be of more value than speculative theory because it would give man a reason for acting, whereas philosophical necessity paralyzes action. "To what extent is illusion necessary to man's life? This is a question in relation to the romantic. How does this go with the theory about the necessary course of the world's development and how may this theory work in life? Might it not paralyze all activity since, while annulling (and rightly so) the egoistical, it also annuls the natural and enthusiastic assurance, at least in the moment of battle, that what one is working for is the only right thing" (*Papers,* I A 205, July 11, 1836).

In order to live—to act at all—one must believe that one can make a difference, that one is free. This freedom is "the cross which philosophy could not bear but remained hanging upon."[16] In that paralyzed position, philosophers cannot explain the riddle of life. They are like the man who went mad while conscious at every moment that the world went round. They are like a person caught in quicksand, who calculates how far he has already sunk, forgetting all the while that he is sinking still deeper.[17]

What value is such philosophy to me personally? Kierkegaard asks. None at all, for it does not help me in my struggle to find personal liberation. It does not even allow freedom as a possibility in the individual, but swallows both freedom and the individual in its monstrous stomach. Kierkegaard concludes that philosophy is to be rejected because it is unedifying: "It is striking how much Hegel hates the edifying (*Opbyggelige*). It shows itself everywhere, but the edifying is not an opiate which lulls to sleep. It is the finite spirit's Amen and is the side of cognition which ought not to be overlooked" (*Papers,* III A 6, July 10, 1840).

During this period, Kierkegaard took notes in a theology course at the University of Copenhagen, given by his tutor Hans L. Martensen, who later became Kierkegaard's opponent. Ironically, Martensen's lectures provided an early formulation of the stages-of-existence concept and the theory of subjectivity. The following entries are two of Kierkegaard's lecture notes: "Only in the same measure that man becomes conscious of himself can he become himself conscious of God; therefore, man must first have gone through the whole of creation's positions, before he finds God. . . . Protestantism's principle is characterized as subjectivity; truth is present in the subject, while in Catholicism it is objectively present" (*Papers,* XIII 31, 36). Here we see themes which will be developed in *Either/Or,* the Climacus writings, and *Stages on Life's Way.* The lecture notes were made, so to speak, in the form of fragments, only the most important ideas being noted. (One wonders how much else was learned from Martensen as Kierkegaard sat at his feet in tutorials or in his classes as a student.)

In another lecture note, we read of the relation of the finite to the infinite which echoes through Kierkegaard's later works. Rationalists assert, according to Martensen, that the world is finite, but "this is at bottom a contradiction, for infinite is finitude's boundary, and I must therefore know something about infinity."[18] The Kantian idea in Martensen's lectures is that reason is limited, that we can critique reason in order to make way for faith. Philosophy, by itself, fails to find truth.

If philosophy fails to find truth, Christianity fulfills its promise in liberating man from his self-imprisonment. It recognizes that redemption must come from outside. Yet Christianity does not paralyze human action, as philosophy does, through a theory of necessity or predestination, but recognizes that paradoxes are the ultimate truth of religious experience. God chooses man in redemption, and yet, at the same time, man's response is made without compulsion.

The position the young scholar comes to is synergism, the view that salvation is finally the result of a cooperative effort by God and the individual, though the initiative remains with God. The following early entry shows the position that Kierkegaard maintains throughout his life:[19]

> There is a major opposition between Augustine and Pelagius. The first will crush all in order to raise it. The second refers itself to man as he is. The first system views Christianity in three stages: creation; the fall through sin and with it a condition of death and impotence; and a new creation, whereby man becomes placed in a position where he can choose . . . Christianity. The other system refers itself to man as he is (Christianity adapted to the world). The importance of the theory of inspiration is seen from the first system. Here one sees the relation between the synergistic and semi-pelagian conflict. It is the same question, only that the synergistic conflict has the Augustinian system's idea of new creation as its presupposition. [*Papers,* I A 101, 1835]

This passage sums up a position which Kierkegaard arrived at through considerable reflection. Apparently, the idea of predestination haunted him, for several entries in the early journals deal with the idea. The compromise he arrived at is again a consequence of Schleiermacher's theology, the concept of 'relative predestination'.

> Here is the real solution to the problem of predestination. When it is said that they are chosen *Quos vocavit,* they are chosen to salvation or are damned, for what else does the expression *quos vocavit* mean than those in whose consciousness Christianity emerged, and thus this view can be united with Schleier-

macher's relative predestination, for those who have lived in this world but to whom no call came are obviously not predestined (since they are not called); nor is it enough to be able to say anyone is called but only the person in whose consciousness Christianity has emerged in relation to the rest of his life views. [*Papers*, I 295, December 1, 1836]

Predestination in the sense of *quos vocavit,* being called by God and elected, is thus transformed from an objective dogma (as may be seen in Calvinism or Luther's writings) into subjective awareness of God's sovereign grace in one's life, which, paradoxically, does not annul the awareness of freedom. The synergistic motif dominates. It is God who acted in procuring our salvation, yet our response is vital to his activity. This is exactly the position Climacus takes in *Fragments.* Grace is the condition which makes the choice of faith possible.

These were the sort of concerns which occupied Kierkegaard during his student days, before and around the time of his conversion on May 19, 1838, when he wrote:

10:30 A.M. There is an indescribable joy which penetrates all through us which is as incomprehensible as the apostle's spontaneous exclamation: "Rejoice and again I say to you, Rejoice!" Not a joy over this or that, but the soul's fullest outpouring, "with tongue and mouth and from the heart's reason"; I rejoice in my joy, in, with, at, on, by, and with my joy—a heavenly refrain which suddenly ends all our other songs; a joy which like a breeze cools and refreshes, a breath of wind from an Etesian gale which blows from Mamre to the eternal dwellings. [*Papers,* I A 228]

We don't know what prompted this ecstatic entry, nor are we certain that this constitutes the actual conversion of Kierkegaard; but we know that Kierkegaard shortly afterward was reunited with his estranged father, resumed communion at the cathedral (next to the university), and continued his theological studies with a view toward the ministry.

The student entries thus reveal some of Kierkegaard's first attempts to deal with issues which were to occupy him during the rest of his life. In them, we find early formulations of the concept of subjectivity, the relation of philosophy to Christianity, a flirtation with speculative philosophy, a suggestion of the stages of existence, based on Martensen's lectures, and a strong leaning toward a synergistic view of redemption, reconciling the ideas of free will and election in a way similar to and based on Schleiermacher's idea of relative predestination. We see the formative influences of Martensen, Hamann (and through him Hume!), Schleiermacher, and Augustine. We see, too, the tension in Kierkegaard's early work between the poetic, personal pole and the speculative and rationalist pole. In these early entries, the subjective or personal pole has hegemony, but the speculative and analytic is never entirely absent. Action is prior to reason in his thought, but action needs reason for its own uses. One sees, too, that Kierkegaard's personal struggles (suspicion that a curse lay on the family because of his father's sins) and vocational uncertainty must have influenced him in the direction of the subjective. It is always difficult to know for certain how seriously to take or how, exactly, to interpret journal entries, but the ones we have looked at give clues to the sources of some of Kierkegaard's most characteristic ideas. We will follow the development of these ideas through the rest of this book, but first we must take a brief look at Kierkegaard's anthropology and his theory of the stages of existence.

Kierkegaard's Conception of Human Existence

A human being is spirit. But what is spirit? Spirit is the self. But what is the self? The self is a relation that relates itself to itself or is the relation's relating itself to itself in the relation; the self is not the relation but is the relation's relating itself to itself. A human being is a synthesis of the infinite and the finite, of the temporal and the eternal, of freedom and necessity, in short, a synthesis. A synthesis is a relation between two. Considered in this way, a human being is still not a self.

In the relation between two, the relation is the third as a negative unity, and the two relate to the relation and in the relation to the relation; thus under the qualification of the psychical the relation between the psychical and the physical is a relation. If, however, the relation relates itself to itself, this relation is the positive third, and this is the self. Such a relation that relates itself to itself, a self, must either have been established by itself or by another. If the relation that relates itself to itself has been established by another, then the relation is indeed the third, but this relation, the third, is yet again a relation and relates itself to that which establishes the entire relation.

The human self is such a derived, established relation, a relation that relates itself to itself and in relating itself to itself relates itself to another. This is why there can be two forms of despair in the strict sense. If a human self had itself established itself, then there could be only one form: not to will to be oneself, to will to do away with oneself, but there could not be the form: in despair to will to be oneself. This second formulation is specifically the expression for the complete dependence of the relation (of the self), the expression for the inability of the self to arrive at or to be in equilibrium and rest by itself, but only, in relating itself to itself, by relating itself to that which has established the entire relation. . . . The misrelation of despair is not a simple misrelation but a

misrelation in a relation that relates itself to itself and has been established by
another, so that the misrelation in that relation which is for itself also reflects
itself infinitely in the relation to the power that established it.

   The formula that describes the state of the self when despair is completely
rooted out is this: in relating itself to itself and in willing to be itself, the self
rests transparently in the power that established it. [*Sickness unto Death*, pp.
13f.]

   In this tortuous passage we have the heart of Kierkegaard's anthropology.[20]
Man is a composite being, a synthesis of soul and body which are related or
brought together as opposing forces, producing an entity (synthesis of spirit)
which is greater than the sum of its parts, a self or spirit. Kierkegaard takes it
for granted that there is a dualism between the physical and the mental
(which gets parsed out as having the properties of temporality, finitude, and
necessity, on the one hand, and eternity, infinitude, and freedom on the
other), which can never be reduced one to another. Despair, he concludes, is a
symptom of the tension between these two disparate aspects. The only important question is whether man is self-constituted or created by another. If
we were really autonomous ("if a human self had established itself"), there
would be no question of despairingly willing to be oneself, for man could
become authentic simply by willing to do so, on his own and without any
outside aid. We would not experience failure and hopelessness in trying to
become ourselves. However, the virtually universal experience is that we
cannot wholly heal ourselves and become fully authentic beings on our own.
Hence, it must be the case that we are not autonomous beings, self-constituted; rather, we owe our being to another who has established (i.e., created) it. This relation of "complete dependence . . . of the self [is] the
expression for the inability of the self to arrive at or to be in equilibrium and
rest by itself, but only, in relating itself to itself, by relating itself to that which
has established the entire relation." If God can be identified with this self-
establishing being, we can infer from this that the fact that we cannot succeed
in healing ourselves (i.e., attaining authentic selfhood) is evidence for a higher
being, a God, who must have established our being in the first place.

   In *The Concept of Anxiety*, Vigilius Haufniensis makes a similar point
regarding the role of dread or anxiety in teaching us that we are not autonomous or dependent on anything finite or temporal, but rather that our beings
are theonomous, having their locus in eternity. "The true autodidact is precisely in the same degree a theodidact. . . . Therefore he who in relation to
guilt is educated by anxiety will rest only in the Atonement." And in a
footnote on the same page as the above, he quotes Hamann, making the same
point even more forcefully: "However this anxiety in the world is the only
proof of our heterogeneity. If we lacked nothing, we should do no better than

the pagans and the transcendental philosophers, who know nothing of God and like fools fall in love with lovely nature, and no homesickness would come over us. This impertinent disquiet, this holy hypochondria is perhaps the fire with which we sacrificial animals must be salted and preserved from the decay of the passing age" (*The Concept of Anxiety*, p. 162; I have corrected the official translation).

If I have understood these passages, the underlying argument is the following:

1. Man must either be constituted by another (superior to himself) or be self-constituted.
2. If he has been self-constituted, he will not be in despair over trying to attain selfhood.
3. But he *is* in despair over willing to be a self.
4. Therefore (by 2 and 3), man cannot have constituted himself.
5. Therefore (by 1 and 4), man must have been constituted by a superior power.

Kierkegaard scholars never tire of proclaiming that he eschewed all proofs for the existence of God, but this seems to have all the earmarks of a proof for something resembling a divine, creative being. Of course, the argument could be sound without the higher power being the Christian God, but something like the Christian God would qualify as a suitable candidate for this higher power. Kierkegaard would, at least, be committed to the idea that belief in God is supported by reason, which I believe he was. This argument is essentially a variation of the argument from contingency, though it substitutes dependency of the spirit for dependency of being. The possibility of our being merely a product of chance and necessity seems to have been rejected without serious consideration in Kierkegaard's thought. The fact of our being conscious of eternity seems evidence enough for 'an eternity'. This seems clear from the above passage, and also from Johannes de Silentio's "Panegyric upon Abraham":

> If there were no eternal consciousness in man, if at the foundation of all there lay only a wildly seething power which writhing with obscure passions produced everything that is great and everything that is insignificant, if a bottomless void never satiated lay hidden beneath all—what then would life be but despair? If such were the case, if there were no sacred bond which united mankind, if one generation arose after another like the leafage in the forest, if the one generation replaced the other like the song of birds in the forest, if the human race passed through the desert, a thoughtless and fruitless activity, if an eternal oblivion were always lurking hungrily for its prey and there was no power strong enough to wrest it from its maw—how empty then and comfortless life would be! [*Fear and Trembling*, p. 30]

But there is a consciousness of eternity in man and, hence, hope for the attainment of salvation. Although Kierkegaard does not tell us how this argument is to be interpreted, I think it is sufficiently clear that it is a variation of the teleological argument. There is a spiritual order of which we are clearly conscious and this order signifies a higher ordering power.

Kierkegaard never shows any doubt about the teleological aspect of human nature. Even though, as Elrod has shown, Niels Treschow had announced a fully developed evolutionary philosophy by 1807, the idea never seems to have affected Kierkegaard as a viable option.[21] I suggest that he held something like the Aristotelian-Cartesian assumption that there must be at least as much reality in the cause as in the effect.[22] Hence our awareness of the concept of a higher power signifies that there must be such a power to have enabled us to have the idea, and our sense that we can become authentic selves (though not by ourselves) is evidence for a higher constituting power to which we owe our being. How self-conscious Kierkegaard was about these matters is unclear, but I suggest that there are assumptions in his work that, if accepted, would lead to the conclusion that a philosopher's God must exist. I leave the exact status of these assumptions in Kierkegaard's thinking open—whether they were self-evident or only the best alternative. For him personally, and apparently in his pseudonymous writings, the former seems to be the case.

If the argument is accepted, it follows that if we are to be healed of our despair at becoming selves, we must have assistance from the higher power which constituted our being in the first place. For Kierkegaard, it seems clear that this higher power is none other than the God and Father of our Lord Jesus Christ. Man, then, has an essence, a telos, and authentic selfhood is found in realizing that telos. Despair, anxiety over the self, and guilt are negative indicators which remind us of our origins and cause a holy home-sickness, until we finally journey back to our Father's home. "By relating itself to its own self and by willing to be itself, the self is grounded transparently in the power which constituted it."[23]

The Stages of Existence

With this religious anthropology in mind, we can understand the role the 'stages of existence' play in Kierkegaard's work. The stages are not equally viable options which are equal in value, none having more warrant than another, as Thompson has claimed.[24] To make them equal in value is to give up the teleological dimension inherent in the religious interpretation of man which informs Kierkegaard's thought. Rather, they are progressive plateaus on a mountainside which each Climacus must ascend if he would attain to the highest point and experience the *summum bonum.*

Exactly how many stages there are is not altogether resolved in Kierkegaard's writings.[25] The main stages are the aesthetic stage, the ethical stage, the religious stage, and the Christian religious stage (sometimes called "religiousness B"). The goal or telos of life is fully realized only in Christian faith, where self-knowledge becomes revealed as necessarily connected to 'God knowledge'.

The importance Kierkegaard attributd to his characterizations of the stages cannot be overestimated; they constitute "my abiding merit to literature."[26] Together with his analysis of the concepts of 'faith' and 'knowledge', they provide a map which will enable any young man to find his way about the conceptual surroundings of existence.[27] He thought he had "nailed down the category relations with regard to Christianity so well that no dialectician would be able to loose them."[28]

According to the theory of the stages of existence, man begins in the aesthetic stage—innocent, amoral, immediate, spontaneous, seeking unlimited self-gratification. Pleasure is the center around which life rotates. (In another publication I have divided this stage into five substages: the immediate aesthetic stage; the reflective aesthetic stage; the crisis of boredom; the flight from boredom through the rotation method; and the end of aestheticism, that is, despair which leads the person out of aestheticism proper into either the demonic or the ethical.)[29] It is not my purpose here to deal with the intricacies of the internal nuances of each stage, but only to set the overall pattern and inherent logic. Essentially, aestheticism fails to satisfy, because pleasure can never be guaranteed, often is balanced with an inverse proportion of boredom and even pain, and in the end cannot satisfy the spirit which begins to awake within the self. The end of aestheticism is despair: "The end of the aesthete is despair. . . . Despair over himself, because he no longer believes in himself. . . . Despair over his human nature, because he no longer believes that any other sort of self is possible for him. . . . Despair over life, because all his tomorrows will be the same as today" (*E/O,* II: 192). But in despair is the possibility of a higher (not just different, as Thompson would have us believe) existence, where choice first genuinely comes into play. "So then choose despair, for despair itself is a choice; for one can doubt without choosing to, but one cannot despair without choosing. . . . So then in choosing absolutely I choose despair, and in despair I choose the absolute, for I myself am the absolute; but in complete identity with this I can say that I choose the absolute which chooses me" (*E/O,* II: 215, 217).

The purpose of the ethical dimension is to lift man, individually and collectively, from the state of nature—with its inherent instability, arbitrariness, and impending destruction—to a higher plane where rationality, stability, and purposeful living are possible, so that the individual can reach his telos, perfect himself, and attain happiness. Ethics, for Kierkegaard, is a rational activity which gives consistency and stability to life. Aesthetic freedom is really enslavement to the passions. The ethical redeems the individual from slavery to the passions and binds him under the law which liberates by setting the individual on the road to true selfhood. By accepting the necessity of the moral law and following it, the individual becomes "the universal man."

Although there is a strong influence of Hegel's thought here (especially in recognizing the importance of the social self), the dominant motif is Kantian. This is especially clear in the light of *Purity of Heart Is to Will One Thing,* which I regard as a clearer description of the ethical motif, the 'good will'. Willing one thing is a necessary and sufficient condition for willing the good, which is purity of heart, necessary not only for moral virtue but for fellowship with God.[30] Sincere intention to do one's duty is the only intrinsic value there is. There is a marvelous passage in *Either/Or* II where Judge William recounts an incident from his childhood, when he was five years old and had just been given an assignment by his teacher of learning by heart the first ten lines in a lessonbook. In what must be considered a classic passage in Kantian earnestness, William concludes that "to me it was as if heaven and earth might collapse if I did not learn my lesson, and on the other hand as if, even if heaven and earth were to collapse, this would not exempt me from doing what was assigned to me, from learning my lesson. At that age I knew so little about duties. . . . I had only one duty, that of learning my lesson, and yet I can trace my whole ethical view of life to this impression."[31]

The ethical stage represents the beginnings of selfhood, where choice or the decision of the will takes over from the pleasure principle. In recognizing the legitimacy of the moral law,[32] in becoming the universal human by subjecting oneself to universally valid principles, in willing with all one's heart to do one's duty, the self begins to appear.

The key idea here is the will. Selfhood is related to the intensity and comprehensiveness of the exercise of the will. As Anti-Climacus says in *Sickness unto Death,* "The more consciousness, the more self; the more consciousness, the more will; and the more will, the more self."[33] That is, the more one's consciousness is raised by anxiety, despair, and guilt, the more one is forced to decide; and in making decisions that issue from the pressure of anxiety, despair, and guilt, the more one attains authentic selfhood. The underlying structure of this argument seems to be the following:

1. What is essential to man, *qua* man, is his freedom. This might be called the image of God in man. Man is the only creature who can truly decide, and in this he resembles God. Here the will replaces reason as the dominant virtue in man.

2. Man is a being who naturally loves himself. It is unnatural not to love oneself. This is part of the divine order of things; a certain self-love is proper as well as a brute fact.[34]

3. If a person rightly loves himself and chooses the good according to his best lights, given a modicum of intelligence and deliberation (which Kierkegaard calls 'reflection'), he will gradually be led from the egoistic hedonism of the aesthetic stage through the ethical stage and, finally, to the religious stages.

4. Therefore, the more one is led to choose for oneself, to exercise one's passionate will subjectively, the more likely one will reach one's telos and become an authentic self.

This sort of reasoning underlies Kierkegaard's task of awakening people in decadent "Christendom" to make a choice about their commitments, for even a "bad choice" is better than no choice at all.

> My either/or does not in the first instance denote the choice between good and evil; it denotes the choice whereby one chooses good *and* evil / or excludes them. Here the question is under what determinants one would contemplate the whole of existence and would himself live. . . . It is, therefore, not so much a question of choosing between willing the good *or* the evil, as of choosing to will, but by this in turn the good and the evil are posited. . . . Here you see again how important it is that a choice be made, and that the crucial thing is not deliberation but the baptism of the will which lifts up the choice into the ethical. . . . If you will understand me aright, . . . in making the choice it is not so much a question of choosing the right as of the energy, the earnestness, the pathos with which one chooses. Thereby the personality is consolidated. Therefore, even if a man were to choose the wrong, he will nevertheless discover, precisely *by reason of the energy with which he chose,* that he had chosen the wrong. For the choice being made with the whole inwardness of his personality, his nature is purified and he himself brought into immediate relation to the eternal Power whose omnipresence interpenetrates the whole of existence. [*E/O,* II: 173, 171]

I have italicized "by reason of the energy with which he chose" to emphasize, once again, the teleological aspect attached to passionate choosing. This is an adumbration of the doctrine to be explored in the third chapter, that subjectivity is truth, that passionately living within one's light or choosing commitments is the necessary and even sufficient condition for knowing the true and good. Choice of the self leads to the becoming of the self in its ideal state.

There is a debate in the literature (begun, I believe, by Elrod's provocative claim that Kierkegaard's conception of the self does not depend upon any Christian world view)[35] over the fundamental basis for Kierkegaard's anthropology. While I am inclined to favor this position over Taylor's Christological account of Kierkegaard's anthropology, I would emphasize the aspect of freedom and the teleological dimensions of the self far more than Elrod does in his first work.[36] Passion has reasons that the mind knows nothing of. Hence it is reasonable to trust one's deepest instincts, even where reason would veto the act.

This deep perception or inner impulse was the cause of the leap into the ethical stage that, once the stage is run to its limit, finally is its demise. There comes a time when the individual perceives another impulse within him which seems to bring him into conflict with the universal command, yet seems to be a genuine call of God. This is the situation described in *Fear and Trembling*. The universal law tells Abraham that he should not murder, that he should nourish his offspring, but Abraham hears another voice, which he identifies with God's voice, instructing him to sacrifice his son Isaac. Likewise, the universal norm is for every man to marry and raise a family, but Kierkegaard perceives that he has a mission to serve God and man as a celibate, as an exception to the rule. One cannot justify oneself before others in adhering to the subjective voice over against the objective command; one cannot even justify oneself to oneself. Kierkegaard thinks the reason for this is that to justify anything is to adhere to or to have recourse to universals; but here it is precisely the universal that one rejects in favor of the singular. The individual who has heard or perceived the call of God to be the exception must live in fear and trembling, because he can never be sure that he is not mad or self-deceived, or simply mistaken, in his lonely existence outside the universal.

Whether Abraham, the hero of *Fear and Trembling,* the knight of faith, ought to be taken as the paradigm for the religious stage, or whether he is simply one possibility of religious existence, is not entirely clear. In the *Postscript* the religious stage is described in somewhat different terms—though not clearly contradicting those of *Fear and Trembling*—suggesting a more general set of conditions: an internalizing of all knowledge, a personal appropriation of all religious assertions. Socrates, the archetype of this way of life, represents the ideal of personally appropriating prescriptive propositions until his life is a reduplication of those propositions. This type of existence is designated 'subjectivity'. The religious stage is characterized by this subjective or intensely inward personalization of religious propositions. We will discuss this stage and the concept of subjectivity in greater detail in chapter 3.

What separates religious existence from Christian religious existence (the fourth and final stage in Kierkegaard's existential topography)? It is the paradox of the Gospel, the message that God, who is wholly Other, becomes man. This, unlike the truths of the ethical and the religious stages, cannot be known intuitively or maieutically. It comes only in revelation. The infinite

qualitative distinction between God and man consists in man's sin, his alienation from God. Sin's corruption is total, affecting not only man's will and
intuition but even his reason. Common sense is non-sense when one judges
divine truth. Even subjectivity is untruth in relation to this highest truth.
Nevertheless, although the Gospel judges all man's efforts severely, bringing
them to nothing, it offers salvation. It reestablishes wholeness and harmony
in man, in that it reunites him to God. Those who receive the condition (the
capacity to believe) as a gift must still exercise their wills and make a 'leap of
faith'. Salvation is a cooperative effort. Kierkegaard is a synergist. God's
grace enables man to choose the Gospel (for all others, it is not even a
possibility), but the individual must make the final decision.

Once the individual has become a Christian, he must necessarily renounce
the world as sin, as opposed to God. He must live at odds with the world, *in*
the world but decidedly not *of* the world. Because of this conflict between the
Christian and the world, the Christian will necessarily suffer, and consistent
witnessing will lead to martyrdom. Indeed, "the Christian should go into the
world in order to be sacrificed."[37] This is, of course, the way Kierkegaard
saw his own struggle with the established church.

Let us sum up our characterization of the theory of the stages. The doctrine
of succeeding spheres of existence constitutes a *scala paradisi,* an existential
chain of being, which, if rightly followed, leads to the *summum bonum,*
blessedness in one's God-relationship. Kierkegaard's entire reflective enterprise can be summed up as a quest for eternity. The stages show that every
human life style must be measured from the viewpoint of eternity. He himself lived and died for what he saw to be the goal of the stages of existence,
eternal beatitude. Unless we see Kierkegaard's work in this light, it is very
difficult to make sense of most of what he did.

2

ATTACK

on

OBJECTIVITY

Essentially, Kierkegaard's strategy uses reason to undermine the sufficiency of reason, to reach the highest metaphysical and religious truth. He gives "reasons why there are no reasons" in showing that reason in these ultimate areas is bankrupt. In this way, he opens the door to his theory of subjectivity as the way to highest truth. We shall examine that theory in the rest of this work, but in this chapter I want to do three things with regard to Kierkegaard's relationship to rationality or objectivity. First, I wish to locate him broadly within the philosophical tradition, examining the sense in which one can call Kierkegaard a philosopher. Second, I wish to examine his rejection of reason, identifying five criticisms I find in his works. Third, I wish to examine in some detail the arguments used against apologetics, the rational defense of the faith, in the first part of the *Concluding Unscientific Postscript*.

Kierkegaard as Philosopher

It is often alleged that Kierkegaard rejected philosophy and philosophical inquiry altogether. According to Josiah Thompson, for example, to seek to elucidate the philosophy expressed in Kierkegaard's pseudonymous works is to miss the point of these works. "They seek to show the vanity of all philosophy and metaphysics." "What they seek to demonstrate is not the adequacy of a new philosophy, but the nullity of all philosophy."[1] Thompson is partly, but only partly, right. Kierkegaard does reject the metaphysical speculations of the Hegelians, and sometimes he uses the term 'philosophy' as a synonym for 'speculative philosophy'. He is not a philosopher in the same sense as Hegel, although, even here, one may note a number of places where Kierkegaard has been influenced by and resembles Hegel.[2]

Nevertheless, it is safe to say that Kierkegaard rejects elaborate system building. His purpose in writing is not primarily theoretical but practical. He wants to help men and women *exist,* not learn to speculate on 'existence'— even though he speculates on the concept a good deal himself. If the terms 'philosopher' and 'philosophy' are given wider scope than 'Hegelian speculative philosophy' and if they include the sort of investigation into the meaning of concepts and validity of arguments that men like Socrates, Kant, Lessing, and Trendelenberg were involved in, then Kierkegaard must be seen as a philosopher.

Thompson and Mackey make Kierkegaard out to be an ironist or poet, rather than a philosopher, and go to some lengths to dismiss all his assertions as instances of irony.[3] This seems to me a gross exaggeration. One need not deny the poetic element in Kierkegaard to affirm the analytic and intellectual. He *is* a poet, but not merely a poet. As he himself wrote in *Point of View,* he was a Christian who subordinated his poetic and philosophic natures to a higher cause, the Christian faith.[4] Throughout his journals, Kierkegaard speaks of himself and his works as dialectical *and* poetic.[5] Even in his rejection of the speculative theology of his day (neo-Hegelian and Martensen's), Kierkegaard recognized that while Christian theology must not allow itself to become subordinate to any philosophical system, there is need for a Christian philosophy, a "Christian epistemology."[6]

Kierkegaard was no friend of sloppy thinking. His criticisms of Grundtvig's "rehetorical shower bath" as a poor substitute for close, critical thinking make it clear how much he valued the analytic role of philosophy. If we can call Kierkegaard a philosopher, it is in the sense that he tried to think hard and consistently about concepts and conceptual constructions. His examination of such concepts as 'dread' (*Angest*), 'despair' (*Fortvivlse*), 'interest' (*Interesse*), and 'freedom' (*Frihed*) are more like phenomenologists' investigations than the Anglo-American analytic philosopher's treatment. The examination focuses on how the concept appears to consciousness, how it is experienced rather than how it is used in ordinary language. Nevertheless, there is clear concern for the logical implications of the concept, and examination of these entailments is what Kierkegaard often refers to as his "dialectical" work.

He seems to have a somewhat Platonic view of language: just as his description of the stages presumes the existence of these ideal types, independent of man's awareness of them, concepts have real existence apart from human convention or discovery. They are eternal verities or realities which we discover by experience, by being forced by experience to introspect. The process seems very much like 'Socratic recollection', on which we will have more to say in succeeding chapters.

That feature of reason which Kierkegaard valued most is 'necessary connection', the aspect emphasized by deductive logic, wherein one proceeds by the "laws of logic" from given assumptions to valid conclusions. Reason or (as he labels reason) 'reflection' cannot ensure that our assumptions are true, nor can it tell us which assumptions to start with; but once we have our assumptions, reason can show the implications in the assumptions. In this respect, he professes to differ radically from Hegel, who thought that reason can somehow bring us to the truth.

Not only does Kierkegaard reject the inflated claims of Hegelian logic, he adheres to traditional Aristotelian canons of logic. Whereas Hegel seems to reject the law of noncontradiction, asserting that contradictions are reconciled in "higher unities," Kierkegaard insists that true contradictions are never united, that the law is always valid. Denial of the principle of noncontradiction rests on the very principle it would deny. "The proposition: the principle of contradiction is annulled, itself rests upon the principle of contradiction, since otherwise the opposite proposition, that it is not annulled, is equally true."[7]

An important early study of Kierkegaard's views and use of the principle of contradiction is Viktor Kuhr's *Modsigelsens Grundsaetning* (The principle of contradiction). Kuhr sets Kierkegaard's comments on this subject within the context of his times, showing that Kierkegaard took sides with Trendelenburg and Bishop Mynster, who held that the principle is universally valid, against the Hegelians, especially Heiberg and Bornemann, who viewed it as abrogated in a "higher unity." Even here, however, Kierkegaard gave the principle an existential emphasis. "Personality" protests against the mediation of "absolute opposites," which "will for all eternity repeat its immortal dilemma: to be or not to be—that is the question."[8] "Life is a contradiction."[9] Such existential contradictions are overcome only in eternity. The principle of identity for existence is "the *terminus a quo* but not the *terminus ad quem.*"

Unfortunately, Kuhr fails to discuss whether Kierkegaard believed that the laws of logic apply to God. Since Kierkegaard treats the doctrine of the Incarnation as a contradiction, it would seem that he, like Descartes, believed that the law did not apply to God; but other interpretations are possible. One might argue that the term 'contradiction' points only to our earthly understanding of the doctrine.

For Kierkegaard, the role of reflective reason is largely negative. By helping us see what a concept is *not,* we may be better able to appreciate what it *is.* (One of his favorite epigrams is Spinoza's dictum, "All determination is negation.") He speaks of negative concepts as being at the heart of human reasoning; they highlight the limits of reason. "Above all it is a fundamental fallacy to think there are no negative concepts. The highest principle for all thinking or the proof for it is negative. Human reason has its limits. There lie the negative concepts."[10] In one way or another, 'irony', 'paradox', 'the unknown', 'the limit', 'dread', and 'guilt' would be considered negative concepts.

Closely related to negative concepts is negative reasoning, a form of dialectics—what we would call *modus tollendo ponens* or 'principle of denying the disjunct'. Given a disjunction and negation of one of its disjuncts, we can affirm the other disjunct. That is, from the disjunction "p or q" (for Kierkegaard, disjunction is invariably an exclusive disjunction: "p or q, not [p and q]"), together with "not-p," we conclude to "q." This form of reasoning is used in several places in Kierkegaard's works. (We have seen one place in the first chapter of this book.)[11] In his private papers, Kierkegaard described this process of negative reasoning as capable of proving transcendental qualities. He calls it "faith's syllogism":

> Faith is, quite rightly, "the point outside the world," which therefore also moves the whole world. It is easy to see that it is the point outside the world which emerges through the negation of all the points in the world. The syllogism that there is no righteousness in the world, but only unrighteousness, *proves* that there is righteousness—indeed, if so, then it *must be* outside the world. Here is the point outside! This is faith's syllogism. Take the absurd. Denying all understanding forces one outside the world to the absurd—and here is faith. [*Papers*, X 2 A 529; my italics]

The argument seems to be: Assume there is some quality which we know as righteousness, and it must either be in the world or in some transcendent (otherworld) domain. We see that every claim to righteousness in this world fails to qualify as a pure case of righteousness; therefore, righteousness must exist in a transcendent world. The argument reminds us of the Platonic arguments for the existence of forms in a transcendent realm. Certainly, Kierkegaard would have to do much more arguing before he convinced us that this syllogism helps us understand faith or "proves" anything about righteousness. What is important for our purposes is the way Kierkegaard sees negative reasoning functioning in a Christian philosophy.

One of the theses I am making, and will try to support in this book, is that Kierkegaard uses such negative reasoning to argue for the reasonableness of the Christian position. That is, one way to read Kierkegaard is to see him set exclusive options, for example, *either* the aesthetic *or* the ethical, then show that one option is somehow impossible, contradictory, or the like, thus leaving the other option as the only way left. It is difficult to be sure just how aware Kierkegaard was of what he was doing. On one hand, as we shall see, he eschews all proofs and demonstrations for faith. On the other hand, he seems to build a case which, given his assumptions, results in something very much like proof—if not for the *truth* of Christianity, at least for the *reasonableness* of the leap into Christianity.

In the next two sections we shall examine his negation of first-order uses of reason to reach the highest truth.

A Critique of Rationality

In this section I shall analyze Kierkegaard's criticism of various uses of reason. Essentially, he makes five contentions against various claims of rationalists:

1. Hegel's dialectical reasoning is confused, and his system is a confused attempt to abstract oneself from existence.
2. Reason, in the general sense, fails as a justification process because of built-in limitations.
3. Reason provides only possibility or probability, whereas certainty is required.
4. Reason, through its instrument, language, distorts reality and is incapable of capturing reality.
5. Reason is not the essence of man, as the philosophers have thought, but a function of the passions, and must be integrated within the whole person to play a valid role in life.

Let us examine these charges separately.

  1. Hegel's dialectical reasoning is confused, and his system is a confused attempt to abstract oneself from existence.

To make Kierkegaard's critique comprehensible, we will make some general comments on Hegel's philosophy as it appeared to Kierkegaard and his contemporaries. Hegel (1770–1831) was seen in his own day as a post-Renaissance Aristotle, a philosopher who had given the world a new encyclopedia of wisdom, a new logic, a unified and systematized philosophy of the spirit, an idealism that incorporated all learning in physics, chemistry, politics, art, history, and religion, weaving these subjects together into a brilliant tapestry of ideas. It was as though one man had pulled his brothers out of the cave of shadows and given them not only a view of the sun but a God's-eye view of all reality, a view *sub specie aeternitatis*. Intellectuals—philosophers and theologians alike—divided into various Hegelian camps: right-wing Hegelians and left-wing Hegelians.

Hegel conceived the task of philosophy to be the attainment of absolute knowledge, freed from the limitations of Kant's critical philosophy. Kant claimed to have shown that man can have knowledge only of things as they appear to him, not as they are in themselves. Knowledge is completely subjective rather than objective, limited rather than absolute. Hegel's philosophy can best be seen as an attempt to counter these claims and restore integrity to our claims to knowledge, which, because he had a coherence theory of knowledge, entailed absolute knowledge. Knowledge of the truth in an infinite sense is the goal of philosophy, and it has always been philosophy's task. "The history of philosophy is the history of the discovery of thoughts about the absolute, which is its object."[12]

Crucial to Hegel's program is the Kantian distinction between understanding (*Verstand*) and reason (*Vernunft*). 'Understanding' involves the proper application of the categories to experience while 'reason' relates to a transcendental application beyond experience. For Kant, understanding is valid for human experience, whereas he denied reason in order to make place for faith. Hegel, however, adopted this notion of reason, associated it with metaphysical speculation, and showed that it not only has the absolute as its object but that it can attain that object.[13]

The law of noncontradiction is fundamental to application of the understanding: two opposed concepts cannot be predicated of any object at the same time. However, Hegel notes that this law seems to be contradicted by the thinking of the understanding in that it produces the antinomies, for by using the understanding we can consistently, and apparently soundly, reason to opposite conclusions about metaphysical issues. For Hegel, the antinomies were evidence that the law of noncontradiction did not apply to metaphysical reasoning. None of the objects of metaphysics is characterized by one and only one category of a pair of putatively contradictory concepts, but each is "essentially the one as well as the other, and thus neither the one nor the other; i.e., such determinations in their isolation are invalid."[14] Since one as well as the other of two opposed categories can be predicated of each object of metaphysics, it must be that in metaphysical speculation the law of noncontradiction breaks down—as well as the law of the excluded middle.

Since, for Hegel, the finiteness of a concept consists in its being excluded from an object by being limited by an opposing concept, the removal of the mutually exclusive character of concepts by his dialectics is precisely the removal of their finiteness. Through an ingenious dialectical logic he presents a series of progressively more refined characterizations of the absolute.[15] In this way he claims to have attained the highest knowledge, his logic being "the account of God, as he is in his eternal essence before the creation of nature and any finite spirit."[16] Of course, Hegel, following Spinoza, is using 'God' as a metaphor for absolute metaphysical reality, but we can imagine how the phrase sounded to pious thinkers such as Kierkegaard.

Other ideas in Hegel also offended Kierkegaard: the retrospective role of philosophy ("The owl of Minerva spreads its wings only with the falling of the dusk"), with its correlative disinterest in the 'edifying'; the view of the State as the embodiment of the Absolute Spirit; the demeaning of Kantian individual ethics (*Moralität*) in favor of a social ethic (*Sittlichkeit*), bound up in objective social structures, customs, and institutions; and, most of all, an apparent subsumption of Christianity to "the System," ending as a religion without revelation. All of this was unacceptable to Kierkegaard.

In spite of the fact that he admired Hegel and had learned from him, he looked upon "the System" as a fraud, as the archexample of hubris. "If Hegel had written his whole logic and had written in the Preface that it was simply a thought experiment, . . . he would have been the greatest thinker who has ever lived."[17] Since he did not write such a preface, he is a comical figure who is unaided by his own philosophy to understand himself. He is like a man who builds an enormous edifice but lives in a hovel next door.

All of Kierkegaard's complaints with Hegel find their final locus in Hegel's inflated claims of reason, the "rose in the cross," which brings us to the final truth in Hegel's system. Kierkegaard objects that, in making such a preposterous claim, Hegel confuses himself with the fourth member of the Trinity.

> An existential system is impossible. An existential system cannot be formulated. Does this mean that no such system exists? By no means; nor is this implied in our assertion. Reality is a system—for God; but it cannot be a system for any existing spirit. System and finality correspond to one another, but existence is precisely the opposite of finality. It may be seen, from a purely abstract point of view, that system and existence are incapable of being brought together; because in order to think existence at all, systematic thought must think it as abrogated, and hence as not existing. Existence separates and holds the various moments of existence discretely apart; the systematic thought consists of the finality which brings them together. [*CUP*, p. 107]

In another place he writes: "Everyone is familiar with the fact that the Hegelian philosophy has rejected the principle of contradiction. Hegel himself has more than once sat in solemn judgment upon those thinkers who remain in the sphere of reflection and understanding, and therefore insist that there is an either/or. . . . Hegel is utterly and absolutely right in asserting that viewed eternally, *sub specie aeterni*, in the language of abstraction, in pure thought and pure being, there is no either/or."[18]

Interestingly enough, Kierkegaard does not reject the idea that motivated Hegel, that there is an absolute truth. Let philosophers who think Kierkegaard lacks a notion of objective truth, let alone absolute truth, take note.[19] There is a coherent, necessary truth about reality—only it is God's possession, belonging to His omnipotence, not man's. God sees reality from eternity, sees it as complete. For man to presume to that vantage point is hubris of the most absurd kind.

One suspects that Kierkegaard has given Hegel too much here, for he may have dealt a devastating blow to his notion of free will when he admits that "Hegel is utterly and absolutely right in asserting that viewed eternally, *sub specie aeterni,* in the language of abstraction, in pure thought and pure being, there is no either/or." Does he mean that, from God's point of view, there is no choice or simply that choice is not part of pure thought? What he should say is the latter, and that God's omniscience in no way precludes human freedom. Otherwise, his philosophy is merely an edifying illusion.

Implicit in these passages are two reasons for rejecting Hegel, and both of them are Kantian. The first reason is signaled by the sentence "It may be seen, from a purely abstract point of view, that system and existence are incapable of being brought together; because in order to think existence at all, systematic thought must think it as abrogated, and hence as not existing." Kant, in his refutation of the ontological argument, had pointed out that 'existence' is not a proper predicate but, rather, a second-order or instantiating predicate. One cannot infer anything at all about reality from the mere thought. Kierkegaard, in *Fragments,* essentially repeats Kant's reasoning in separating 'ideal essence' from 'factual being', showing that we cannot go from one to the other. "A fly, when it is, has as much being as God; with respect to factual being the stupid remark I here set down has as much being as Spinoza's profundity, for factual being is subject to the dialectic of Hamlet: to be or not to be. Factual being is wholly indifferent to any and all variations in essence, and everything that exists participates without petty jealousy in being, and participates in the same degree. . . . But the moment I speak of being in the ideal sense I no longer speak of being, but of essence."[20]

The second reason for rejecting Hegel's claims is found in Kierkegaard's adherence to Aristotelian logic, which precludes abrogation of the law of noncontradiction, even with regard to metaphysical truth. Again in *Fragments,* he points out that the claim that this principle is annulled depends on the validity of the principle, since otherwise both it and its denial are equally true.[21] In this he shows that he accepts the Kantian antinomies as well as Kant's category of the understanding as appropriate for human existence. However, it could be asked whether Kierkegaard's statements about reality being a system for God, and there being no either/or in eternity, imply that God is a super-Hegelian for whom the antinomies are mediated? This would explain why Climacus can view the Incarnation as containing a contradiction and still being true: contradictions are annulled in a higher unity by the absolute, God.

There is a final reason for rejecting Hegel's system—a practical one. It is unedifying. It doesn't help; and we, in the crucible of suffering and sorrow, desperately need a philosophy we can live by. "Only the edifying is true for you." I shall show (in the next chapter) that the edifying is not necessarily a denial of objective truth for Kierkegaard, but at times he seems to emphasize it to the neglect of any objective-truth connection.

I turn now to the other criticisms Kierkegaard levels against the claims of reason.

2. Reason, in the general sense, fails as a justification process because of built-in limitations.

Kierkegaard's critique of reason goes further than a mere polemic against Hegel. He points out that the very notion of proving a theory or a metaphysical proposition is fraught with severe difficulties. One cannot even logically justify an action. Justification of theories and propositions breaks down because the process has no natural resting place. In a deductive argument, one can always question a premise and ask for a justification of it; when one is given, one can always question that justification; and so on. This is called an infinite regress. There is no logical reason to stop asking for a reason for our reasons. Or justifying involves a vicious-circle argument; for example, *Question:* Why do you believe in God? *Answer:* Because the Catholic Church teaches me there is a God. *Q:* Why do you believe what the Catholic Church teaches? *A:* Because it is based on belief in God.

Not only is reason helpless in offering final justification regarding any metaphysical or theoretical proposition, it can't even offer justifications of right action. Concerning any action, I can find as many reasons *for* as *against* it. It is not reason which decides what I shall do, but my will. "If I really have reflection [reason] and am in the situation in which I must act decisively . . . my reflection will put forth as many possibilities *pro* and *contra*, exactly as many."[22] This is an absurd situation. My reason says to me: "You can just as well do the one thing as the other"; that is, my reason places me in a state of indifference, where I have no rational justification to act but nevertheless *must* act. In such a situation, a leap of faith is necessary. "Only when reflection comes to a halt can a beginning be made, and reflection can be halted only by something else, and this something else is something quite different from the logical, being a resolution of the will" (*CUP,* p, 103).

Kierkegaard isn't altogether rejecting practical reasoning, in the sense that if one has decided what he wants, reason may help him get it. For example, if I want to get rich and if I am offered a job which pays a high salary, reason can show that I ought to take the job. The sort of questions Kierkegaard is concerned about includes: "Should I continue to endure the pain of existence or end this life of suffering?" Sometimes, however, his skepticism becomes all embracing and he seems to say that life is so contingent and unpredictable that, considered in the long run, we never can be sure any action is the right one. This leads into Kierkegaard's third criticism of reason: whether probability is a sufficient guide to action and belief.

   3. *Reason provides only possibility or probability, whereas certainty is required.*

Deductive reason can show that a proposition is not contradictory or inconsistent, if it is possible, and inductive reasoning may tell how probable certain propositions are; but neither deductive arguments nor inductive reasoning can guarantee truth, can give us the certainty we would like to have, and sometimes need to have, in order to function properly.

With regard to induction, Kierkegaard asserts that it always goes beyond the evidence. "As soon as I form a law from experience, I place something in which is more than there is in the experience."[23] Inductive reasoning has neither the rigor nor reliability of deductive reasoning; it is merely approximative, depending on a leap of faith for its conclusion. Deductive reasoning, on the other hand, is more secure as a method, but it cannot provide an initial set of premises or assumptions. It cannot even guarantee that our basic beliefs are true: that the laws of logic have universal applicability; that other persons exist; that the world was not created five minutes ago, with false memories already present; that the laws of nature will be the same tomorrow as they are today. These are all basic beliefs, which are fundamental to our noetic structure (our rock-bottom conception of reality). We know these things intuitively and feel certain about them. Yet the certainty does not come from reasoning these propositions out, but from something prerational.

Kierkegaard believed beliefs about God, moral absolutes, immortality, and free will are like these foundation beliefs. They cannot be deduced rationally, but anyone who looks deep within himself will find these beliefs *self-evident*. Kierkegaard does not argue for this—how could he? He simply finds it so and assumes that others will have the same experience if they think passionately about the subjects. The point is that these moral and religious truths are discovered by intuition, not conclusions at the end of syllogisms.

What of scientific and historical reasoning? They, too, fail to offer certainty. Science can experiment and provide lawlike generalizations, but future experiments can modify or change these results. History is more crucial for Kierkegaard, because Christian faith—which he found so vital—is based on historic documents: the Old and New Testaments. What can historical scholarship guarantee? Can it give certainty that the documents are altogether reliable and hence trustworthy?

It depends on how they are interpreted. One scholar can argue that the documents are replete with error and inaccuracy, that we know very little about the historical Jesus, and that we do not have enough hard evidence to believe in the miracles or the resurrection. Another scholar can assert an opposite assessment of the documents. Whom are we to believe? Is there a consensus of scholarship, making it—on the basis of scholars' opinion—slightly probable that most of the documents *are* reliable? Suppose there is, and we place our faith in that scholarship, and next week one of the scholars changes his mind, shifting the balance of probability; or a new consideration is offered that throws new light on the problem. Ought one's faith in God and Christianity rest on such shifting sands of research and consensus?

Faith demands an inner certainty, which scholarship can never satisfy. The probability of researchers is entirely incommensurable for faith. We will examine this aspect of Kierkegaard's thought in further detail in the next section, under "Faith and History."

> *4. Reason, through its instrument, language, distorts reality and is incapable of capturing reality.*

That which annuls immediacy is speech. If man could not speak, then he would remain in immediacy. Johannes thought this might be expressed by saying that immediacy is reality and speech is ideality. For when I speak, I introduce opposition. If, for example, I want to express the actual world which I perceive with my senses, then opposition is present. *For what I say is quite other than what I want to express.* Reality I cannot express in speech, for to indicate it I use ideality, which is a contradiction, an untruth. . . .

How does the Word annul reality? By talking about it. For that which is talked about is always presupposed. Immediacy is reality. Speech is ideality. Consciousness is the opposition or contradiction. The moment I express reality the opposition is there. For what I say is ideality. [*JC*, p. 148f.]

Kierkegaard is saying that language is inadequate in capturing reality (immediacy); yet, in a sense, we can never be conscious of reality apart from language or a system of symbols. We judge things within a linguistic framework, yet the reality at the bottom of the judgment transcends language.

There seems to be a Kantian notion here, for Kant distinguished between the phenomenal and noumenal worlds. We can know only the phenomenal aspects of the world, reality as it presents itself to us in space and time; we can never get behind the veil of space-time to see things-in-themselves. Kierkegaard is saying that, in language, we know the world as phenomena, but we can never completely know what the world is in itself. But he also seems to be saying that we *can* have some knowledge of this world, "for what

I say is quite other than what I want to express." That is, we can know things that we cannot express.

This is a difficult thesis, which Bergson, coming after Kierkegaard, also held. What sense can it be given? How do we know we know something if we cannot express it, not even to ourselves? It does not seem to make sense to speak of propositions that we know but cannot express, for to know a proposition seems to entail that it is expressible, since a proposition includes the notion of asserting beliefs. But propositional knowledge is not the only kind of knowledge. We can also know how to do things and have a knowledge of particulars, knowledge by acquaintance.

I cannot express (put into propositional form) all that my senses take in at any given moment, partly because too much information is coming in at once, partly because I don't have a way of measuring qualities and quantities of experience (e.g., "I'm now feeling ten units of boredom" or "I'm now smelling five degrees of odor, type K"), and partly because the experiences seem to converge into a whole, continuous experience which cannot be discretely separated. All this seems true—but this has little to do with the sort of knowledge with which reason has to do. Language, as a function of reason, predicates universals of particulars so that we can communicate and structure our world.

Perhaps what Kierkegaard had in mind is that language is an artificial tool; but if so, it is highly necessary. Perhaps, further, Kierkegaard wanted to tell us that the language we choose (or are born and raised into) has enormous influence in shaping the way we see the world. If so, he's right, and perhaps we often forget this; but he seems to be saying more: that language can never express the reality we know.

The question is, "Is there any underlying reality in the first place, or is all reality (in any significant sense of that word) a construction of language?" If there *is* independent reality, "Is it not the case that we can name it and speak of it?" Kierkegaard has again raised an important question, but his solution seems inadequate.

> 5. *Reason is not the essence of man, as the philosophers have thought, but a function of the passions, and must be integrated within the whole person to play a valid role in life.*

Traditionally, man has been defined as a rational animal, reason being his "true self." As Aristotle put it, "Reason is the true self of every man, since it is the supreme and better part. It will be strange, then, if he should choose not his own life, but some others. . . . What is naturally proper to every creature is the highest and pleasantest for him. And so, to man, this will be the life of

Reason, since Reason is, in the highest sense, a man's self" (*Nichomachean Ethics*, X:7).

Kierkegaard denies that reason is the person's true self. The will, the emotions, the imagination, as well as reason, must all work together in harmony if a person is to live authentically. Reason cannot be separated from the whole person. A person is a unitary being, whose springs of actions lie deep within, bound up with the intuitions and passions. Elevation of reason where it does not belong produces deceptive rationalization. "In existence thought is by no means higher than imagination and feeling, but coordinate. . . . In existence all factors must be co-present."[24]

Basically, reason is to be subordinate to the passions. Kierkegaard agrees with Hume, who said: "Reason is, and ought only to be the slave of the passions, and can never pretend to any other office than to serve and obey them."[25] Kierkegaard writes in a similar vein: "Reasons are in general very curious things. If I lack passion, I look down on them with contempt. If I have passion, they grow up into something immense."[26]

Both Hume and Kierkegaard are skeptical about reason's power to judge impartially. We usually do what we want to do, finding reasons to support what we desire to do, or find ourselves valuing, or instinctually believing. From a rational point of view, there is not more reason for valuing life rather than nonexistence, but most of us find we have a high regard for life, especially our own. In any situation where we must make a moral decision and there are considerations on both sides (pro and con arguments), not reason, but intuitive weighing processes—the passions—decide the issue. Reason only brings us to a dilemma, given classical description in the story of Buridan's hungry ass, which found itself equidistant from two equally desirable stacks of hay. Because there was no rational way of deciding which stack to prefer or choose, the ass remained in place and starved to death. Thus reason's self-proclaimed equanimity. In itself, it leads to immobility, paralysis—a paralysis of analysis. Hence the passions are needed to give reason focus and direction.

Again, I think Kierkegaard put his finger on a limitation of pure reason, but has he not exaggerated? Aren't there times when reason changes our passions and helps us get through the fog or thicket of emotions and immediate instinct? It is true that we need passion to *motivate* us to think, but, as motivated thinking, this need not be emotional thinking or mere rationalization of our prejudices. It is hard to know to what extent even our finest justifications partake in self-deception, but I think a good case can be made that, without impartial or rational judgment, self-deception (and all forms of irrationality, for that matter) becomes endemic. However, I think he has a valid point in relating reason to the whole person, including his passions, and the subjective side of man.

Let us turn now to a more detailed critique of objectivity in the first book of the *Postscript*.

The Failure of Objectivity: Analysis of Book 1 of *Concluding Unscientific Postscript*

The objective problem consists of an inquiry into the truth of Christianity. The subjective problem concerns the relationship of the individual to Christianity. . . . In order to make my problem clear I shall first present the objective problem, and show how this is dealt with. In this manner the historical will receive its just due. Then I shall proceed to present the subjective problem. [*CUP*, p. 20]

Introduction

Is there any point in objective inquiry into the credentials of religious beliefs? According to Climacus, such an inquiry is not only useless but undesirable, a temptation to be avoided at all costs.

If a naked dialectical analysis reveals that *no approximation to faith is possible,* that an attempt to construct a quantitative approach to faith is a misunderstanding, and that any appearance of success in this endeavor is an illusion; if it is seen to be a *temptation* for the believer to concern himself with such considerations, a temptation to be resisted with all his strength, lest he succeed . . . in transforming faith into something else, into a certainty of an entirely different order, *replacing its passionate conviction by those probabilities* and *guarantees* which he rejected in the beginning when he made the leap of faith, the qualitative transition from non-belief to belief—if this be true, then everyone who so understands the problem, insofar as he is not wholly unfamiliar with scientific scholarship or bereft of willingness to learn, must feel the difficulty of his position, when his admiration for the scholars teaches him to think humbly of his own significance in comparison with their distinguished learning and acumen and well merited fame, so that he returns to them repeatedly, seeking the fault in himself, until he is finally compelled to acknowledge dejectedly that he is in the right. [*CUP*, p. 15; my italics]

This long sentence sums up what Kierkegaard wishes to show in the first part of the *Postscript*:

1. No approximation to faith is possible. That is, faith does not rest upon probability calculations of evidence.
2. Objective inquiry is not only useless but undesirable.

It is "a temptation to be resisted with all his strength." We may call the first thesis the 'uselessness thesis' and the second the 'undesirability thesis'. If either thesis can be sustained, it would follow that the objective way fails and that the subjective way is the only option for anyone concerned with metaphysical or religious truth. In the first two chapters of book 1 of the *Postscript*, Climacus argues that both in the form of empirical (historical) inquiry and in the form of speculative (dialectical) reasoning, the objective way completely fails to satisfy the requirements that any conscientious person would place upon it.[27]

In this case, "conscientious person" refers to one who is infinitely concerned with eternal happiness. Johannes Climacus is not a Christian, but wants to know how he can become one. He wants to become a Christian because it promises eternal happiness, and he wants to be eternally happy. "I, Johannes Climacus, born in this city and now thirty years old, a common ordinary human being like most people, assume that there awaits me a highest good, an eternal happiness, in the same sense that such a good awaits a servant-girl or a professor. I have heard that Christianity proposes itself as a condition for the acquirement of this good, and now I ask how I may establish a proper relationship to this doctrine" (*CUP*, p. 19).

This is an important statement: it reveals that Climacus is already involved in religious ideas. He assumes there is such a thing as eternal life, and passionately wants what religion has to offer. He is even willing to "join up" without investigating the credentials. There must be good reason for this decision, but what can it be? Either passion to start on the way to eternity is too great to allow time for investigation into credentials or investigation is a nonstarter, and it turns out that both answers are correct. In the first book in *Postscript*, Climacus gives an objective case to explain why objectivity fails; he gives reasons why there are no justifying reasons for or against faith. *Book Two: The Subjective Problem: The Relation of the Subject to the Truth of Christianity; The Problem of Becoming a Christian* deals at length with the aspect of infinite passion that motivates the believer. (We will look at this aspect of religious consciousness at the end of the next chapter.)

For Climacus, then, there is a disjunctive relationship between objective and subjective inquiry, an exclusively (as opposed to inclusively) disjunctive relationship. One asks about the truth either objectively or subjectively; but he cannot do both at the same time. Every moment he does so, the person who asks objective questions is denying the subjective.[28] The objective inquirer is basically disinterested in the results of the inquiry; interest may be a relative, motivating factor, but the inquiry must be impartial, disinterested. Passion is to be excluded from the process, as a fog which blurs our mental vision. For the subjective inquirer, on the other hand, interested in the results, the inquiry is more than an intellectual exercise; it is a matter of utmost importance. "The inquiring, speculating, and knowing subject thus raises a question of truth. But he does not raise the question of subjective truth, the truth of appropriation and assimilation. The inquiring subject is indeed interested; but he is not infinitely and personally and passionately interested on behalf of his own eternal happiness for his relationship to this truth. Far be it from the objective subject to display such presumption, such vanity of spirit" (*CUP*, p. 23).

The subjective inquirer seeks to appropriate and assimilate possibly true propositions into his life. Religious assertions become necessary postulates for him.[29] The passionate exigencies of his existence find resolution only in the message of religion.

For future reference, we will call the thesis we have been discussing the 'cognitive disjunct thesis', or CD: *There is an exclusive disjunctive relationship between a subjective inquiry and an objective inquiry.* The CD rests on the observation that one cannot be both interested and disinterested in the same object in the same respect and at the same time.

This is not formally asserted by Climacus, but is implied in what he says about the mutual exclusiveness between objective and subjective inquiry. Apparently, he would admit that in every act of knowing both an objective factor and a subjective factor are involved. The difference is that in 'objective knowing', the object is the governing term, whereas in 'subjective knowing' the subject is the governing term. Some things can only be known if the objective factors are given prominence. For example, it does not matter how I feel about a mathematical sum for it to be known to be true or false; but other things can only be known if I am in a certain condition, have a certain interest and training. For example, only the person who looks for the clue finds it; only the person who has persevered to expertise can appreciate or understand the subtleties of a subject matter. This is not a logical but a psychological point. Human nature could have been such that things were different, that no training, no passion or interest was required in knowing anything. Perhaps in heaven, where (*pace,* Kierkegaard) faith is no longer required, passion is also abolished.

Climacus' point is that there are things, or truths, which can only be known objectively, and there are truths which can only be known subjectively. Among things which can only be known objectively are the sciences and mathematics. Among things which can only be known subjectively are ethical and religious truths. He thinks it can be shown that objectivity fails in these areas.

The implications of Climacus' thesis (CD) seem disturbing. Surely, we may object, most of our activities involve highly complicated subjective interest *and* objective evaluation. The neat either/or seems to falsify what most of us feel to be the case. We try to make objective assessments of each case and then proceed to act accordingly. The objective seems to precede the subjective: "Because I believe a proposition to be objectively true, I feel passionately about it." Climacus would no doubt reply that it is only because I am already interested in this kind of proposition that it can have any meaning for me.

However, our unsureties about the cognitive disjunct principle may be settled, one way or another, by investigating how it is used. We turn now to Kierkegaard's rejection of two types of objective inquiry: historical research (into both the documents and history of the faith) and speculative inquiry.

Faith and History

For Kierkegaard, history constitutes both a necessary aspect and an embarrassing distraction to Christian faith. On one hand, he recognizes the necessity of the Incarnation as the basis for Christian faith: God entered history as a human being. On the other hand, he regards any preoccupation with historical inquiry as both useless and harmful for faith. That is, while Christianity needs a minimum of historical data, inquiry into the credibility of those data will necessarily fail to establish anything, one way or another, and may even result in turning the believer aside from obedient discipleship.

In this section I will discuss these two theses. First I will analyze the claim that a historical point of departure is necessary for faith; then I will discuss Kierkegaard's claim that historical investigation is unnecessary, and even harmful, for faith. Then, I will offer a brief evaluation of this aspect of Kierkegaard's thought. On these issues, I believe, there is no substantive difference between Kierkegaard's beliefs and those set forth by Climacus—but nothing hangs on this point. If readers disagree, let them take this section as a critique of Climacus' ideas, since nearly all the material comes from *Philosophical Fragments* and *Concluding Unscientific Postscript*.

Necessity of History for Eternal Happiness

Johannes Climacus (John the Climber) begins *Philosophical Fragments* with a series of questions concerning the relationship between faith and history: "Is an historical point of departure possible for an eternal consciousness? how can such a point of departure have any other than merely historical interest? is it possible to base an eternal happiness on historical knowledge?" (From title page of *Fragments*). In other words, what is the relationship between faith (the eternal consciousness) and history, between eternal truth and contingent historical information?

Climacus sets a thought experiment, juxtaposing two opposite ways of answering this question. One way represents the Socratic-Platonic theory of knowledge; the other is merely called "B" but is a version of orthodox Christianity. Schematically, these opposing epistemologies can be thus classified:

Socratic Way	*Christian Way*
1. Truth is within man and man is open to that truth.	1. The truth is not within man; rather, man is in error, closed to the truth.
2. The teacher is incidental to the process of discovering the truth.	2. The Teacher is necessary to the process of discovering the truth; he must bring it from without and create the condition for receiving it within man.
3. The moment of discovery of the truth is accidental. The opportunity is always available; we must merely use our innate ability to recover it.	3. The moment is decisive for discovering the truth. The Eternal must break into time at a definite point (the fullness of time) and the believer must receive the condition in a moment of contemporaneity with the Teacher.

The essential truth is already within man, in the Socratic view of reality, so that history is only of accidental importance. It is only an occasion for making explicit what is already implicit. Through introspection, one recovers knowledge. In the Christian view, however, history is of decisive importance, for God becomes man in history and reveals the truth to the disciple in a moment of history. The questions posed on the first page of *Fragments* are answered, for the most part, negatively for Socrates and positively for the Christian.

1. Is a historical point of departure possible for an eternal consciousness?
   Socrates: Only accidentally, as an occasion for recalling the truth.
   Christian: Yes, in the moment of personal revelation, the truth that God entered history is received.
2. How can such a point of departure have other than merely historical interest?
   Socrates: It cannot have any other interest.
   Christian: By being accepted through an act of will (you have the option of receiving or rejecting the revelation).
3. Is it possible to base an eternal happiness on historical knowledge?

Socrates: No, eternal happiness resides precisely outside of history. Time and eternity are absolutely separate.

Christian: Yes, receiving the truth of the Incarnation is the only way to attain eternal happiness. In the Incarnation, eternity breaks into time and in conversion (the moment) eternity joins the individual in time with the Eternal.

According to Climacus, man is so devoid of truth that only God's power is sufficient to bring the truth to man. However, the Teacher must be man in order to put man in possession of the truth, which is so 'absurd' that natural man could never, self-consciously, believe it: that God became man. That proposition is sufficient for faith to base its eternal happiness on, and not much else is necessary. It need not be Jesus of Nazareth that one believes in. All that is needed to get faith "off the ground" is for a group of people to assert that they have believed that one of their contemporaries is God and to leave a testimony for others to believe. Climacus gives an example:

> If the contemporary generation had left nothing behind them but these words: "We have believed that in such and such a year that God appeared among us in the humble figure of a servant, that he lived and taught in our community, and finally died," it would be more than enough. The contemporary generation would have done all that was necessary; for this little advertisement, this *nota bene* on a page of universal history, would be sufficient to afford an occasion for a successor, and the most voluminous account can in all eternity do nothing more. [*F*, p. 130]

This simple statement, that God has become man and has been seen to serve humbly, is *more* than enough to "get faith going." Never has Occam's razor been more ruthlessly applied to the *depositum fidei*!

The first thing to notice about the *nota bene* is what is omitted. What does the name 'God' stand for? Do the witnesses mean the same thing by 'God' as we do? What would an adequate definition be? Would it have to include omnibenevolence, or could the deity be *mostly* good? Would this God have to be a creator God? Would it (he or she?) have to be all powerful, or would something like Plato's demiurge suffice? Presumably, 'paradoxicality' is important here: the deity, who is decidedly not man, becomes man without ceasing to be the deity. Climacus seems to want a high (or maximal) paradox sufficient to cause the passion of faith to rise to its maximum. As Climacus says in the *Postscript:* "Subjectivity culminates in passion. Christianity is the paradox; paradox and passion are a mutual fit; and the paradox is altogether suited to one whose situation is to be in the extremity of existence."[30]

Leaving aside the criticisms that this seems bad psychology (it is not necessary to have a paradox to raise the passions to their height, not even the passion of faith) and that the Incarnation of God as man is not the only way to build a maximal paradox (God could have become an ape or a mouse), Climacus' *nota bene* seem inadequate for anything that even approximates Christian faith.

But perhaps Climacus could defend himself by asking us to state exactly what is necessary for a faith to be salvific. Perhaps he could set criteria for separating nonsense paradoxes from justified paradoxes and show us that only the Christian message adequately fulfills those criteria. Suppose that to be the case; then the question arises: "What role does historical investigation play in deciding whether So-and-So is really the God-man, and whether the record left by the contemporaries is authentic and reliable?" We turn to the general question of the relation of faith and history to answer this question.

Historical Investigation Is Useless and Harmful for Faith

For Kierkegaard, faith is a passionate matter, and only lovers and haters have any chance of comprehending what it is all about. Anyone who understands what Christianity is about cannot but be offended by it. It is a judgment of our ordinary understanding. The point is to get over the offense, into a state of "happy passion," acceptance, and trust.

With this radical and passional interpretation of Christianity before us, we can best consider Climacus' attack on historical inquiry. This attack is sharpest in the opening pages of *Concluding Unscientific Postscript* and forms part of a general polemic against all forms of objective investigation into the credentials of Christianity. Kierkegaard's thesis is: A Christian should have nothing to do with historical research into the materials which involve the articles of Christian faith. There are two basic reasons for this:
  1. The results of such objective inquiry do not matter for faith in the least.
  2. The process of inquiry involves a temptation, an infidelity to the Gospel.

We turn now to the arguments Climacus uses to support these two claims.

'Uselessness of Investigation' Thesis. Climacus' reasons for regarding historical research as useless turn on the thesis that historical evidence and faith are incommensurable.
  1. All historical inquiry gives, at best, only approximate results.
  2. Approximate results are inadequate for religious faith (for faith demands certainty).
  3. Therefore, all historical inquiry is inadequate for religious faith.

When Christianity is viewed from the standpoint of its historical documentation, it becomes necessary to secure an entirely trustworthy account of what the Christian doctrine is. If the inquirer were infinitely interested in behalf of his relationship to the doctrine he would at once despair, for nothing is more readily evident than that the greatest attainable certainty with respect to anything historical is merely an *approximation*. And an approximation, when viewed as a basis for an eternal happiness, is wholly inadequate, since the incommensurability makes a result impossible. [*CUP*, p. 25]

The first premise seems unarguable. Historical research never provides absolute knowledge or absolute certainty. However slight, there is always some chance of error. The chance of error may seem ridiculously small, but it is nevertheless present.

The second premise, that approximation is wholly inadequate for faith, is more debatable. For Kierkegaard, religious faith is absolute in that it is the kind of certainty which excludes all doubt. "The conclusion of belief is not so much a conclusion as a resolution, and it is for this reason that belief (*Tro*) excludes all doubt."[31] Approximate knowledge, however likely, cannot give the absolute conviction that is necessary for faith.

Take any historical example—for instance, that Nixon was president of the United States during the Watergate scandal. One might immediately object to Climacus that this proposition is virtually certain; the chance of error is so small as to put this statement beyond reasonable doubt.[32] However, it would not be too small if our eternal happiness depended upon it—if we had the sort of infinite, passionate interest in the truth about Nixon and Watergate that Kierkegaard requires. If our interest is infinite, any chance of error is enough to cause infinite concern. "In relation to an eternal happiness, and an infinite passionate interest in its behalf (in which latter alone the former can exist), an iota is of importance, of infinite importance."[33]

More historical evidence will not remove our doubt about Nixon's being president during the Watergate affair. Because the resolution of faith entails the decision to disregard all possibility of error, Kierkegaard seems to be right at this point.

There is something incommensurable between the absoluteness of the kind of faith Kierkegaard sees as adequate and the relativity of historical knowlededge. Consider the believer who is at the mercy of historical evidence (supposing it possible), who bases his confidence in Christianity on certain sources which today seem more or less established. So he decides to believe the Gospel; but tomorrow the evidence takes on a new dimension and he is forced to withdraw his confidence in that evidence and change his commitment, suspending his faith. Can one really subject faith and commitment to the changing shifts of evidence in this way? Climacus believes that faith safeguards the believer from the uncertainties of scholarship, the ingenuity of the clever, and the luck of archeologists. The metaphysical assertions of

Christianity must be beyond the threat of the empirical (and the speculative, too, for that matter).

Kierkegaard illustrates this thesis of the incommensurability between faith and scholarly inquiry by considering the doctrine that the Scriptures are inspired by God. He asks: "What can scholarship show with regard to this assertion?" The objective inquiry must make sure of the Scriptures, historically and critically, before it can conclude that they are or are not inspired. The scholar must consider the canonicity of the individual books, their authenticity, their integrity, and the trustworthiness of the individual authors before he can even begin to think about the possibility of their being divinely inspired. This is an enormous undertaking, and just when one feels he is beginning to see daylight, a little dialectical doubt may set the whole project in doubt.[34]

But even if scholars could come to a consensus on all of these matters, inspiration could not be inferred from the results, for the proposition that the Bible is inspired by God is not arrived at by adding up the accumulated evidence. It is solely a matter of faith, a subjective matter. Anyone who believes the Bible to be inspired "must consistently consider every critical deliberation, whether for or against, as a misdirection.[35] On the other hand, anyone who begins the investigation without faith "cannot possibly intend to have inspiration emerge as a result."

Who, then, is interested in this sort of inquiry? No one. If a person has faith, he has the inner certainty about inspiration. If a person does not have faith, he will never be led to it by scholarship and the approximations of scholarship. Therefore, such scholarship is useless. Hence anyone who engages in such an enterprise is involved in a practical contradiction. He purports to be doing something which makes a difference to faith that cannot possibly have anything to do with faith.

To see this point about the total incommensurability between faith and historical inquiry, Climacus invites us to consider the following thought experiment. Imagine what it would be like if the investigation were maximally favorable to theologians' deepest hopes. Then imagine what it would be like if the results of the inquiry were as negative as any enemy of Christianity could desire.

First we imagine the positive situation: the canonicity of the sixty-six books of the Bible has been established; the authors have been shown to be entirely trustworthy and their accounts authentic; all apparent contradictions in the Bible have been satisfactorily resolved. What follows from this? Has anyone who previously did not have faith been brought closer to its acquisition? "No," says Climacus, not a single step, for "faith does not result simply from a scientific inquiry; it does not come directly at all. On the contrary, in this objective inquiry, one tends to lose that infinite personal interestedness in passion which is the condition of faith."[36]

Now imagine the opposite situation, that opponents have proved their case against the Scriptures. The sources are demonstrably unreliable and contradictory; the writers are not trustworthy; the accounts are shown to be false. Have the opponents abolished Christianity? No. Has the believer been harmed? No, says Climacus. Has the opponent acquired the right to be relieved of the responsibility of becoming a believer? The answer, again, is no. "Because these books are not written by these authors, are not authentic, are not in an integral condition, are not inspired (though this cannot be disproved, since it is an object of faith), it does not follow that Christ has not existed. Insofar, the believer is equally free to assume it" (*CUP*, p. 31).

Even if it were established that the sources are unreliable, what they reported could still be true. Even if the Bible were not inspired by God, what the Bible affirms could nevertheless be the case. The faithful believer cannot conceive of seeing things differently than from the Christian point of view. Faith is not corrigible, is not based on evidence, but is a resolution of the will to accept what it believes to be a gift of God, a miracle. The argument is admittedly circular: faith is its own authentication. There is no way to attack it from without.

Let us pause at this point to consider Climacus' contention. While we may admit that he has put his finger on a certain phenomenological feature of faith—that it goes beyond the evidence and seems certain to the believer—we would question whether faith is absolute in the way he claims. It is one thing to admit that faith goes beyond the evidence; it is a different thing to claim that it is impervious to rational inquiry.

For example, Climacus says that even if it were proved that the Scriptures are unreliable documents, the proposition that Christ existed (viz., that God became man) is not falsified. It is, of course, notoriously difficult to falsify existential propositions. How would one go about proving that God never became man (assuming we could annul the logical difficulties)? If not Jesus of Nazareth, why not someone else? "Insofar, the believer is equally free to assume it." But one might as well assume that God became a rattlesnake and build a system around that "truth."

Perhaps no single bit of evidence or the sum of all the evidence can enable us to infer a metaphysical proposition, for example, that God raised Jesus from the dead, the Scriptures are divinely inspired, Jesus is perfect God and perfect man; but the opposite situation may not be ruled out. Evidence can disconfirm metaphysical propositions. The assertion that Jesus was raised by God from the dead is falsified by proof that Jesus never lived and/or never rose from the dead. The assertion that Jesus is the Son of God is falsified, if he never existed or if he went around doing evil.

Even Climacus' *nota bene* could be seriously infirmed. According to his account, all that is necessary for faith is the confession by some people that they believe one of their contemporaries to be God. This, presumably, is necessary for faith; but if it is, then faith can founder, for we could imagine that the note was proved a forgery. It was not written by a group of people but by a man who believed he was God and wanted to gain support for his belief, and so attributed it to others. Or it could have been a product of an accident—a historian was writing about one of his contemporaries, a man named Gade, but wrote illegibly: "We have believed that in such-and-such a year Gade came among us, served us, and taught in our community." When someone else read what he had written, the reader misread *God* for *Gade* and so mistranscribed the sentence: "We have believed that in such-and-such a year God came among us, served us, and taught us." Later, when the original writer showed the transcriber the document again and explained what had happened, everyone had a hearty laugh. Would Climacus want to maintain that no one's faith would be affected, or should be affected, by such a discovery?

The second reason Climacus gives for rejecting historical inquiry into the articles of faith is that such an inquiry constitutes a temptation, a distraction from discipleship. It can be harmful to the believer's deepest duty to be faithful no matter what.

> Here is the crux of the matter, and I come back to the case of the learned theology. For whose sake is it that the proof is sought? Faith does not need it; aye, it must even *regard proof as its enemy*. But when faith begins to feel embarrassed and ashamed, like a young woman for whom her love is no longer sufficient, but who secretly feels ashamed of her lover and must therefore have it established that there is something remarkable about him—when faith thus begins to lose its passion, when faith begins to cease to be faith, then a proof becomes necessary so as to command respect from the side of unbelief. [*CUP*, p. 31; my italics]

If we substitute 'evidence' for 'proof', we still retain the meaning of Climacus' critique. The argument for this position presupposes that one cannot evaluate evidence (or construct proofs) and be entirely (absolutely) committed to Christianity at the same time. One can do only one thing at a time. Either you are infinitely interested in Christianity, in which case inquiry is meaningless, or you are not infinitely interested in Christianity, in which case you are not properly a Christian.

The inquiring, speculating, and knowing subject thus raises a question of truth. But he does not raise the question of subjective truth, the truth of appropriation and assimilation. The inquiring subject is indeed interested; but he is not infinitely and personally interested in his own eternal happiness. . . . The inquiring subject must be in one or the other of two situations. *Either* he is in faith assured of his own relationship to it, in which case he cannot be infinitely interested in all the rest, *since faith itself is the infinite interest in Christianity, and since every other interest may readily come to constitute a temptation.* Or, the inquirer is, on the other hand, not in an attitude of faith, but objectively in an attitude of contemplation, and hence not infinitely interested in the determination of the question. [*CUP*, p. 23; my italics]

The argument seems to be that all inquiry involves interest, which is either infinite or finite. Being finitely interested in something involves placing a relative or nonabsolute value upon it. One cannot place relative *and* absolute value on something at one and the same time and in the same respect; hence one cannot be both absolutely and relatively interested in anything at the same time and in the same respect. All objective inquiry is finite or relative inquiry and, thus, is relative to some higher interest; but Christianity demands infinite interest: absolute and total involvement of the subject in one's eternal happiness via the Paradox. Hence if one is infinitely interested in Christianity, one cannot be finitely interested in it. Therefore one cannot inquire whether Christianity is true and, at the same time, be totally committed to Christianity. If one is totally committed, he has ruled out further inquiry into its truth value; its truth is assumed as basic for every other inference and action. If this is so, any suggestion that one become interested in objective inquiry into the truth of Christianity must be regarded as a temptation, to be rejected automatically.

I think this is an insightful and valid argument. If one believes that the proposition that God has become man in order to save man is the foundation of all other knowledge or if, at least, it is part of one's foundational set of beliefs, then the sort of attitude Kierkegaard advises seems appropriate. It is no use arguing that such an attitude disregards human fallibility, because the argument supposes that God has revealed this truth to the believer. It is no use arguing that this is a circular argument, for the believer will admit as much and point out that all metaphysical argument ends either in infinite regress or in something intuitively self-evident. It is no use pointing out that this sort of logic could lead to fanaticism, for the believer will acknowledge that possibility and insist that this is exactly the weakness of all reasoning. It is really—*pace,* Hume—a slave of the passions. Other belief systems must be preached against, not argued against.

Plantinga has advocated that the theist place the proposition that God exists in the foundation of his noetic structure, thus escaping most of the arguments against theism as well as the need to find arguments in support of theism.[37] In a similar way, I think, Kierkegaard advocates putting the idea of the Incarnation in the foundation of one's noetic structure, thus escaping the arguments for and against Christianity, as well as the need to find arguments. In this sense, Kierkegaard thinks philosophy of religion of little use, besides showing that there are reasons why there are no reasons.

Evaluation

I think Kierkegaard puts his finger on an important feature of Christian belief as it has traditionally been manifest: the sense of its absoluteness. If Christian faith is as absolutely important as he says it is and in the way he says it is, then much of what he says about the unimportance (and even sheer danger) of apologetics seem plausible, if not convincing. This attitude could also be applied to the proofs for God's existence, *mutatis mutandis.*

There are problems, however, which need to be considered, the first of which is the relation between faith and reason. The second is in terms of the ability of a human being to live up to Kierkegaard's volitional standard. The third is the problem of subjectivity and objectivity in general, as set forth by Kierkegaard.

What sort of religion does Climacus' bare minimum leave us with? Is not the essence that results a mere abstraction? Does not salvation come down to the ability to perform an enormous mental exercise, of believing that, at some time and place, God became man? But what does making that mental leap over reason have to do with eternal happiness? Does believing paradoxes denote or produce some special virtue?

Kierkegaard's thought experiment seems to suggest its own deficiency. It may be juxtaposed not only with Socratic theory but with historic Christianity, of which it claims to be a genuine representation. Christianity purports to be about not just the Incarnation but a specific era in history, where a particular person is said to be the Savior of the world. There are background conditions (the history of Israel) and a set of supporting evidences (Jesus' teachings, miracles, resurrection, as well as the changed lives of the disciples) for the doctrine of the Incarnation. There is a "cloud of witnesses" who claim to offer evidence. While all this may not solve the problem of the place of apologetics in religious faith, it seems to suggest that the pure abstraction in Climacus' formulation of faith differs fundamentally from the religion he thought he was defending. Historical investigation seems of vital importance to the spirit of New Testament Christianity.

It might also be argued that Kierkegaard has a confused idea of faith as unduly volitional. "Belief is a resolution of the will." Somehow, according to

Kierkegaard, we can choose to believe propositions and by grace can decide whether to believe the apparent contradiction of the Incarnation.

I think an argument can be made to show that beliefs are events, not actions, and that, as such, we are not directly responsible for our beliefs or doubts. If this is so, it seems unreasonable to demand that absolute commitment means that the believer always overcomes doubt by a leap of believing. Beliefs and doubts are not things we have direct control over. It is true that if we are successful in avoiding certain evidence, we are more likely not to have doubts; but, given the fact that we cannot easily shelter ourselves from untoward evidence, there is no way of assuring against doubt. If absolute commitment means refusal to doubt, Kierkegaard has laid an impossible burden on the believer.

In general, I think Kierkegaard lacks sufficient distinctions with regard to possible attitudes toward truth. There are too many sweeping "either/ors"— either objectivity or subjectivity. "Abstract thought is disinterested, but for an existing individual, existence is the highest interest."[38] According to him, such questions as "Is there eternal life?" "Does God exist?" "How shall I live?" can only be answered subjectively. On the opposite side of subjectivity, he sets the foes of this virtue; objectivity, disinterestedness, neutrality, and abstract thought. These are inappropriate attitudes toward existential and religious questions.

I think there is a fundamental confusion here. Disinterestedness or impartiality is not necessarily opposed to subjectivity (*qua* passionate interestedness). The opposite of interestedness is the spirit of neutrality. Both impartiality and neutrality imply conflict situations, for example, war, competitive sport, argument; but 'to be neutral' signifies *not* taking sides, doing nothing to influence the outcome, remaining passive in the struggle, refusing to make a decision toward one side or the other, whereas impartiality *involves* one in the conflict in that it calls for a judgment in favor of the party which is in the right, based on objective criteria. To the extent that one party is right or wrong, measured by the appropriate standards, neutrality and impartiality are incompatible concepts. To be neutral is to detach oneself from the fray; to be impartial (rational) means to commit oneself to a position—not partially (i.e., unfairly or arbitrarily) but in accordance with an objective standard.

The model of the neutral person is an atheist, indifferent about football, watching a Notre Dame versus Southern Methodist football game. The model of the impartial person is the referee in the game, who, though knowing that his wife has bet their life savings on the underdog (Southern Methodist, of course), still manages to call what any reasonable spectator would judge to be a fair game. He does not let his wants or self-interest enter into the judgments he makes. The model of the partial person is the coach, who always sees the referee's decisions against his team as entirely unfair and the decisions against the other team as entirely justified. The atheist spectators are neutral and impartial; the coaches are interested and partial; the referee is interested and impartial.

On Kierkegaard's analysis, the referee's position is either impossible or is classified with the spectators' as undesirable and entirely inappropriate for faith. He does not seem to notice that one can be passionate and impartial at the same time, and that to be rational does not commit one to give up passionate concern. The rational believer, who seeks good grounds for his or her faith, is no less likely to be deeply committed to the object of faith than the partial and passionate believer. It is true that the rational or impartial believer seems to have a prior commitment to truth or justified belief, rather than the object of faith, for he or she will modify beliefs in the light of new evidence; however, the commitment to the existential aspects of life seems equally serious. Both are passionately concerned to will the good and live within their lights. Only the impartial person believes that reason can and ought to play an important role in guiding us in these matters. Regarding religious belief, the impartial believer seeks to have his beliefs based on the best evidence available, and where that evidence is not available, he or she modifies the belief or the strength of the belief, though (note well!) not necessarily the strength of interest in the question itself.

However, it might be objected that my analysis is one sided. "Isn't the *Postscript* precisely an effort to be objective precisely about one's subjectivity, and this is an exceedingly tall order that involves the strategy of indirect communication, pseudonymity, etc.?" I admit that Kierkegaard may be fully aware of the radicality of his notion of faith here, but I don't think the appeal to indirect communication or pseudonymity will explain his position (see the appendix on these items). I find nothing in his work to give us reason to doubt that this is exactly Kierkegaard's position. But even if it isn't, he has given us the argument through his pseudonym, Johannes Climacus, and it is this argument I challenge, whether or not Kierkegaard seriously held it himself. If one objects that this undermines my thesis that Kierkegaard is a rationalist of sorts, I would reply (as should become clear in what follows) that the rationalism built into Kierkegaard's (or, at least, Climacus') schema involves acceptance of the 'cognitive disjunct thesis' and is very much a matter of practical reason. Given the logic of the situation, the rational thing to do is become a believer with all one's might. (These matters will be elaborated in the last three chapters.)

It seems that Kierkegaard fails to take sufficiently into account the possibility that one can be both objective (impartial) and subjective (passionately interested) at the same time. Herein, I believe, is his greatest weakness, a weakness that mars an otherwise insightful understanding of religious existence.

Critique of Objectifying the Church

Climacus applies essentially the same criticisms (mentioned above) to theologians who base their faith on the authority of the Church. Those who replace the authority of the Bible by the authority of the Church are on no firmer ground than the Biblicists. Climacus has in mind Grundtvig, his courageous and influential contemporary, who did so much to reshape the religious, educational, and social life of Denmark in the first half of the nineteenth century. Indeed, Grundtvig's influence in Denmark today far outweighs Kierkegaard's.

Grundtvig and his followers had responded to attacks on the books of the Bible by elevating the Church as the "living witness." It is true, they conceded, that the Bible could be doubted. It is uncertain even whether Jesus existed, let alone that he claimed he was the Son of God or that he rose from the dead. Placing one's faith in the unsureties of historic documents is very risky; but, the Grundtvigians argued, the Church exists. That cannot be doubted. A battery of arguments issues from this fact, to the effect that the living Church is a true witness to the truth of Christianity.

Climacus shows that the same sort of questions raised against the Scriptures can be raised against the Church theory. Is the church based on the truth? Has its nature changed through the ages? Grundtvig claims that God would preserve the truth in the Church; but this only begs the question. One might just as well say that if there is a God, he could preserve the record of Jesus in the Gospels. To seek to substitute the Church for the Bible is not only an escape from dialectical doubt, it is to miss the point of Christian faith altogether: to quit playing the game of seeking for objective certainty. Not only is it not possible, it is not even desirable.

> If truth is spirit, it is an inward transformation, a realization of inwardness; it is not an immediate and extremely free-and-easy relationship between an immediate consciousness and a sum of propositions, even if this relationship, to make confusion worse confounded, is called by the name which stands for the most decisive expression for subjectivity: faith. The unreflected personality is always directed outward, toward something over against it, in endeavor toward the objective. The Socratic secret, which must be preserved in Christianity unless the latter is to be an infinite backward step, and which in

Christianity receives an intensification, by means of a more profound inwardness which makes it infinite, is that the movement of the spirit is inward, that
the truth is the subject's transformation in himself. [*CUP*, pp. 37, 38]

Christian faith is not a mere intellectual assent to a set of propositions. The
"Socratic secret" is inherent in the Christian idea of faith; that is, one must
transform an objective idea into a personal principle. The process is the
opposite of Kant's categorical imperative. For Kant, one must test the subjective maxims on which one's actions are based by a universality rule: the
individual must abstract the lawlike principle from what he is inclined to do
in order to see whether it is in line with practical reason. For Climacus, one
must take the universal abstract and judge it by one's interests and inclina-
tions. He must take the 'law', the objective norm, and make it into his
personal maxim.

The Church theory has no advantage over the Bible theory as the basis for
religious authority, for both involve us in endless approximation. The point is
to be done with the quest for objectivization altogether. For if one has an
objective authority, whether through the Church or the Bible theory, one is
still a pagan, "for Christianity is precisely an affair of spirit, and so of subjectivity, and so of inwardness."[39]

One argument that Grundtvig seems to have put forward as a proof that
the Church is God's witness in the world is that it had endured, in spite of all
opposition, for eighteen centuries. The argument, stated formally, is this:

1. If the Church is God's witness, it will withstand all opposition.
2. The Church has withstood all opposition.
3. Therefore, the Church is God's witness.

This, of course, is an obvious case of the fallacy of affirming the consequent
(from "If p, then q, and q." I cannot infer p, but only q).

Climacus comments further: "Eighteen centuries have no greater demon-
strative force than a single day, in relation to an eternal truth which is to
decide my eternal happiness."[40] The whole Church theory, but most obviously the 'endurance argument', is as "slender as toothpicks."

The same criticisms we made of Climacus in the earlier section apply here.
He unwarrantedly asserts the 'radical disjunct thesis', to the effect that because objective and subjective inquiry are different, they are eternally antag-
onistic. One has to choose one or the other and live with his choice. This, we
concluded, is unreasonable.

There seems good reason to take the witness and influence of the Church
into account in assessing the merits of Christian faith. If the Church that is
named by Christ's name had done nothing but persecute heretics, exploit the
poor, impede political and scientific progress, this would certainly cast doubt
on its claim to be God's witness. Climacus may be right to insist that the

matter is ambiguous, but this is not the same as saying it does not matter at all.

Critique of Speculative Point of View

In the short second chapter of the first part of *Postscript,* Climacus considers the failure of objectivity, in terms of speculative reason, to come to grips with the truth of Christianity. The argument is brief and not fully developed, perhaps because it rests on the sort of premises discussed in the earlier sections, and part of the discussion leads into the next part of the *Postscript* ("Book Two, The Subjective Problem"). Our discussion of this section will be correspondingly brief.

The argument rests on the 'cognitive disjunct principle', that an object must be known either subjectively or objectively (but not in both ways at the same time). There is such a thing as being in a subjective condition and such a thing as being in an objective condition. If, and only if, a knower is in the right condition will he know (observe) certain objects. Where the object is subjective, it is necessary for the knower to be in a subjective condition; where the object is objective, it is necessary to be in a correspondingly objective condition. If Christianity were essentially objective, it would be necessary for the knower to be in an objective condition to know what Christianity is. "But if Christianity is essentially subjectivity, it is a mistake for the observer to be objective."[41] He must be in a subjective condition. If Christianity is subjectivity, then only two kinds of people know anything about it, "the happy and the unhappy lovers."

Climacus thinks it is obvious to anyone who takes the time to reflect that Christianity is a species of subjectivity. The essence of Christianity is the 'God relationship' and the related thought that the believer will enjoy eternal happiness in His presence. This 'God relationship' and the idea of eternal happiness appeal to one's interests, to something inward. The 'God relationship' is a love relationship. Only those who have loved can appreciate what love is or correctly identify it when they see it. Likewise, only those who see the point of Christianity, who have felt the force of the questions it tries to answer, will understand what Christianity is about. The conclusion is that the objective way completely fails. "Christianity does not lend itself to objective observation, precisely because it proposes to intensify subjectivity to the utmost; and when the subject has thus put himself in the right attitude, he cannot attach his eternal happiness to speculative philosophy."[42]

Again, I am dissatisfied with Climacus' use of the 'cognitive disjunct principle'. Are subjective and objective inquiry so entirely separate from one another? Or is it not the case that both subjective and objective factors play important roles in every kind of inquiry? What does it mean to be in an 'objective' or a 'subjective' condition? If one is subjective about a religious belief, does this mean that objective factors cannot influence the matter at all? Kierkegaard's answers to these questions seem to leave much to be desired.

3

SUBJECTIVITY

and

EPISTEMOLOGY

The only fundamental basis for understanding is that one understands only in proportion to becoming himself that which he understands. [*Papers,* V B 40]

Here is such a definition of truth: holding fast to an objective uncertainty in an appropriation process of the most passionate inwardness is the truth, the highest truth available for an existing individual. [*CUP,* p. 182]

The thesis of this chapter is that within the structures of Kierkegaard's work, both implicitly and explicitly, are epistemological theories which are related to his ideas of subjectivity. Indeed, the epistemology defines the concept of subjectivity—but I shall point out three notions of subjectivity which seem mutually incompatible in the works of Kierkegaard. In the first section I shall examine the concept of subjectivity as it appears in Kierkegaard's writings, pointing out two fundamental aspects in that concept and that scholars have concentrated on one to neglect of the other. In the next section I shall examine some aspects of an epistemology to be found in Kierkegaard's works. In the third section I shall examine the three incompatible theories on the relation between subjectivity and knowledge which emerge in the writings. In the conclusion, I will endeavor to resolve the issue pertaining to these conflicting theories.

The Domain of Subjectivity

On the surface at least, it would seem that the term 'subjectivity' in Kierkegaard's work signifies not a simple concept but a set of concepts, related to each other but not identical. At various times, the term stands for inwardness in general, passionate striving for some object, the emotions, the action of the will, acquiring a belief, the act of faith, the voice of conscience, the process of reduplicating an ideal, and the process of introspection, as well as intuition.[1] Perhaps these concepts can be worked into a unified theory, or perhaps Kierkegaard simply wants to call our attention to a special dimension in life (as Robert Roberts claims),[2] but it is often difficult to get precise meaning from Kierkegaard's uses of the term. One isn't quite sure which of the above meanings is signaled.

Earl McLane argues that the dominant characteristics in his usage juxtapose it with 'scientific spirit':

1. its reliance on inner experience versus public observation;
2. a reliance on a limited perspective versus an openness and pursuit of pluralistic perspectives; and
3. a preference for an emotional or passional manner of seeing versus an objective or disinterested manner of seeing.[3]

McLane doesn't claim this is all there is to the idea of subjectivity, but he thinks it is a significant part of it. I agree. Placing this in wider context, one might say that a core meaning of the term in Kierkegaard emphasizes the thesis that the springs of action and knowledge lie deep within a person, within his essential or transcendental self, and that unless a person gets in touch with that self, there is little hope that he will ever reach his proper destiny, his telos.

McLane's characteristics, however, are unduly passive ("experience," "seeing," "perspective"). Most of Kierkegaard's uses of 'subjectivity' emphasize the will as the vital organ for spiritual development. "The essential thing about subjectivity is that in resolution and decision of choice one takes a risk. This is the absolute decision."[4] It is an experiencing, a seeing, and a perspective which involves decision at every step. Whether we consider subjectivity as reduplication of an ideal, believing a proposition, or introspecting, the will is ubiquitous. Every instance of subjectivity involves the will, though every act of the will need not involve subjectivity. Subjectivity may be a subcategory of the will's activities, having to do with only those activities perceived to be vital to the spiritual life. Choosing a secondhand Buick over a

new Ford would probably not constitute a subjectively significant act, but
deciding whether or not to marry probably would (or should).

Although the emotional and conative aspects of subjectivity are dominant,
the concept has a cognitive dimension as well. At least some instances of
subjectivity have as their object a proposition. For example, Kierkegaard
treats such statements as "God exists," "The soul is immortal," and "God
became man" as objects of belief which affect one's inner being. Subjectivity
is intentional; it always takes some object, which need not be a proposition. It
may be an ideal which the subject wishes to exemplify in his or her life, but
even here a proposition is implied. For example, to make Christ's character
my ideal implies such propositions as "It would be a good thing if my
character were like Christ's."

Commentators have treated Kierkegaard as uninterested in propositions
and argument, but it can be shown that every ideal implies a propositional
aspect. Although this is true, there is a difference between appropriating an
ideal and claiming to know that a proposition is true. In the first instance, the
emphasis is on bringing a possibility to actuality. It is a practical task, requir-
ing imagination and creativity; it is a doing. In knowing, conversely, no
action is necessary. I can know the good without doing it, or I can believe that
some action would be good without being motivated to do it. Sometimes,
however, one may have to exercise one's will in order to believe a proposition
which is not apparent to reason alone. That is, subjectivity may enter in to
decide whether to believe what the evidence, by itself, does not warrant.
Indeed, Kierkegaard believes that all nontautological believing involves the
will in going beyond the evidence.[5] In the *Postscript,* belief in the Incarnation
becomes the *sine qua non* to a special type of life.

There seem, then, to be two senses or aspects to the concept of subjectivity,
one focusing on appropriating an ideal and the other on believing a proposition, and they are reflected in the two quotations cited at the beginning of the
chapter:

> The only fundamental basis for understanding is that one understands only in
> proportion to becoming himself that which he understands. [*Papers,* V B 40]

and

> Here is such a definition of truth: holding fast to an objective uncertainty in an
> appropriation process of the most passionate inwardness is the truth, the high-
> est truth available for an existing individual. [*CUP,* p. 182]

Notice that the language of the second quote resembles that of the creative
or practical type of subjectivity. It speaks of an "appropriation process" and

"the most passionate inwardness" as though one were going to do something, master some activity, change one's character in some way. But "objective uncertainty" seems to imply that a proposition is involved in the process.
Was Kierkegaard aware of the fundamental ambiguity in passages such as
these? (I suspect he was, though not fully.) The context, however, makes it
clear that a proposition is involved, that God's existence is the content which
must be believed, and that truly believing involves objective uncertainty, a
resolution of the will to accept the proposition, and a further passionate
resolution of the will to let the implications of that proposition dominate
one's life at every moment.

Later in the *Postscript,* and in *Training in Christianity,* Climacus and Anti-
Climacus each applies this dual aspect of subjectivity to Christian faith, making it clear that Christian subjectivity involves (1) having this "insane" belief
and (2) living according to an otherworldly pattern, as Christ. This double
thrust of subjectivity constitutes a complete offense to, as well as a complete
rejection of, the standards of secularity, the ways of this world. With regard to
cognitive standards and to behavioral goals, there will be an infinite gap
between the Christian and the non-Christian member of 'Christendom'.

To sum up the distinction we have been making, we can say that, for
Kierkegaard, subjectivity is a process of volitional appropriation in either or
both of two ways, which we may designate the 'reduplication way' and the
'cognitive way'. In the reduplication way, the accent falls on the ideal or
pattern to be instantiated; in the cognitive way, the accent falls on the proposition that is to be wrestled with until one believes it. Reduplication represents a movement from the proposition or ideal to life, while cognitive
subjectivity represents the movement from my life as a cognitive subject to
the ideal (the truth) or proposition. In the first case, I bring something that is
outside myself inside myself so that I may reflect it. In the second case, I go
outside myself, as it were, and choose to regard the world in one way or
another. It is a strikingly volitional interpretation of believing, a radical version of what William James called "the will to believe." (We shall examine
this radical volitionalism in chapter 5.)

If we are to understand Kierkegaard's concept of subjectivity, we must
contrast it with its opposite, objectivity. Kierkegaard paints in broad strokes,
as though he saw the issue not in any detailed defense of subjectivity but in
the battle between two fundamentally opposed ways of relating to reality.
'Objectivity' stands for a composite of attitudes, including unemotionality,
disinterested evaluation, neutrality, impartial judgment, which leaves the interested subject out of the scene, and consensus, based on the public's assessment of the situation. In all these attitudes, the individual's deepest
evaluations and aspirations are set aside as very secondary. The motivation
for the idea of subjectivity is to counter this exaggerated view of man, where

the person is cut off from his inner depths, where the true springs of action lie.

Objectivity is not necessarily a bad thing. There are times when disinterested evaluation is required (e.g., the referee in a sporting event) and when public consensus may be safer than individual opinion (e.g., deciding on which side of the road to drive one's carriage); but it is catastrophic to allow that attitude to encroach on the spiritual dimension of life, to suppress the individual's deepest instincts with regard to the imagination, the realm of values, and the possibility of the supernatural. It is not simply, as Louis Mackey implies, that objectivity doesn't get us where we want to get because we can't get there *any* way (to some objective set of truths or values).[6] Rather, the point is that it is positively wrong to treat the spirit of man as a subject for science and objective scrutiny. It is not simply a category mistake (though it is that, too). It is morally evil—a perversity of the first order—to treat the mystery of personhood as an artifact on a par with other artifacts, to apply objective modes of assessment where subjectivity is the proper mode.

Juxtaposing objectivity with subjectivity may be outlined as follows: Subjective reflection yields subjective understanding; that is, deep introspection produces self-knowledge whereas objective reflection yields objective understanding. That is, by using the methods of rationality (deductive and, especially, empirical induction), one arrives at objective knowledge. Objective reflection involves disinterestedness in the pursuit of truth in a way that subjective reflection does not, in that the former leaves out the individual's deepest feelings and sense of self-development in the process. In objective reflection, the emotions and passions function as a fog which clouds the deliberation process.

Objective understanding is arrived at through the process of objective reflection. At its best, the result is knowledge, a conscious possession of true propositions, to be contrasted with merely true *beliefs*. (Kierkegaard would reject the modern definition of knowledge as 'justified true belief', for belief and knowledge have different phenomenological aspects. Knowledge or objective truth is the goal of objective reflection.)[7]

On the other hand, subjective reflection means the process of introspecting with significant interest (passionately). The area of life for which subjective reflection is most appropriate is ethical-religious thinking, sometimes called the 'existential': "All existential problems are passionate problems, for when existence is interpenetrated with reflection, it generates passion. To think about existential problems in such a way as to leave out the passion, is tantamount to not thinking about them at all, since it is to forget the point, which is that the thinker is himself an existing individual" (*CUP*, p. 313).

Subjective understanding results from subjective reflection. I begin to understand myself as I really am—a creature related essentially to God, before whom I have infinite responsibility—and because of my failure to live in perfect obedience, I am infinitely guilty. Because of my infinite guilt, I discover an alienated self, unable to cure itself.

There is another distinction which seems implicit in Kierkegaard's works, which Stephen Evans makes explicit: between subjective understanding, on the one hand, and existential understanding on the other.[8] While I may look within and attain a modicum of subjective understanding, there is no guarantee that I will act on my knowledge; but existential understanding is that understanding I receive *in* becoming some sort of person or *in* deciding to act in a certain way. For example, I can have an understanding of what Christianity is all about by reflecting on it passionately as a possibility, but I can understand what it is to *be* a Christian only by becoming one, through an act of the will.

Finally, there is the concept of subjective truth, a special kind of existential understanding that results from maximal subjective reflection. Where the passion of subjectivity reaches its apex, resulting in a decision, we have a state of subjective truth. There are some qualifications on the appropriate object in such a state (Climacus offers criteria for distinguishing madness and nonsense from subjective truth), but for our purposes we can say that subjective truth is a specific type of existential understanding. There is something teleological in the process which makes subjective truth necessary for spiritual health or whatever true fulfillment humans may find in life. The schema, then, is the following:

Types of Reflection	Results
1. Objective reflection	a. Objective understanding
	b. At its maximum, objective truth
2. Subjective reflection	a. Subjective understanding and, if sufficient,
	b. Existential understanding, which at its height becomes
	c. Subjective truth

In addition to the above categories, one more needs to be mentioned: eternal, essential knowledge, or eternal truth (ET), the complete, comprehensive knowledge of existence which Hegel pretended to have but which only God has.[9] Only a being who is outside time could have this kind of knowledge of the temporal domain, for humans, in time, cannot find the necessary place from which to survey the whole *sub specie aeternitatis*. From the vantage point of objective knowledge and eternal knowledge, subjective truth is precisely untruth. From the point of view of objective knowledge (OT), it is untruth because it seems to defy the standards of reason and can be attached to a false belief. From the point of view of eternal knowledge (ET), it is untruth because it is infinitely removed from the realm of the eternal. However, subjective truth seems to be a dialectical denial of the sufficiency of objective truth and so, in a sense, an advancement of truth. And, one may say, using this same Hegelian dialectic (which I suspect to be implicit in Climacus' work), that eternal truth subsumes the antinomies within a higher unity. Something like the following results:

Objective knowledge (OT)	Subjective knowledge (ST)
(Accidental knowledge)	(Essential knowledge)
Knowledge related to science, common sense, mathematics, etc.	Knowledge related to the ethical-religious dimension of life

Essential eternal knowledge (ET)
(Absolute knowledge)
   The objectively true, comprehensive knowledge
   that God possesses

Whether Kierkegaard consciously used such a schema, I am unsure (I suspect he was conscious of doing so in the *Postscript*). What is interesting about this schema is that Climacus seems to end up (via the back door) with a result not very far from Hegel. In the end, it seems there is the possibility of scaling the heavens and arriving at essential, eternal knowledge—not through objective reflection but through subjective reflection. Because of our finitude and temporality, we cannot see the whole *sub specie aeternitatis*. We need to spend our whole effort existing, internalizing our beliefs and ideals. If, however, we could transcend ourselves, we could have the eternal truth in some measure. Kierkegaard, then, allows his pseudonym to say something startling, which has gone unnoticed by his commentators; a particular individual may attain such a state "in the moment of passion": "It is only momentarily that the particular individual is able to realize existentially a unity of the infinite and the finite which transcends existence. This unity is realized in the moment of passion" (*CUP*, p. 176).

What is wrong with Hegelian philosophy is not that it strives for truth, but that it strives in the wrong way, through objectivity, holding passion in contempt. "In passion the existing subject is rendered infinite in the eternity of the imaginative representation, and yet he is at the same time most definitely himself." We will come back to the relationship of subjectivity to knowledge, but first we must look at a few principles of epistemology outlined in Kierkegaard's work.

Kierkegaard's Epistemology

Kierkegaard was not especially interested in epistemology, though it is vital to his work. There is a section in the "Interlude" (in *Fragments*) where he sets out a brief description of an epistemology wherein the will plays a significant part. In each case of propositional belief, the will must decide whether to accept the proposition or withhold judgment. "Believing is not so much a conclusion as a resolution."[10] We will discuss this aspect of Kierkegaard's thought in chapter 5, when we look at the problem of volitionalism, but for now, suffice it to say that acquiring a belief is not merely an event for Kierkegaard; it is an action. Hence it involves the will, and when the "candidate" for belief is perceived as momentous, as crucial for the self's fulfillment, the "candidate" is perceived as a means to subjective truth.

In this section we want to look at a set of principles, found mainly in the early sections of *Postscript,* which throw an interesting light on the relation between subjectivity and knowledge. These principles, which have been neglected by Kierkegaard scholars, follow from the subjective and existential understanding mentioned above. Only by appropriating the knowledge one has can one receive more knowledge, and this is especially applicable to the progress of the individual along the stages of existence. Unless one lives to the fullest degree within the stage where one finds oneself, one cannot understand the next stage. This principle, which I call the 'appropriation principle', involves the person's total immersion in his values, ideals, and background beliefs in order to become what he understands. "The only fundamental basis for understanding is that one understands only in proportion to becoming himself that which he understands."[11]

On further analysis, this principle breaks down into two principles, suggested (but not developed) by Climacus, which we may designate the 'adequacy-to-subject principle' (ASP) and the 'adequacy-to-object principle' (AOP). They are derived in part from the analytic insight that, in every instance of knowing, both the objective and the subjective factors are present. ASP states that whatever is known must be known in a way peculiar to the knower. "*Quidquid cognoscitur per modum cognoscentis cognoscitur.*"[12] Everything one knows one knows by virtue of personal conditions—one's particular situation, innate capacities, previous choices, the theoretical framework within which one thinks; all these affect what is known. All knowing is perspectival, theory laden, from a particular point of view. It follows that everyone knows what he knows in a unique way and that every instance of coming to know something involves personal interpretation, and that every personally interpreted and appropriated bit of knowledge involves one in a new choice, a personal decision with regard to how one will accept, then use, the putative knowledge. "It depends, then, not only on what a man sees, but what a man sees depends on how he sees it; for all observation is not only a receiving, a discovery, but also a creation, and insofar as it is that, the crucial thing is what the observer himself is" (*ED,* I:67).

This is of relative importance for accidental (nonethical-religious) knowing, but it is of vital importance for essential (ethical-religious) knowledge, for that sort of knowledge is a creation of freedom. "For all things spiritual are appropriated only in freedom; but what is appropriated in freedom must also be produced in freedom."

The second epistemological principle to be derived from the appropriation principle, the 'adequacy-to-object principle' (AOP), focuses on the nature of *what* is known. It states that all that is known must be known in a mode appropriate to the thing known. 'Knowing that' requires 'knowing how'. The principle draws attention to objective structures in reality. Each subject matter involves requisite skills or states of mind in order to be mastered. If I am to understand mathematics, I must master whatever principles and skills are required. If I am to understand what it is to ride a bicycle, I must obey certain laws of nature, correlating my innate capacities and personal peculiarities with a specific, two-wheel machine. Unless I apply certain attitudes of attentiveness and obedience that are appropriate to the object, I will never learn, say, to ride a bicycle. All knowing, then, demands a certain conformity to the structure of the object: "Only the like is understood by the like. . . . In the case of observation where it is requisite that the observer should be in a specific condition, it naturally follows that if he is not in this condition, he will observe nothing" (*CUP,* p. 51).

If I understand Kierkegaard correctly, he believed that different objects of knowledge deserve and require different levels of interest in order to be understood. Accidental (nonethical-religious) knowledge properly requires a sort of detached attentiveness (an interested impartiality); essential (ethical-religious) knowledge, because it more intimately relates to one's self, one's telos, requires more intense and personalized interest, culminating in decision; for unless a decision results from subjective contemplation, the process is incomplete. "In subjectivity what is important is resolution and choice, the decision to run a risk. This is the absolute decision."[13]

The idea is that knowledge in the ethical-religious sphere demands action, a choice. "The real action is not the external act, but an internal decision in which the individual puts an end to the mere possibility and identifies himself with the content of his thought in order to exist in it."[14]

With AOP and ASP in mind, we can understand how Kierkegaard tried to develop his concept of subjectivity to distinguish it from both subjective madness ("aberrant inwardness") and nonsense.[15] In subjective madness, a state of relating incorrectly to the object, the object is finite, clearly (objectively?) having nothing to do with spiritual development of the self, yet the person treats it as having infinite importance. In the case of nonsense the situation is similar, except that some internal incoherence disqualifies the object. The proper "fit" of subject with object in subjectivity occurs when the subject is suitably related to the object. Minute subjectivity for things of minute value, absolute subjectivity for that which is of absolute value; hence the proper relationship to God is absolute, involving absolute passion.

With these categories in mind, we can examine the relationship between subjectivity and truth.

Subjectivity and Truth

In a recent article on Kierkegaard's theory of subjectivity, "Thinking Subjectively," Robert Roberts concludes: "If my analysis is right, it should be obvious that the concept of subjectivity is very far from being the foundation for a general epistemology, and almost as far from being a special epistemology for religion and ethics. Its concern is to diagnose and forestall the various ways in which the life of learning can deflect a person from a genuine personal employment of the concepts of morals and of Christian faith."[16] In a paper delivered at a meeting of the American Philosophical Association, Louis Mackey stated that Kierkegaard's concept of subjectivity has no relation to objective truth. It is a noncognitive doctrine, directing us not to an object but to ourselves:

> The way is the truth, and the truth is . . . a life. Portentously enough. For— and we ignore this at our peril—the passage above [*CUP*, p. 182; quoted in chapter 5, below], like everything else in Climacus' text, is a piece of rhetorical exhortation masquerading as discursive presentation. It is a solemn admonition: whatever you believe, remember that your creed has no objective warrant, no *fundamentum in re* save the reality it has in your life. "The passion of infinity is itself the truth" [*CUP*, p. 181]. There is no objective state of affairs by conformity to which our thoughts and words are authenticated. Truth is precisely the venture—the awful risk and the awesome responsibility—that translates objective uncertainty into the decisiveness of infinite passion. Appropriately, Climacus' definition of truth does not direct us to an object, but recalls us to ourselves. ["Subjectivity Is Something or Other"]

I think that these two representatives of the anti-epistemological interpretation of Kierkegaard's theory of subjectivity fail to see the complexity of that theory, or fail to take sufficiently into account that at least three versions of subjectivity with regard to truth can be attributed to Kierkegaard. Both of these scholars, focusing on the reduplicative aspect of subjectivity, fail to note the epistemological aspect. Therefore, I shall outline the three positions on the relationship between subjectivity and knowledge, but, since I have developed some of this material elsewhere, I will not give as detailed an argument as might otherwise be desired.[17]

My thesis is that in Kierkegaard's works, including his private papers, there are at least three views on the relationship of subjectivity to eternal objective truth, or to knowledge of the highest truth. The first view, the reduplicative model of subjectivity or Socratic subjectivity, states that subjectivity has no special epistemological relevance. It is the view adumbrated in the quotations from Roberts and Mackey above; it is also held by Gregory Schufreider, Benjamin Daise, and Paul Holmer.[18] The second view, the necessary-condition model of subjectivity, states that subjectivity is a contributing factor but not a sufficient condition for the acquisition of truth. (This view was held by my teacher, Gregor Malantschuk.)[19] The third view, the Platonic model of subjectivity, states that subjectivity is a sufficient condition for truth. (I have discussed this view elsewhere; Evans seems to be aware of it also.)[20]

Before I discuss these versions, I will give an outline of the arguments for each, and in order to be schematic, I will abbreviate: 'subjective truth' = ST; 'objective truth' = OT; subjective reflection' = SR; 'objective reflection' = OR; 'eternal truth' = ET.

   A. Reduplication Argument for Subjectivity (Socratic Subjectivity)
      1. One may choose either SR or OR regarding ET, but not both, for they are mutually incompatible.
      2. But OR is wholly inappropriate to the goal, ET.
      3. Therefore, we must use SR, which leads to ST.
      4. But ST is eternally removed from ET. ST is merely about how we should live; it doesn't pretend to bring us to ET. We can never have any justification about our metaphysical beliefs, let alone knowledge.
   B. Platonic Argument for Subjectivity
      1. One may choose either SR or OR regarding ET, but not both.
      2. But OR is wholly inappropriate to the goal, ET.
      3. Therefore, we must use SR, which leads to ST.
      4. But ST by itself cannot guarantee ET.
      5. However, *maximal* ST over the right object (metaphysical and ethical propositions) will guarantee ET. Maximal subjectivity is a sufficient condition for attaining the highest truth. No one who is sufficiently subjective can fail to know the truth about metaphysics and ethics.
   C. Auxiliary Argument (Necessary Condition) for Subjectivity
      1. One may choose either SR or OR regarding ET, but not both.
      2. But OR is wholly inappropriate to the goal, ET.
      3. Therefore, we must use SR, which leads to ST.
      4. But ST cannot guarantee ET.
      5. However, there seems to be some connection between ST and attainment of ET. If anything will get us to ET, it will be ST. We can be sure that no one who is not in ST understands the truth about ultimate reality in the least. ST is a necessary, but not sufficient, condition for ET.

All three views agree on the first three premises; disagreement comes on whether there is an object to subjective appropriation. For Mackey, there is no object. The best we can do is construct a "kind of redemption myth." For others, we can never know whether the beliefs we attain in a state of deep subjectivity are true. This is the position of Roberts and Holmer. But all three of these scholars agree on the lack of any epistemological connection between subjectivity and truth: Mackey because there is no 'truth', Roberts and Holmer because it is without guarantee.

To repeat, I have called the position espoused by these scholars (who otherwise disagree about the meaning of Kierkegaard's thought) the 're-duplication model of subjectivity' because the emphasis is on the manner of relating to one's ideals. I have called it 'Socratic', in opposition to the more extravagant 'Platonic' version of subjectivity, because it places the accent on ethical existence—the opposition being suggested by Climacus himself, who wrote: "Socrates concentrates essentially upon accentuating existence, while Plato forgets this and loses himself in speculation."[21] In the Climacus writings and in Kierkegaard's private papers, the accent is usually on the existential, but from time to time there is more than a touch of speculation, pointing toward a doctrine of recollection with implications more far reaching than, and even contrary to, some of the more existential phases of his work.

The third (auxiliary) model is more difficult to locate precisely, but seems to mediate the first two positions, recognizing an epistemological core to the idea of subjectivity but rejecting the more extravagant speculations of the Platonic view as an overliteral reading of Kierkegaard.

These three views seem incompatible. Since one can find evidence for each in the works of Kierkegaard, it would seem that either two of the views are misreadings or that Kierkegaard is inconsistent. Let us examine each view.

Reduplication Model of Subjectivity (Socratic Concept)

When subjectivity is truth, the definition of truth must also include an expression for the antithesis to objectivity, a reminiscence from that parting of the ways, and this expression then also indicates the elasticity of inwardness. Here is such a definition of truth: the objective uncertainty held fast in the appropriation of the most passionate inwardness, is the truth, the highest truth there is for one who exists. There where the way swings off (and where that is cannot be said objectively, for that precisely is the subjectivity) objective knowledge is put in suspension. Objectively then he has only the uncertainty, but it is just this that intensifies the infinite passion of his inwardness. And truth precisely is this venture, to choose the objectively uncertain with the passion of the infinite. [*CUP*, p. 182; my translation]

The emphasis here is on existing, against speculating. Socrates is contrasted with Plato and, more specifically, Hegel, who has no ethics inasmuch as his system annuls existence through a synthesis of all human experience and thought. The Kierkegaardian-Socratic position is that an existential system cannot be formulated by man. "Reality itself is a system—for God; but it cannot be a system for any existing spirit. . . . Existence separates, and holds the various moments of existence discretely apart."[22] The existentialist position does not deny objective truth in the sense that there is a correct explanation to the world, a metaphysical answer to all our questions; it denies that we are in a position to *know* that explanation. Being finite and not infinite (i.e., able to view things *sub specie aeternitatis*), we ought to turn from idle speculation and, with Socrates, devote ourselves to the problems of existence: ethics and religion.

'Truth', then, takes on a new look. It becomes redefined for existing subjects in terms of the way we appropriate our beliefs. The focus is on the relationship, not on specific content. "If only the mode of this relationship is in the truth, the individual is in the truth, even if he should happen to be thus related to what is not true."[23] Climacus illustrates this with his parable of the two worshipers: a believer in the Christian God prays insincerely in church while a pagan worships with the entire passion of the infinite. The former, even though he is praying to the true God, is praying falsely. The latter, even though he is praying to a false god, is worshiping *in truth* the true God.[24]

There is no guarantee that the worshiper will ever realize that his religion is false. Likewise, there is no guarantee that Socrates will ever have a true conception of God, no matter how subjective he becomes. In fact, none of us, as believers, can claim any knowledge about religious belief. This is where faith differs from knowledge. We can only be *maximally sincere* about our beliefs and values. But uncertainty is a necessary condition of our predicament.

The important thing in subjectivity is *appropriation*, the resolution and integration of an idea in one's life. If I understand Kierkegaard correctly, all learning requires decision, the focusing of interest. What he calls 'accidental knowledge' (nonethical-religious knowledge) properly requires a detached attentiveness (an interested impartiality). 'Essential knowledge' (ethical-religious knowledge), because it is more intimately related to one's self, requires more intense and personalized interest, culminating in higher-order decisions; for unless a decision on how I am to live results from subjective contemplation, the process is incomplete. Subjective understanding gives rise to existential decision. "In subjectivity what is important is resolution and choice, the decision to run a risk. This is the absolute decision."[25] "The real action is not the external act, but an internal decision in which the individual puts an end to the mere possibility and identifies himself with the content of his thought in order to exist in it."[26]

Through concentration on the object and willing one's self into conformity with it, one transforms one's self (we have already referred to this as 're-duplication'). One incarnates an idea, one's life becomes the exemplification of the idea, one becomes "himself that which he understands." One may call this personal appropriation of the idea the 'correspondence theory of subjective truth'. Whereas the correspondence theory of *objective* truth states that truth consists in the correspondence of a proposition with a state of affairs, the correspondence theory of *subjective* truth states that truth is a correspondence of a state of affairs (my life) with an idea which it aims to reproduce. 'True' takes on its primitive meaning of 'faithful' ('troth'; in Danish, *Sandhed* has the same double meaning as our word 'truth'). The most notable instance of this interpretation of subjectivity as truth is the conforming of the believer's life unto Christ's.

It is not to be inferred from this type of subjectivity as truth that Kierkegaard—or Climacus, for that matter—is unconcerned about objective truth. Of course, that is desirable. It's simply that it will never be reached and that our task is to live within our lights. We still ought to seek to have as many truths as possible, but it's in the quest that we realize ourselves, not in the attainment. Kierkegaard quotes Lessing approvingly at this point: "If God held all truth in His right hand and in His left the life long pursuit of it, and said to me, 'Choose!', I would deferentially touch His left hand and say, 'Father, give me this! The pure truth is for You alone!'" (*CUP*, p. 97). The point is to exist, to act, to become what one understands, for it is only to the extent that one becomes what one understands that one can be said to understand the object.

We see, then, that this concept of subjectivity has to do with a relationship to one's beliefs. It is not a relationship to facts or true propositions, even though the beliefs may by chance be true. We will always be uncertain; there is no guarantee of objective truth. The very idea of a guarantee would militate against the process of personal development, which only comes through risk in uncertainty, through overcoming doubt where evidence is equally distributed on both sides of an issue, or where evidence is pitted against one's intuitions. In the end, subjective passion and paradox are a mutual fit.

It would seem that subjectivity is neither a necessary nor a sufficient condition for truth, neither in the Hegelian sense of coherent truth nor in the more modest sense of correspondence truth. One never knows when one's belief in religious–ethical matters is true. Or, perhaps more accurately, one can be sure that, in the Hegelian sense, one's beliefs are false, while one can never know whether they are true in the correspondence sense of truth (*adaequatio intellectus et rei*). The subjective person may just as likely be objectively wrong as right about metaphysical–ethical beliefs. One never knows when one is right or believing truly. We may wonder if Kierkegaard meant to embrace such all-encompassing skepticism, but it seems to be the implication of his Socratic concept of subjectivity.

Metaphysical Model of Subjectivity (Platonic Concept)

In Socratic subjectivity, one never knows whether one has a true belief. 'Truth' is defined as sincere faith, passionately becoming conformed to the object of one's faith. In what I call 'Platonic subjectivity', subjectivity seems to be an instrument for arriving at the objective, metaphysical truth. No one who is suitably subjective over an appropriate proposition will fail to have knowledge or a true belief (conviction) with regard to that proposition. This is clearly the case with 'immanent truth', which is not contrary to reason. The individual can introspect or recollect and come to an apprehension of the truth. In this, Kierkegaard clearly accepts Plato's doctrine of recollection for learning first principles.

The evidence points to the fact that Climacus' thought experiment in *Fragments* is more than a thought experiment and that Kierkegaard believes that the doctrine of recollection is a true theory. There is evidence for this in the *Postscript* but the main evidence is in Kierkegaard's private papers, where he comments on what he has done in the Climacus writings and what he means by 'indirect communication.' In his comments on the latter, he clearly embraces the maieutic method as the proper way to elicit truth from people, for everyone really knows the ethical.[27] His comments on the Climacus writings make it clear that he believed all immanent metaphysical truth could be gained through recollection. What has been overlooked by commentators on Kierkegaard's rejection of the proofs in the third chapter of *Fragments* is that it is foolish to seek objectively for what is available, and available only subjectively, through recollection.[28] Socrates knew that God exists, and so can we if we rightly introspect. No leap of faith is needed for knowledge of God.

Kierkegaard wrote in his papers, commenting precisely on this point made in *Fragments*:

> Both [proving and being convinced by an argument for the existence of God] are equally fantastic, for just as no one has ever proved the existence of God, so no one has ever been an atheist, although many have never willed to allow their knowledge of God's existence to get power over their mind. It is the same with immortality. . . . With regard to God's existence, immortality, and all problems of immanence, recollection is valid; it is present in every man, only he is not aware of it; however, this in no way means that his concept is adequate. [*Papers*, V B 40]

And he says, "I do not believe God exists. I know it, but I believe that God existed [the historical]."[29] Proofs are simply redundant and improper objective ways to get to the truth, to metaphysical truth.

Likewise, one can discover ethical truth through properly willing the good. By following one's deepest conscience, one will inevitably be led to do what is objectively right, and at the same time will develop his character toward his ideal or telos:

> In making a choice it is not so much a question of choosing the right as of the energy, the earnestness, the pathos with which one chooses. Thereby the personality is consolidated. Therefore, even if a man were to choose the wrong, he will nevertheless *discover, precisely by reason of the energy with which he chose, that he had chosen the wrong.* For the choice being made with the whole inwardness of his personality, his nature is purified and he himself brought into immediate relation to the eternal Power whose omnipotence interpenetrates the whole of existence. [*E/O,* II:171]

There is, then, something self-corrective about intense subjectivity, so that by a process of elimination false goals and actions are annulled and only the true goal and/or act remains. The process is reminiscent of the promptings of Socrates' divine daimon, who only spoke negatively, thereby leaving the good to stand by elimination of the bad. Right and wrong do not have merely subjective value for Kierkegaard. There is an objective 'good', of which it may be said that he who truly seeks it will become it and, in so becoming, will be put in touch with an eternal power and, as such, will do good. To deeply will the 'good' is to be on the way to becoming good and doing good.

This process of discovering ethically right acts through subjectivity is illustrated in the *Postscript*, where Climacus writes that had Pontius Pilate been sufficiently subjective, he would not have condemned Jesus Christ to be crucified. "Had not Pilate asked objectively what truth is, he would have never condemned Christ to be crucified. Had he asked subjectively, the passion of his inwardness respecting what he had in truth to do, would have prevented him from doing wrong" (*CUP,* p. 206).

The thesis seems to be the converse of Socrates' doctrine that virtue is knowledge: to know the good is automatically to do it whenever the occasion arises. For Kierkegaard, the slogan "Knowledge is virtue" would be more fitting: if a person wills to do the good, he will come to know it. I suspect that a verse from the Gospel of John confirmed this view in Kierkegaard's thought: "If any man's will is to do God's will, he shall know whether the teaching is from God" (John 7:17). Maximal subjectivity seems sufficient to bring one to the truth.

It is hard to be sure exactly how Kierkegaard would have explained this apparent switch from his Socratic version of subjectivity, but I think we get some hints in his writings. He seems to hold the proposition that passionate inquiry will result in not merely right action but true belief or knowledge, "that only he who works gets the bread"[30] and that, in these matters, "truth manifests itself to the ones who love truth."[31] Divine law and order prevails in the world of spirit, so that seekers after truth and righteousness gradually approach their object.[32]

If this is true, it would appear that not only can we be assured of finding immanent truth, we should also be granted revelatory truth. The truly passionate person should finally have truth manifested to him, and—presuming Christianity is true—should come to see that the doctrine of the absolute paradox is the truth. Given a good God, this would seem a reasonable doctrine; but God's ways also are inscrutable. Nevertheless, it would seem that the principle that "truth manifests itself to the ones who love truth" should apply to both immanent and transcendent truth. If we live within our lights, more light will be given.

This seems to me the essence of the stages of existence in Kierkegaard's thought. Each stage represents a preparation for the next, a necessary condition for attaining the higher stage. The stages depict the personal development of the individual, rather than his beliefs, but beliefs cannot be left out. For Kierkegaard, true belief seems connected to a certain type of life, relevant to developing capacities and dispositions which will result in action; for example, witnessing for the truth. But to say that the accent is on the 'existential' aspect of life is not to dismiss the cognitive factor entirely. Beliefs are vital 'action-guides', and true beliefs are a necessary part of realizing the highest good.

One of the puzzling elements of Kierkegaard's work is the way he differentiates 'knowledge' from 'conviction'. 'Knowledge' for him means something self-evident, which cannot seriously be doubted. The truths discovered by recollection are like this; they are self-authenticating: "I know I am free, if I only introspect sufficiently." (If anyone disagrees, it follows that he hasn't introspected sufficiently.) But how is this different from having a 'conviction' that Christ is God incarnate?

Granted, the message may come differently—through direct communication instead of indirect or maieutic communication, as immanent knowledge must. How are these states of mind to be distinguished? How do I know when I know, rather than simply believe absolutely (without doubt)? Isn't my belief in Christ as self-authenticating as my belief in God or free will? If self-authentication works in one case, why not in the other? It may well be that Kierkegaard is committed to saying that both types of propositions (immanent and revelatory) can be known through subjectivity to be true, though revelatory propositions require maximal subjectivity and more grace.

A passage in Kierkegaard's private papers may suggest that something like the above is indeed the case. Here, some years after writing the *Postscript*, he reacted to those who labeled him a subjectivist: "In all that is usually said about Johannes Climacus being purely subjective and so on, people have forgotten . . . that in one of the last sections he shows that the interesting thing is that there is a 'how' which has the property that when it is present the 'what' is also present; and that this is the 'how' of faith. Here quite certainly, we have *inwardness at its maximum proving to be objectivity once again*" (*Papers*, X A 299; my italics).

It would seem, then, that if a person is maximally subjective over some proposition, he can be sure that the proposition is true. That is, maximal subjectivity is a sufficient condition for having metaphysical knowledge, even when it is of the highest kind, centered on the absolute paradox.[33] The believer can know that he has a true belief. All he has to do is recognize that he is in a state of maximal subjectivity. I don't know how anyone would *know* when he is in such a condition, but I suppose it follows that if you're not sure you are in such a state, you're not. But does it follow that if you are sure you are in such a state, you must be?

It would seem, then, that maximal subjectivity is both a necessary and a sufficient condition for arriving at some ethical, metaphysical, and theological truths. It is a necessary condition, for "only he who works gets the bread," and it is also a sufficient condition, for "truth manifests itself to the ones who love truth." Unless someone is searching for it, he will not recognize it when it appears; but if one is properly searching, sooner or later God will reveal it to him. There is the suggestion that this process will go on in the next life, so that such sincere people as Climacus' pagan worshiper will receive the revelation of Christ.[34]

Necessary-Condition Model (Auxiliary Concept)

Midway between the reduplication and the Platonic model is what one may call the 'necessary-condition model' (for want of a more imaginative label). This view denies or withholds judgment on the proposition that subjective earnestness is sufficient for eternal truth. It states that if the truth is attainable, it must be attained through subjectivity and not objectivity. Subjectivity doesn't guarantee truth (ET), but is a necessary condition for it. "Only he who works gets the bread," says Kierkegaard, but that doesn't imply that *all* who work will get the bread. The person who works through the stages toward the telos is closer to ultimate truth than the pleasure-seeking aesthete and the self-satisfied egoist. And yet, if the idea of sin is taken seriously, it may be truly said that *all* are infinitely far from the highest truth ("subjectivity is untruth").[35] And yet it may be the case that some metaphysical truth may be attained through subjectivity, for example, God's existence and the truth of immortality, truths of immanence, though there is no guarantee that everyone who is subjective will receive a clear understanding of these truths. There is a difference between immanent metaphysical truths and the absolute truth, which is transcendent. But, even regarding this highest truth, it may be said that the subjectivist is closer to it, in the sense that he is closer to the place where the revelation will be forthcoming.

On the other hand, it may simply be that knowledge of the truth is not that important in Kierkegaard's eyes. What really is important is a "quality of life," living within one's light. It is the way, the striving, that is important, not results, though the striver, the sensitive person who is attentive, is incidentally more likely to have more true beliefs and, perhaps, even knowledge in matters that count than the uninvolved objectivist. However, we ought not put the accent on knowledge, but on subjectivity. The pagan worshiper described by Climacus is in maximal subjectivity, 'in truth', but he still has a false belief: that his idol is God. Apparently, Climacus wants to say that subjectivity is not a sufficient condition for knowledge or true belief.

However, the issue is not decided, for there may be only a time lag between the state of maximal subjectivity and the apprehension of truth. A revelation may be just around the corner, or it may come after death. In the *Fragments*, Climacus suggests that those who lived within their lights during this life will be given the "good news" after death and allowed to make a choice.[36] If this is the case, it would seem that subjectivity is more than merely a necessary condition for knowledge. The thesis that subjectivity is merely a necessary condition, but not a sufficient one, though initially plausible, seems inadequate. The connection between subjectivity and the truth seems much stronger in Kierkegaard.

Conclusion

It seems we have three incompatible theses about the relation of subjectivity to objective, eternal truth in the works of Kierkegaard. Subjectivity is, or is not, a *necessary* condition for the highest truth; it is, or is not, a *sufficient* condition for such truth. The simplest explanation for this discrepancy is to concede that Kierkegaard was not terribly interested in logical connections. He was concerned to promote the value of subjectivity, and as he concentrated on it, he sometimes made claims which are inconsistent with what he said elsewhere. If he had been asked which theory was his, he might have replied that all of these theories were merely possibilities. He wasn't interested in a detailed theory—only in an imaginative set of descriptions to awaken us to the need for looking inward and acting on the basis of that vision. In this sense, writers such as Mackey are correct to emphasize the poetic tone of what may mistakenly be taken for straightforward philosophy.

I think there is a good bit of truth to this interpretation of Kierkegaard. The religious-poetic motif is very strong in his work, and it is helpful to view his theories as 'thought projects'. However, another side to his work (a side we noticed in the second chapter) reveals a striving for consistency and comprehensiveness, an attempt to map reality for the Christian. There is the attempt to unveil a Christian epistemology.[37] Paul Sponheim was one of the first to note the tension between these two motifs in Kierkegaard's works: the motif of dispersion, the breaking up of all system and cohesion, and the motif of synthesis, regathering the pieces into a comprehensive Christian philosophy.[38] Sponheim's insight remains in spite of his critics. Kierkegaard is thoroughly dialectical; the conflicting movements compete at every point.

An illustration of this tension as applied to our topic, subjectivity and epistemology, is in *Training in Christianity* (1850), written four years after the *Concluding Unscientific Postscript*, the locus of most of the debate on subjectivity. In a seven-page section (pp. 198–205), Anti-Climacus (the ideal Christian, according to Kierkegaard) attempts something of a reconciliation of the reduplication and cognitive models of subjectivity. Anti-Climacus tells us that, essentially, Christ is the truth, and knowing the truth is to know a person; it is knowledge by acquaintance, which must be reduplicated in one's life. "Christ is the truth in such a sense that to be the truth is the only explanation of what truth is." So defined, the truth is not propositional; it is not "a sum of sentences, not a definition of concepts, etc., but a life."

> Truth in its very being is not the duplication of being in terms of thought, which yields only the thought of being. . . . No, truth in its very being is the reduplication in me, in thee, in him, so that my, that thy, that his life, approximately, in the striving to attain it expresses the truth, so that my, that thy, that his life, approximately, in the striving to attain it, is the very being of truth, is a *life*, as the truth was in Christ, for He was the truth. And hence, Christianly understood, the truth consists not in knowing the truth but in being the truth. [*TC*, p. 201]

Anti-Climacus contrasts the sort of truth he is looking for with that which involves results. When truth is defined as a way, one is never finished producing it. When it is defined as a result, one can use it, but there is nothing further to be done with it *qua* truth. He illustrates this with the invention of gunpowder, which probably involved great struggle and mental effort for the inventor, but once he had produced the formula, it was easy for anyone to copy him. Likewise the results of a scholar whose entire life has been spent on research; once he has established his hypothesis, it is a given, something his disciple takes for granted and, *qua* researcher, goes beyond the teacher. But in the realm of the spirit, it is not thus. Each generation, each individual, must begin anew and accomplish the task of self-knowledge and appropriation of a form of life. Truth is a reduplication, brought about through acquaintance. It is an original effort for everyone who seeks truth.

However, Anti-Climacus does not leave the matter in a noncognitivist state. He says that although truth is first to be defined as 'the way', it becomes knowledge afterward. Commenting on Christ's silence before Pilate when he was asked "What is truth?" Anti-Climacus says:

> Not as though Christ did not know what the truth is; but when one is the truth, and when the requirement is to be the truth, this thing of knowing the truth is untruth. For knowing the truth is something which follows as a matter of course from being the truth, and not conversely; and precisely for this reason it becomes the truth, or when knowing the truth is separated from being the truth, or when knowing the truth is treated as one and the same thing as being the truth, since the true relation is the converse of this: to be the truth is one and the same thing as knowing the truth, and Christ would never have known the truth in case He had not been the truth. Indeed, properly speaking, one cannot know the truth; for if one knows the truth, he must know that to be the truth is the truth, and so in his knowledge of the truth, he knows that this thing of knowing the truth is an untruth. . . . That is to say, knowledge has a relation to truth, but with that I am (untruly) outside of myself; within me (that is, when I am truly within myself, not untruly outside myself) truth is, if it is at all, a being, a life. Therefore it is said, "This is life eternal, to know the only true God and Him whom He hath sent," the Truth. That is to say, only then do I truly know the truth when it becomes a life in me. [*TC*, p. 201]

If I understand this difficult passage correctly, Anti-Climacus says that we can approximate the truth (as a process) and, in so doing, come to know the truth cognitively, but we can never attain the perfection of Christ and so never become the truth, nor know it perfectly. Nor can we go from knowledge to being. The order of priorities is clear: being, then knowing. Still there is a necessary connection between subjectivity and knowledge. To the extent that I become what I know, to that extent do I come to know the truth. "For knowing the truth is something which follows as a matter of course from being the truth."

In less extravagant prose, we might say that the only criterion for testing this special kind of truth claim is to try to live by it. In living by this world view, one will discover its truth value. If we live by the light we have, we will be given more light so as to understand that light more fully. In sum, subjectivity seems to be both a necessary and sufficient condition for eternal truth, but because of the process nature of reality, we will never have a complete understanding of the truth.

Another passage in the religious writings of Kierkegaard confirms this interpretation, linking subjectivity with epistemology:

> But verily, as little as God lets a species of fish remain in a particular sea unless the plant also grows there which is its nutriment, just so little shall God leave in ignorance of what he must believe the man who was truly concerned. That is to say, the need brings with it the nutriment, the thing sought is in the seeking which seeks it; faith, in the concern at not having faith; love, in the concern at not loving. The need brings with it the nutriment, not *by itself*, as though it produced the nutriment, but by virtue of God's ordinance which joins together the need and the nutriment, so that when one says that this is so, he must add, "as certainly as God exists"; for if God did not exist, it would not be so. [*CD*, p. 248]

In the end, we have affirmation of an epistemological theodicy. Subjectivity, by the providence of God, leads to knowledge of the highest truth. Subjectivity is the means by which God brings us to the *summum bonum*, which includes both a vision (knowledge) of the good and the true as well as rapturous experience of it. But we are getting ahead of ourselves, for the *summum bonum* is not to be experienced in this life, except proleptically. In this life, the proper task is to struggle subjectively in faith.

We now turn to an examination of the meaning and role of faith in Kierkegaard's thought.

4

FAITH

and the

STAGES

of

EXISTENCE

On the whole question of faith (*Tro*) . . . I venture to declare that in my writings there have been advanced precise dialectical qualifications on particular points which hitherto have not been known. [*Papers,* X² A 597]

Kierkegaard, passionately concerned with faith, looked back on his authorship in 1850 and wrote that he believed he had made a substantial contribution toward analysis of the concept. In Chapters 4, 5, and 6 we shall examine in detail Kierkegaard's treatment of faith (*Tro*) in order to decide what that contribution amounts to and whether it deserves to be seen as a significant contribution to our understanding. First, I shall list the main ways in which the concept(s) is used in Kierkegaard's works; I shall then examine them within the contexts in which they appear.

In this chapter, I shall examine the concept as it unfolds within the stages of existence. In chapter 5 I will examine the concept as it is developed in *Philosophical Fragments* and I will offer a critique of the volitional aspect attached to the concept. In chapter 6 I will examine the concept as it appears in *Concluding Unscientific Postscript*, and I will offer summation criticisms of Climacus' use.

First, we must point out that the Danish word for 'faith' is the same word used for 'belief': *Tro*. One must be especially attentive to the context, therefore, to distinguish the proper use. Fortunately, the Danes have a word for 'weak belief' or 'opinion', *Mening*, which is used by Kierkegaard to signify ordinary, common–sense believing. Accepting *Mening* as a doxastic term (a technical term for study of the concept 'belief'), I have located seven main concepts of 'belief/faith' in the works of Kierkegaard:

1. Aesthetic faith: immediate, animal intuition or primitive trust. This is not faith proper, but the stuff from which genuine faith grows.

2. Ethical faith: commitment to the moral law and the ethical way of life in general. This type is more properly described as 'faithfulness' or 'commitment'.

3. Religious or existential faith: a second immediacy, an attitude of passionately holding onto its object in spite of apparent evidence. This type of faith is immediate like aesthetic faith—spontaneous—but it appears after a certain sophistication or maturation has been attained in the ethical-rational realm; so it is a *second* immediacy. It is characterized as a leap into the unknown or swimming over 70,000 fathoms of water.

4. Ordinary belief (usually *Mening* is used): commonsense, propositional belief. Kierkegaard takes this type of belief for granted—says little about it and is not very interested in it. He is scornful of those who equate it with the highest type of faith. A good translation of *Mening* is 'opinion'.

5. Faith as an organ for apprehending the past or history: the function or process of making the past present (to use Kierkegaard's word, "contemporary"). The believer, through resolution of the will, appropriates the testimony of others for his own purposes. It is volitional, acquisitional.

6. Salvific faith: a combination of miraculous grace and effort of the will (discussed in *Fragments*). Grace must be present as the condition enabling the subject to believe, but the will must decide whether it will believe.

7. Faith as hope: a modified form of religious faith, found in Kierkegaard's later papers, which suggests living *as if* an important proposition were true—of risking one's life on behalf of an idea, even though one's mind is not convinced of the truth of the idea.

These are the main types of belief/faith that we find in Kierkegaard's works. Essentially, Kierkegaard views *Tro* as a species of subjectivity, that deep, passionately introspective striving which we discussed in the preceding chapter. The rest of this chapter will analyze these concepts and the role they play in Kierkegaard's Christian philosophy.

Faith in the Stages of Existence

For Kierkegaard, concepts have life; they also die. They have birth, grow through levels of progressive unfoldings of meaning, and finally die—that is, enter a zone where they no longer play a role, but give themselves over to new concepts. Also, they can be transformed.

In *Works of Love*, Kierkegaard explains that all spiritual language is essentially metaphorical (overførte).[1] Man is spirit from birth, but becomes self-consciously spirit only much later, after he has experienced a sensual–psychical existence, has suffered and been forced to make crucial decisions. When finally he becomes aware of himself as spirit, he does not cast out the intervening sensual–psychical sector of his life, but subsumes (*aufheben*) it by transferring (*overførte*) its experience into the realm of spirit. In the process, he also transfers the secular meaning of words to the realm of the spirit, so that a "leap" is the signal of spiritual becoming, "repetition" the symbol for the eternal's encounter with existence, and "paradox" the sign of that divine contradiction which is the proper object of faith.

The same transformation characterizes *Tro*. It is, first of all, a secular/psychical word with a secular/psychical history, and is converted by regeneration of the spirit to serve a peculiarly Christian function. Kierkegaard describes development of the concept of *Tro* within the stages of existence. We outlined these stages in chapter 1, and what follows takes place within the structure described in that chapter.

In the first stage of existence, the aesthetic, faith is defined as 'intuition'. It is an immediate instinct, a sort of sixth sense with which we are born—animal faith. It is not faith proper, but a sort of embryonic trust, a protofaith, the stuff from which faith may develop. Kierkegaard's point of departure for aesthetic faith is Hegel's comments on the religious thinker, Jacobi.

In his attack on Jacobi's definition of faith as intuitive knowledge, Hegel devalued such a concept as "nothing but the shapeless abstract of immediate knowledge." Such a quality is to be identified with "the heart's revelation, the truths implanted by nature, and also, in particular, healthy reason or common sense."[2] Such immediate knowledge is unreflective and must finally be subsumed (*aufgehoben*) by a process of mediation under a higher form of knowledge.

When Hegel came to the Christian idea of faith, he distinguished it from this intuitive knowledge. Christianity has a definite content; it is not formless and amorphous, like intuition. Christianity is the highest of all non-philosophical forms of truth. Its content is semirational; it is true to a certain degree. However, because Christianity, *qua* religion, is not absolutely rational, it is philosophy's job to bring out the latent absolute truth, which it does by separating the idea from the encumbering mythical forms. Christianity must finally be subsumed under the higher unity of speculative philosophy. "Faith already has the true content. What is still lacking in it is the form of thought."[3]

Kierkegaard emphatically rejects Hegel's diagnosis of Christian faith, but he agrees with Hegel that Jacobi's idea of faith is deficient for full understanding of the concept. However, Kierkegaard takes Jacobi's idea to signify a protofaith, an animal instinct, which all men possess simply as members of the higher animal species.[4] The undeveloped human being, not yet a full person, together with other higher forms of life possesses this trait.

Kierkegaard relegates the entire Romantic movement's notion of faith to this primitive dimension, as well as Schleiermacher's treatment. Schleiermacher described faith as a spontaneous feeling of dependence upon an ultimate source within the universe; it is the vital *fluidum*, "the spiritual atmosphere we breathe in."[5] There is this characteristic in man, Kierkegaard agrees, but it is not faith in the proper sense.

An illustration of aesthetic faith is given in *Either/Or,* where the aesthete answers the charge of the ethicist that he does not possess faith:

> What! Am I supposed not to have faith? Why, I believe that in the inmost depths of the stillness of the forest, where the trees are reflected in the dark water, in its mysterious darkness, where even at midday there is twilight, there lives a being, a nymph, a maiden; I believe that she is more beautiful than anyone can conceive, I believe that in the morning she plaits garlands, that at midday she bathes in the cool water. . . . I believe that I should be happy, the only man deserving to be so called, if I could catch her; I believe that in my soul there is a longing to search the whole world, I believe that I should be happy if that longing were satisfied; I believe that after all there is some meaning in the world if only I could find it—do not say, then, that I am not strong in faith. [*E/O*, II:204]

By the standards of mature faith, aesthetic faith is whimsical, imaginatively rich, but frivolous, lacking in seriousness, in depth; a mere visage of reality. It is play, which may anticipate reality, but it lacks the necessary seriousness. "Faith is . . . not an aesthetic emotion but something far higher, precisely because it has resignation as its presupposition; it is not an immediate instinct of the heart, but it is the paradox of life and existence."[6] Even as one might argue that a fetus or infant is not yet truly a person, but a potential person, Kierkegaard would say that aesthetic faith is not faith but the potential for faith.

The modern reader of Kierkegaard may be puzzled by his scant attention to the relation between ordinary belief and evidence. Ordinarily, we speak of a belief being justified if there is good evidence for it; conversely, a belief is unjustified if it is not based on evidence. This type of common-sense belief Kierkegaard, with many of his Idealist contemporaries, relegated to a very low level. Generally, 'evidence' in this usage is taken to mean *empirical* evidence. Kierkegaard, with his Germanic contemporaries, believed intuition, pure reason, or *synthetic a priori* knowledge is available to man. Compared with this, ordinary empirical knowledge is simply taken for granted, as relatively uninteresting. Kierkegaard had little affection for the man who cautiously proportions his beliefs to empirical evidence, to probability.

This sort of belief is placed within the class of aesthetic faith, a more refined type than that of the simple aesthete, but of the same quality. However, Kierkegaard sometimes discussed this type of common-sense individual as 'neither/nor', neither aesthetic nor ethical-religious: "I have not [discussed duty] with the wild alarm which sometimes is displayed by men in whom *prosaic common sense* has first annihilated the feelings of immediacy and who, then in their old age have betaken themselves to duty, men who in their blindness cannot express strongly enough their scorn of the purely natural" (*E/O*, II:155; my italics). Kierkegaard says: "They do not live aesthetically, but neither has the ethical manifested itself in its entirety, so they have not exactly rejected it either."[7]

In *Fear and Trembling*, Johannes de Silentio berates these cautious calculators. "These slaves of paltriness, the frogs in life's swamp, will naturally cry out [against a love which has no likelihood of succeeding], 'Such love is foolishness.'"[8] Prudentialist faith, the trust in probabilities, is inadequate because it cuts man off from the deep springs of action. Such faith may be appropriate to the unimportant things of life, which may be important in routine experiences but are inadequate for our deepest strivings; and we must never let prudential faith encroach where it does not belong. It is one thing to learn not to put your hand in a fire in the physical world; it is another thing to risk putting your life on fire in the spiritual realm.

Perhaps we can categorize this probabilistic type of believing as ordinary common-sense believing, what Climacus later calls 'opinion' (*Mening*). Kierkegaard, who says little about it, takes it for granted, but is anxious that it not dominate the spirit of man. It is the spirit of science, but not religion or even morality. Kierkegaard's ethics have little room for prudence or the shrewd calculations of consequentialism, and no one could be further from the spirit of Utilitarianism. Ideals, not consequences—except consequences brought about by God's power—concerned him. When one follows ideals and reasons deductively from them, empirical evidence about the likely consequences of an act is of secondary importance.

This brings us to an account of 'ethical faith', or faith as it develops within the stages to the ethical level of existence. The ethical stage is characterized by acceptance of universal moral principles, rules that are binding on all persons everywhere, that have their source in God, the supreme lawgiver.

Kierkegaard's understanding of ethics is deontological, being based broadly on natural law, and, as such, ethical living is rule-governed living, a life of reason, of justifying actions by principles which either are self-evident or, in turn, are justified by more self-evident reasons. In spite of his reputation for leaps into the "absurd," Kierkegaard never disowned a generally rational view of morality; he simply recognized its inability to motivate. In most cases our duty is clear, if we but pay attention; it is another matter whether we will *do* our duty. The will is finally decisive. But he recognizes a need to justify oneself within the social domain. Within the ethical stage, then, faith manifests itself as a commitment to this rationalization or justificatory process, centered on the moral law. "The ethical thesis that every man has a calling is the expression for the fact that there is a rational order of things in which every man, if he will, fills his place in such a way that he expresses at once the universal-human and the individual" (*E/O*, II:297).

According to Kierkegaard's ethical pseudonym, it is obvious to every clear-headed person that there is a rational, moral order, and every person has a place, a calling, in it. He is to be the particularized universal, the combination of accidental and universal. That is, the universal (requirement) commands him abstractly; for example, "Thou shalt marry," "Thou shalt obey the laws of the State"; but it does not tell him how he is to fulfill these requirements. He is free to marry whom he will or become a member of whatever State he chooses.[9]

There may be conflicts of duty within this moral scheme of things, but they are only apparent, readily resolvable in virtue of the fact that duties are arranged hierarchically in logical order. For instance, there may be a conflict between one's duty to his family and his duty to the State (e.g., Brutus' situation with his traitorous sons). This is resolved by noting that the institution of the family is "logically" dependent on the institutions of the State, the ultimate expression of the "concrete ethical" (following Hegel). Without the State, the family has no value.

An exception to the universal—a person whose actions are based on maxims which do not fall within this moral scheme—is an unjustified anomaly. He stands outside the security, protection, and benevolence of the rational universe. Since God has established the moral order in which universal duties have their necessary place, to violate one of these duties is to sin against God.[10] The only way of finding forgiveness is by recognizing one's sin and repenting oneself back into the universal. Outside the universal there is no justification, because justification implies appeal to the universal, which is the one thing the exception cannot do.

Kierkegaard substantially accepts this Hegelian view of the moral order. His dilemma, however, is that it sometimes happens that a person hears another command of God which contradicts a command in the universal moral order—not simply breaking one moral rule for the sake of a higher one (as Brutus), but of rejecting the moral order altogether. It is a case of suspending the moral order for the sake of a higher order. That is, a direct mandate from the source and author of the moral order takes precedence over the moral order.

This state of feeling oneself an individual, standing above the universal in a personal relation to God, is what Kierkegaard calls the *'religious stage'* of existence. His primary example of someone who lives this way is Abraham, who believed himself called by God to sacrifice his son, thus violating the universals regarding murder and protection of one's offspring. Kierkegaard, of course, felt himself to be an exception, called to reject the universal of marriage and the universal of having a socially approved vocation. It is to this lonely state of exception that faith seems particularly suited.

One might argue that, on Kierkegaard's terms, our apprehension of the universals involves not faith but knowledge. The moral order is intuitively and rationally ascertainable; its edicts are self-evident truths. In the ethical stage, faith is defined as obedience to these truths, but the situation is different in the religious stage. The (religious) moral 'truth' (the command to be an exception) is not known. It cannot be deduced rationally from other premises, nor is its content *a priori* knowledge. There is no way to justify its content because the process of justification appeals to the very universals which are rejected or suspended.

Processes of reason fail here, and yet the individual feels intense conviction about what he ought to do. He cannot do otherwise, and yet he questions the morality and sanity of his action. Hence the fear and trembling. Faith, in this sense, is risking one's whole being on a course of action without the slightest objective warrant. It is the very opposite course of the prudentialist, who tailors his beliefs, including his beliefs about right actions, according to testable evidence. Kierkegaard's "knight of faith" seems a reckless gambler, with almost limitless trust in the reliability of intuitions.

In dialectical terms, aesthetic immediate faith is abrogated by both resignation and ethical faith, and then restored in a higher form (a second immediacy), in the religious stage, by virtue of the absurd.[11] In this mediated form, faith is to be understood as holding a conviction without sufficient evidence—even *against* what would normally count as good evidence. It hopes for its object after (humanly speaking) having resigned itself forever from obtaining it. Yet 'hope' is too weak a word, for faith conquers the indecision of doubt and has a positive attitude of expectancy.

This is the faith of Abraham, who was willing to sacrifice his son, Isaac, to prove his love to God, believing all the while that Isaac would somehow be given to him again. This is the faith Kierkegaard strove to emulate when he believed, against all reasonable evidence, that he would be once more united with his beloved, Regina. This sort of faith is not merely immediate intuition or instinct (as in the aesthetic stage); it is a reflected, second intuition.

The process is as follows. First, there is the naive, immediate belief, for example, about the future. Second, one reflects on the possibility of that state of affairs occurring and realizes that the probability is very low, or even zero. Third, one chooses that belief in spite of the evidence. One believes in the same thing as in the aesthetic stage, only now it is after one has reflected and resigned oneself to never attaining one's object. It is this doubly reflected belief over an issue of existential import that Johannes de Silentio calls 'proper faith'. A distinctly religious concept, it implies a 'God relationship', for while, humanly speaking, such-and-such may be impossible or improbable, with God all things are possible.[12] "By faith Abraham went out from the land of his fathers and became a sojourner in the land of promise. He left one thing behind, took one thing with him. He left his earthly understanding behind and took faith with him. . . . It is great to give up one's wish, but it is greater to hold it fast after having given it up, it is great to grasp the eternal, but it is greater to hold fast to the temporal after having given it up" (FT, pp. 31f.).

Kierkegaard's point is that the God relationship is unique, unlike any other relationship. It involves its own standards, which must be judged irrational—even immoral—by human standards. I will examine this claim at the end of the chapter; in his view, however, because of the deep mystery of the self and its essential freedom, our intuitions are useful here in a way they are not in other areas.

In ethics, intuitions may give us knowledge, but a knowledge which everyone has. But religious intuition is a conviction the individual shares by himself, which he cannot communicate, which sets him off from the normal affairs of life. Faith is an infinite risk in which one exists in fear and trembling. We see now why Kierkegaard calls this type of faith 'second immediacy': it resembles the intuitive immediacy of the aesthete, but it is reflective, fully aware of its rejection of normal standards of rationality. Faith sees that its object is improbable or impossible, whereas the aesthete has not got that far; and yet the believer believes by virtue of the absurd. He reflects on the absurdity of the proposition, realizes it is "incredible," judged by ordinary standards, but perseveres, and somehow, through an act of will, believes it. (I will say more about volitionalism in the next chapter.)

The final stage of faith is within the Christian religious sphere of existence. Essentially, it is like religious faith, only the object is unique, the 'Paradox', and grace is necessary for the individual to experience this sort of faith. However, we must wait until we examine the concept of faith in the Climacus writings before we can be satisfied with our understanding of this highest expression of the concept (which we will do in the next chapter).

It remains for us to evaluate Kierkegaard's analysis of faith through the stages up to this point. We see the heavily Hegelian coloration of his treatment, the dialectical neatness that somehow seems contrived: immediacy—the annulment of immediacy in ethical resignation—the synthesis of the process in a second, postreflective immediacy, the religious expression of faith. However, this was the thought form of the times, and the analysis should not be dismissed because of the unnaturalness of the expressions. There is also a tendency for Kierkegaard to treat concepts as things rather than as abstract characterizations of types of functions and experiences. Faith and love (two of his favorite concepts) take on an almost Platonic dimension, become substances in his work. However, I think there is something phenomenologically on target in his analysis.

We feel there is something deep within us that is transcendental, the source of free actions. This 'essential self' (I cannot find a better phrase for it, unless we use 'soul') cannot be reduced to physicalist descriptions without significant loss of meaning. There seems to be something mysterious within us which both strives for some obscure telos and is the basis for choices that would bring us to that telos. Faith is a composite of believing intuitively when there is insufficient evidence and of trusting in or commiting the self to the conclusions of its judgments.

Whether these rather intuitive beliefs can hold up to rigorous analysis is a question for philosophy of mind to deal with. In the next chapter we will take a closer look at some of the inherent problems, but I want to end this chapter with a different criticism—whether Kierkegaard is correct in characterizing the faith of Abraham as irrational and whether his own analysis of faith is correctly characterized as irrational. I also want to question his notion of ethics and universality.

As we have noted, Kierkegaard views the highest (and lowest) types of faith as going beyond and against the canons of rationality. Abraham, the knight of faith, acted "in virtue of the absurd," against normal standards of reasonable conduct. In the *Papers*, Kierkegaard speaks of this type of faith as "divine madness."[13] Abraham "left his earthly understanding behind and took faith with him."[14] "Faith is the paradox that the particular is higher than the universal."[15] Nevertheless, all of Kierkegaard's assurances that this type of religious faith is above and against reason seem to me dubious.

It seems that Kierkegaard was laboring under an unduly rigid understanding of a universal, as an objective absolute of the most general sort: any judgment can be universal as long as it has universal application. For example, the principle "Always tell the truth" is no more universal than the principle "Always tell the truth, except when a lie can prevent enormous suffering"—though the first is more general than the second. Kierkegaard, like his mentor Kant, seems to have missed this distinction. He seems to have assumed that the most general judgment is automatically the universal. This was perhaps due to the fact that he believed that moral law is a system of simple, synthetic *a priori* truths. In a nonconflicting hierarchical system, simple absolutes work better than complicated principles.

Applying this criticism to Kierkegaard's interpretation of Abraham, we may question whether his rendition is accurate. The reader will recall the story: God told Abraham to go to Mount Moriah and sacrifice his son, Isaac, to prove his love for God, and Abraham proceeded to carry out the command; but at the last moment an angel stopped him, showing him a ram in the thicket to be used for the offering. This has usually been taken as the height of religious faith: believing God where it really affects one's deepest earthly commitments; and is taken to prove that faith is irrational: believing against all standards of rationality.

Many Old Testament authorities simply dismiss the literalness of the story and maintain that it must be read in the context of Mideastern child sacrifice. The story provides pictorial grounds for breaking with custom, but, even leaving this plausible explanation aside, we might contend that some sense can be given to the episode. Seen in a broader context of Abraham's life, one might make a case that even in this citadel of the incommensurabilist, the Bible exhibits respect for rationality.

To make this point, let us imagine that the philosopher W. V. Quine happened to be strolling along the ridge of Mount Moriah (perhaps looking for gavagai) when Abraham was tying up Isaac and aiming the knife at his breast. Quine, a good friend of Abraham, shouts to him to stop, but Abraham takes no notice and proceeds with his task. Quine, of course, does not have eyes to see the angel who appears to Abraham, but he sees Abraham untie Isaac and slay the ram instead, and mistakenly thinks he has saved Isaac's life. Some years later Quine questions his old friend Abraham about this.

Quine: Abraham, there is, as you must be aware, one thing I have always wanted to ask you. Whatever inspired you to try to kill Isaac on Mount Moriah that day so long ago? I thought you were mad, clear out of your mind.

Abraham: God commanded me to sacrifice my son. It was a case of testing my devotion to Him. I wrestled with the idea for a long time. I wondered whether I was losing my mind. But finally I felt I simply had to do it—in spite of the unthinkableness of the deed.

Quine: But how did you know that God told you that? How do you know it wasn't Satan, or simply your imagination?

Abraham: I didn't *know* it was God who commanded me—and I still don't know whether I was right to do what I did. I simply believed—and still do— that God spoke to me.

Quine: But surely you must have some grounds for such a strange belief. Why did you—and do you still—believe that it was God's voice you heard?

Abraham: I heard a voice. It was the same voice (or so I believed) that commanded me years before to leave my country, my kindred, and my father's house and venture forth into the unknown. It was the same voice that promised me that I would prosper. I hearkened, and though the evidence seemed weak, the promise was fulfilled. It was the same voice that promised me a son in my old age and Sarah's old age, when childbearing was thought to be impossible. Yet it happened. My trust was vindicated.

My whole existence has been predicated on the reality of that voice. I became an exception by hearkening unto it the first time, and I have never regretted it. The tone of this last call was similar to the other calls; the voice was unmistakable. To deny its authenticity would be to deny the authenticity of the others; I should be admitting that my whole life has been founded on an illusion. But I don't believe it has, and I prefer to take the risk of obeying what I take to be the voice of God, and disobey certain social norms, than obey the norms and miss the possibility of any absolute relation to the Absolute. What's more, I'm ready to recommend that all men who feel so called by a higher power do exactly as I have done.

It seems to me that even if we accept at face value the story of Abraham's offering up his son, we can give it an interpretation that is not inconsistent with a rational account. Abraham has had inductive evidence that following the voice is the best way to live; so we can generalize the principle on which he acted: If one acts on a type of intuition (I) in an area of experience (E) over a period of time (t) and with remarkable success, and no other information is relevant or overriding, one can be said to have good reason for following that intuition (I_n—an instance of type I) the next time it presents itself in an E-type situation. Given the cultural context of Abraham's life, his actions seem amenable to a rationalist account.

If the reader objects that I am supposing a standard of induction to be imposed on our intuitions, I plead guilty to the charge. Kierkegaard can respond that sometimes we choose that which is counterinductive, and that that is the point of the Abraham story—his version, not mine. I admit this is possible. The difference between us is that it is difficult for me to make any sense or see any virtue in going against all that experience has taught us; but this does not seem difficult for Kierkegaard to envisage. The source of action is not in experience but in the depths of a mysterious self which has purposes of its own.

5

'FAITH'

in

PHILOSOPHICAL

FRAGMENTS

The Climacus Writings

Our analysis in this and the next chapter will center on two pseudonymous works of Kierkegaard: *Philosophical Fragments* (1844) in this chapter and *Concluding Unscientific Postscript to the Philosophical Fragments* (1846) in chapter 6. Kierkegaard published these works under the name of Johannes Climacus, a seventh-century monk who wrote the *Scala Paradisi* (Ladder of divine ascent). The pseudonym—literally, John the Climber—suggests the theme of the books: the quest for eternal happiness, the striving for that life and truth which transcend the world. The books may be seen as examinations of the various 'ladders' men have used in their attempt to ascend to this higher realm: the Socratic, Hegelian, Christian, and so forth. In his *Papers*, Kierkegaard speaks of Hegel as a sort of "Johannes Climacus, who did not, like the giants, storm heaven by setting mountain upon mountain but entered by means of his syllogisms."[1] Climacus thinks he can show this 'ladder' is too short for the ascent.

Kierkegaard began one other work in the name of Johannes Climacus, *Johannes Climacus or De omnibus dubitandum est* (1842), in which he depicts a young man (himself, no doubt) trying to doubt all—and failing. (This work is probably a satire on his teacher, Professor H. L. Martensen.) One of the conclusions of the young Johannes is that if his teacher has taught him to doubt everything, then he must certainly doubt the words of his teacher and everything he utters, including the statement about universal doubt. The work was never completed, and although it contains some fascinating ideas, it is not central to our study.

Both of the works under discussion are 'thought experiments', written not so much as offering the last word in orthodox theology as helping the reader see the inherent problems more clearly. The central problem is the individual's relationship to Christianity:

> To put it as simply as possible, using myself by way of illustration: I, Johannes Climacus, born in this city and now thirty years old, a common ordinary human being like most people, assume that there awaits me a highest good, an eternal happiness, in the same sense that such a good awaits a servant-girl or a professor. I have heard that Christianity proposes itself as a condition for the acquirement of this good, and now I ask how I may establish a proper relationship to this doctrine. [*CUP*, p. 19]

Johannes Climacus already assumes (for the thought experiment, at least) that Christianity is possibly objectively true. He has heard that there awaits every individual the possibility of an eternal happiness, and Christianity claims to be the sufficient condition for attaining this highest good. That is, if the individual becomes a Christian, he acquires the promise of eternal happiness. Climacus' question is simply, "How do I join up?" However, in spite of this desire for eternal happiness, even at the end of these works Climacus seems no nearer to becoming a Christian. The leap of faith is indefinitely postponed.

Johannes is not a Christian philosopher, but a humorist or a religious person with humor as his incognito.[2] He does not make the leap of faith necessary to become a Christian, but "he is completely taken up with the thought how difficult it must be to be a Christian." His purpose is to understand how difficult it is "for every man to relinquish his understanding and his thinking, to keep his soul fixed upon the absurd."[3]

Climacus, then, is a humorist; humor for Kierkegaard is the perception of incompatible opposites that are juxtaposed; and a humorist is one who has an eye for the 'incommensurable' in life.[4] In a religious sense, 'humor' is the insight that God is wholly other, and if His truth is to break into the sphere of human activity, it will surely appear different from our finite expectation of it. That is, because divine reason is disjunctive with human reason, it appears to man ridiculous, absurd. In this sense, 'humor' signifies the attitude for the divine–human encounter. It is not offended by the apparent absurdity of a union between two absolutely different beings, but judges it is altogether natural that divine truth should appear bizarre to us.

In Climacus' division of life spheres, the religious-humor life style is the penultimate sphere, just preceding the Christian-religious sphere.[5] In this penultimate sphere, the person is no longer surprised or offended (as one is in the ethical and religious spheres) by the paradox of the Incarnation, the juxtaposing of the temporal and the eternal. But he hesitates to make the leap into Christian faith.

There is a challenge in this use of humor. Considered in this light, one is not sure whether what is 'humorous' is ridiculous after all, or whether Climacus' description is really the way things are: truth appears absurd to mortal man.

One final word of introduction to the works under consideration, which concerns Kierkegaard's relationship to Johannes Climacus. Some writers have taken Kierkegaard's disclaimer at the end of the *Postscript* seriously and concluded that Kierkegaard did not take the content of his pseudonymous writings seriously.[6] That is, he had "no opinion" on the matters expressed therein. The passage is the following (which appears unpaginated).

> So in the pseudonymous works there is not a single word which is mine, I have no opinion about these works except as third person, no knowledge of their meaning except as a reader, not the remotest private relation to them, since such a thing is impossible in the case of a doubly reflected communication. One single word of mine uttered personally in my own name would be an instance of presumptuous self-forgetfulness, and dialectically viewed it would incur with one word the guilt of annihilating the pseudonyms.

The difficulty with Kierkegaard's disclaimer is that it contradicts what he later asserts in *Point of View,* where he embraces the pseudonymous works. Furthermore, it is clear from Kierkegaard's journals that he believed the substance of the Climacus writings to be correct interpretations of the Christian faith. His ideal Christian, Anti-Climacus, says of the disputed writings, "I gladly take upon myself the endorsement of what the other pseudonymous writers have enjoined."[7] A possible explanation of the discrepancy is that Kierkegaard, in the heat of battle, denied adherence to the ideas in the pseudonymous works so that the reader would be forced to consider the ideas on their own merits and not as belonging to the ill-reputed Kierkegaard, who at that moment was undergoing public ridicule. It was at the critical stage of abuse by the scandal-inventing magazine, *Corsair,* that Kierkegaard submitted the additional, unpaginated pages disclaiming his works.

In *Point of View* (as we noted in a previous section) Kierkegaard revealed his intentions in using pseudonyms: to make the familiar (i.e., the claims of Christianity) unfamiliar, so that those who deceive themselves into thinking they are Christians might be reawakened to what Christianity is really all about. By hearing the Gospel proclaimed from a different vantage point, by "non-Christians" (the pseudonymous authors), they would be forced to reexamine their relationship to Christianity. Hence when Kierkegaard disclaimed his pseudonymous authorship, it would seem he was not rejecting the ideas therein but only the way the writers view Christianity—from the outside rather than inside. In his papers, Kierkegaard put the matter this way: "Anti-Climacus has something in common with Climacus, but the difference is in Johannes Climacus' having placed himself so low that he even declares himself to be a non-Christian whereas Anti-Climacus declares himself to be a Christian in an extraordinary degree. . . . I consider myself above Johannes Climacus but below Anti-Climacus" (*Papers,* X^1 A 517).

I think a case could be made that almost every proposition on the Christian faith in the Climacus writings can be found in some form in Kierkegaard's nonpseudonymous writings, religious writings, or private papers—although this claim would require a thesis of its own to be sustained. I hope, however, that I have given enough reasons why we should consider the Climacus writings as Kierkegaard's thought. What distinguishes Climacus from Kierkegaard is simply perspective. Kierkegaard writes about Christianity as insider; Climacus writes about it from the outside, as something to be entertained; but both agree on how one becomes a Christian and on the content of Christianity.

I have spent some time on this issue because I believe there is a basic unity to the Kierkegaardian literary corpus. It may not be as united as Kierkegaard supposes in *Point of View,* but it is sufficiently united that the student can use passages from various writings in the corpus to throw light on other passages, without having to justify himself each time he does so.[8]

Now we may analyze the role of 'faith' in *Philosophical Fragments,* after which we will look at its role in *Concluding Unscientific Postscript* (chapter 6).

'Faith' in *Philosophical Fragments*

Introduction

The basic problem of *Fragments* is the relation between faith and history: "Can there be a historical point of departure for an eternal consciousness?" "How can such a point of departure have more than historic interest?" "Can one build eternal happiness on such historical knowledge?" The first question may be rephrased: "Can history be a basis for faith in the Eternal?"

We have noted part of Kierkegaard's treatment of faith and history in chapter 2, examining his rejection of historical research as useless and undesirable for faith, but at the same time noting the necessity of a core of historical data for faith. In this section we will examine the meaning of 'faith' in the *Fragments,* whose basic plan is simple but whose argument is anything but simple. The basic question is how can eternal truth be known (or learned).

Climacus sets two ways he deems exhaustive: the Platonic way (represented by philosophical Idealism, especially Leibniz and Hegel) or the revelational way (represented by Christianity). Kierkegaard seems to assume the truth of Plato's assertion: one cannot seek or find the truth, for if one does not know it already, one does not know what to look for; and if one knows it already, there is no need to look for it (*Meno,* 80). The Socratic-Platonic solution to this dilemma is that we learn by recollection; we have the truth within us in the form of innate ideas. We simply need an occasion to become conscious of these ideas. Essentially, the historical moment of discovery is of no importance (being accidental), nor is the teacher of decisive importance. It could as well have been Prodicus as Socrates who served as the occasion for the slave's learning to do geometry.

The revelational way solves the dilemma posed by Plato in an opposite manner. Truth is not innate within man, who is in untruth or error. Truth must come *to* man, if it comes at all, as a gift, bestowed from without. In this way the teacher is decisive; without him there is no learning. He is not merely a teacher but a benefactor, in that he freely gives what we would not otherwise be able to obtain. Likewise, in distinction to the Platonic way, the moment of discovery is of essential importance: it marks the distinction between untruth and truth, the passage from ignorance to knowledge. The difference between not possessing the truth and possessing it is so important that we can speak of the passage as a "new birth." He who has come to know eternal truth has passed from nonbeing to being, or from ordinary being to new being. The rest of the *Fragments* is analysis of implications if the revelational way is correct.

The first condition is that a capacity corresponding to the truth must be given along with the truth. If man is void of truth and in untruth, there is no possibility for learning or receiving the truth. He must be given a new organ, a capacity for receiving the truth, a receptacle for containing the truth. This organ is faith.

Climacus argues that man originally lost this capacity due to his own fault and misuse of freedom, but his argument suffers from all the problems of having to explain the rationale of original sin, which need not delay us here. Our interest is in the nature of faith as the capacity for receiving eternal truth.

Faith is not the truth, nor is the capacity for faith a guarantee of possessing the truth. It is the necessary, but not sufficient, condition for possessing or knowing the truth. That is, knowledge of the truth in the revelational sense involves choice, a decision to live entirely according to this truth. The process of receiving the truth is traditionally known as 'synergism', so that salvation is a cooperative venture between God and man. The capacity for divine truth, as well as a revelation of the truth, is given freely by God, but the individual must choose whether or not to accept it. Rejection is possible. Grace does not force man against his will. "If I do not have the condition . . . all my willing is of no avail; although as soon as the condition is given, the Socratic principle [the power to will] will again apply."[9]

Exactly how the will works is left a mystery. In a journal entry, Kierkegaard discussed the dialectic of free will—grace—showing that every instance of free will regarding the good can be seen as a gift of grace. Even our willingness to will the good, or a knowledge of the truth, can be analyzed as an instance of grace; but at bottom, freedom (the subjective) must be insisted upon. "There are many, many envelopings, but they must at one point or another be stopped by the subjective. That man makes the scale so great, so difficult, can be praiseworthy as majesty's expression for God's infinity; but however, do not allow yourself to exclude the subjective; unless we want to have fatalism."[10]

It would seem, then, that the thesis that man is somehow free to accept or reject grace is necessary to preserve a person's essential humanity, which Climacus identifies with the truth of Socratic humanism. Without freedom of the will, man is not a man. With freedom of the will, a man takes responsibility for his decisions—yet (Christianly speaking) in such a way as to make God responsible for all his correct choices. This is the paradox of grace, a paradox endemic to all deep religious experience.

Climacus' use of 'faith' *(Tro)* at first sight looks ambiguous. Sometimes it seems to mean the capacity to believe;[11] sometimes it seems to mean a knowledge of the truth.[12] The word is sometimes used to describe the vision of God.[13] It is a miracle which opens the "eyes of faith."[14] Faith is contemporaneity with its object.[15] It is the organ for apprehending the historical, and, in its eminent sense, the organ for apprehending the Eternal's appearance in history.[16] It is a "happy passion."[17] It is not a form of knowledge.[18] It is an act of the will, a volition.[19] It is not an act of the will, but a gift.[20] It is anti-inductive.[21] Some of these uses can be easily reconciled, but the reader may be forgiven if he wonders whether Kierkegaard could not have done more to reconcile his categories.

In the subsections which follow I will try to analyze some prominent uses of 'faith' in the *Fragments,* drawing occasionally from other writings to illustrate the point. First, however, I will distinguish what one might call 'existential faith' from 'ordinary belief' in *Fragments.* 'Existential faith' is almost identical to what I have referred to as 'religious faith' in the preceding section; the difference is simply that when Kierkegaard uses the concept of existential faith in the Climacus writings, it is applicable to a wider scope than simply the religious stage of existence.

Existential Faith and Ordinary Belief

We have noted the regrettable fact that Danish has only one word for the English 'faith' and 'belief', the word *Tro*. Two words hardly seem adequate to convey the variety of meanings suggested by these words. It helps somewhat, however, that both English and Danish have an additional word which is related to, but different from, these words ('belief', 'faith', and *Tro*). We have the additional word 'opinion', which in Danish is *Mening*. Kierkegaard distinguishes between one type of belief (*Tro*) and opinion (*Mening*): "To have an opinion is both too much and too little for my uses. To have an opinion presupposes a sense of ease and security in life, such as is implied in having a wife and children; it is a privilege not to be enjoyed by one who must keep himself in readiness night and day, or is without assured means of support. Such is my situation in the realm of the spirit" (*F,* p. 6).[22]

'Opinion' signifies a settled, ordinary judgment about the truth of a proposition or body of propositions (an ideology or theory). 'Belief', in an existential sense, means an unsettled, extraordinary judgment about propositions. The difference lies in the importance of the proposition to the subject. In a faith situation, the subject regards the proposition as crucial for his life; in an opinion situation, this is not the case. Whereas objectively a person may judge two propositions (p and q) equally probable, if one proposition (p) is life crucial and the other (q) is not, then the uncertainty attaching to p will be more important than the uncertainty attaching to q. The uncertainty of p will arouse the passions in a way that the uncertainty of q will not. Belief in p will involve risk in a way that belief in q will not, as if one's whole existence were put at risk. We may call this life crucial type of belief 'existential faith' (or 'existential belief'), leaving 'belief' to cover 'opinion', which is ordinary, nonexistential, propositional belief.

The reader will note that even as 'existential belief' is similar to what was designated 'religious belief' in the last section, 'ordinary belief' is similar to the 'prosaic common sense' with which mediocre minds are satisfied. It is clear that Kierkegaard has little interest in ordinary, propositional belief, that he thinks philosophy has been too preoccupied with it at the expense of existential faith. "What modern philosophy understands by faith is what properly is called 'opinion', or what is loosely called in every-day speech, 'believing'."[23]

Existential faith is not merely propositional belief, but neither is it Christian faith. In the *Postscript,* Climacus identifies existential faith with passionate commitment to uncertain, action-guiding propositions. It is a persistent clinging to a proposition in spite of all hazards. "Sitting quietly in a ship while the weather is calm is not a picture of faith; but when the ship has sprung a leak, enthusiastically to keep the ship afloat by pumping while yet not seeking harbor: this is the picture. And if the picture involves an impossibility in the long run, that is but the imperfection of the picture; faith persists" (*CUP,* p. 202n.).

Trusting in the ship in calm weather is the picture of ordinary belief, opinion, taking-for-granted belief. Existential faith involves wrestling with the evidence; it involves the deepest structures of the self, the passions as well as the volition. It struggles to keep the ship afloat, even when all seems lost, and it succeeds.

We turn now to a related but somewhat different account of 'belief' as the organ for apprehending the past, that is, history.

Belief as the Organ for Apprehending History

Kierkegaard's treatment of belief and history occurs in the "Interlude," the section of *Fragments* between chapters 4 and 5, one of the most difficult sections in Kierkegaard's writings. The "Interlude" opens with a question about the modal status of past events: "Is the past more necessary than the future? or, When the possible becomes actual, is it thereby made more necessary than it was?"[24] Kierkegaard's answer, in brief, is that the transition from possibility to actuality does not occur by necessity (logical necessity) but by nonnecessity.

All natural becoming ('coming-into-being') comes into being because of a cause. The first cause is the Creator of all else, an agent who acts freely. All history is imitative of this creative causality in that free agents bring possibles into existence. In arriving at this conclusion, Climacus analyzes the concepts of becoming (*Tilblivelse,* 'coming-into-being'), the past, actuality, necessity, and apprehending the past. Through analysis of these concepts, Climacus purports to reveal the "autopsy of faith," from which we can understand Christian faith, faith *sensu eminentiori.*

'Coming-into-Being' (*Tilblivelse*)

Climacus' idea of becoming or 'coming-into-existence' derives from Aristotle's concept of *genesis,* which divided all change (*kinesis*) into four categories: quantitative change (increase and decrease [*auxesis-phthisis*]), qualitative change (*alloiosis*), change of place (*phora*), and the change of 'coming-into-being' from nonbeing and 'ceasing-to-be' (*genesis-pthora*).[25] Climacus takes Aristotle's framework, but alters it to his own understanding. He divides all change into two fundamental categories: (1) change from nonbeing to being (*genesis*), which he identifies as *kinesis* or *Tilblivelse* ('coming-into-being'), and (2) all other changes (*Forandring*), which he identifies with the Greek *alloiosis*.

In the second form of change, existence is presupposed; the existing subject simply changes its features or place. If I understand Climacus rightly, this sort of change may be called 'natural change'. It can be explained or described in language that omits all reference to agency (human or divine). 'Coming-into-existence' change, on the other hand, presupposes an agent who creates reality. An idea in the agent's mind is actualized through the agent's action. Only this kind of change can be described as 'free' or as 'done in freedom'. All natural change can be subsumed under the category 'necessity'.[26]

'Actuality' (*Virkelighed*), 'Possibility' (*Mulighed*), and 'Necessity' (*Nodvendighed*)

These words and their German equivalents played an important role in nineteenth-century Idealist thought. Hegel had written in his *Wissenschaft der Logik,* "The Necessary is, and this Being is itself the Necessary . . . . Thus Actuality is in its differentiation with the Possibility, identical with itself. As this identity, it is Necessary."[27]

'Necessity', for the Hegelians, is the unity which subsumed (*aufgehoben*) the difference between 'actuality' and 'possibility' within itself, the higher unity of these lower categories. 'Necessity' is the continual process of the Absolute, which moves inexorably through history, determining what shall be. But Kierkegaard rejected this ordering of the categories, in particular the notion of 'necessity's' *doing* anything at all. To speak of 'necessity's' subsuming 'actuality' and 'possibility' within its higher unity was to confuse logical categories with movement and action.

Harkening back to Aristotle, Kierkegaard defined 'necessity' as 'logical necessity', sometimes called '*de re* necessity'.[28] It is connected with a thing's essence, its 'whatness'. 'Possibility' (*dunameion*) and 'actuality' (*energeia*) are defined as the two modes of being which any essence may have. 'Possibility' is that which has the potentiality to be; 'actuality' is the realized potentiality. Thus 'necessity' cannot be a synthesis of 'possibility' and 'actuality', for 'actuality' and 'possibility' do not differ at all in 'necessity' (essence) but only in being (*Vaeren*). The problem is how to get potential being ('possibility') into existence ('actuality').

Here Kierkegaard rejects the idea of gradations of being, of a quantitative increment from nonbeing to a 'little bit of being', to being, to absolute being. "Factual being is wholly indifferent to any and all variation in essence, and everything that exists participates without petty jealousy in being, and participates in the same degree. . . . A fly, when it is, has as much being as God."[29] Instead of a quantitative increment via necessity, in which the possible is made actual, Kierkegaard asserts that the change from nonbeing to being (possibility to actuality) takes place by a leap (*Spring*). It is an act of creative will, for which agency is required.

The 'necessary', then, is that which remains unchangeable throughout the change from possibility to actuality. It is the constant self-identity of the subject (the thought) throughout the process of change from nonbeing to being. In this sense, nothing ever happens by necessity, for the necessary simply *is*, logically *is*. The necessary cannot come into existence, because only that which can change can come into existence. "The necessary is a category entirely by itself. Nothing ever comes into existence with necessity; likewise the necessary never comes into existence and something by coming into existence never becomes the necessary. Nothing whatever exists because it is necessary or because the necessary is. The actual is no more necessary than the possible, for the necessary is absolutely different from both" (*F*, p.92).

Kierkegaard's point is simply that logic and existence are separate realms. Logic (necessity) never brings anything into existence. Coming–into–existence is a contingent matter; it could have happened otherwise. Kierkegaard calls this it–could–have–happened–otherwise character 'freedom'. "All coming into existence takes place with freedom, not by necessity. Nothing comes into existence by virture of a logical ground, but only by a cause. Every cause terminates in a freely effective cause."[30]

'The Historical'

Everything which has 'come into existence' is 'historical'. Nature, as the opposite of history, is not something which comes into existence. Its change is the ordinary change (*alloiosis*), which we noted above. The changes are not brought about by free agents. However, there is a sense in which even nature is a coming–into–existence type of change. In the sense that it is originally an act of God, a *creatio ex nihilo*, nature represents a possibility made actual. Seen *sub specie aeternitatis*, the original change from nonbeing to being is the creation. This is the absolute coming–into–being, within which all other coming–into–being (history) takes place.

In this higher sense, only God has no history, for only He never underwent the transition from nonbeing to being via agency. Human history is analogous to God's creative activity, because human beings imitate God. As free agents, they create actuality. As relatively free agents, they point back to an absolute free agent. "The more specifically historical coming into existence occurs by the operation of a relatively freely effecting cause, which in turn points ultimately to an absolutely freely effecting cause."[31]

'The Past'

Climacus' idea of 'the past' is the historic past in the broadest sense: any event brought about by human agency. Nature is "too abstract to have a dialectic with respect to time in the stricter sense."[32] The past is immutable; it can no longer change into something else. But this is so *not* because the past (history) became such by necessity (logical necessity is excluded at every point). "If necessity could gain a foothold at a single point, there would no longer be any distinguishing between the past and the future."[33] On the contrary, the past has been brought about by freedom. Its unchangeableness has been caused by human action and not by any immanent logical necessity. History *could* have been otherwise. Kierkegaard is not speaking about causal necessity here; however, it is clear that what he says is not compatible with any determinist account of agency.

The past partakes of a duality. Something actually happened; and while the event was present, the witness knew what was happening, but now that it is past, it is uncertain exactly *how* it occurred and *what* occurred. This conflict (Climacus calls it a 'contradiction', *Modsigelse*) between certainty *qua* present and uncertainty *qua* past is the distinguishing mark of all coming-into-existence.

Climacus states that only immediate sensation and immediate knowledge are to be called 'knowledge'—that which is beyond the possibility of deception. What is past is no longer immediately present; hence it cannot be known. Even when I behold a phenomenon of nature—for example, a star— this relation holds. I confine myself to the given sense data, but I may be said to know I am seeing what appears as a star. However, when I ask *how* it came into existence or whether the star is an instance of coming-into-existence (actualization of a thought in the mind of God), the star "becomes involved in doubt." "It is as if reflection took the star away from the senses."[34]

How do we come to apprehend the past, the historical? Climacus says we must have a faculty (an organ) within us which has the appropriate structure for grasping this elusive quality. The structure must be analogous to the historical itself ("only like can know like"). This faculty functions in such a way that it brings the past event into the person's presence and, in so doing, makes it immediate cognition. The faculty for grasping the past negates the uncertainty in coming-into-existence. "It must comprise a corresponding somewhat by which it may repeatedly negate in its certainty the uncertainty that corresponds to the uncertainty of coming into existence."[35]

This faculty which annuls the uncertainty of the past and makes history immediately present is belief, which is the required faculty for apprehending the past. It is a function which makes the objectively uncertain subjectively certain. The believer believes what he cannot see. (He does not *believe* he sees a star, for he *sees* it. Immediate sensation is infallible.) He believes that the star has come into existence and that this has come about by divine agency. It was not eternally there. Climacus seems to conflate perception and sensation here and seems to assume that the beholder also *knows* he is seeing a star. However, the discussion in *Fragments* is unclear at this point.

Suppose, however, that we can be said to know that what we are seeing is a star. We still cannot *know* that the star has come into existence, is a product of divine agency. There is always the possibility that it is a result of natural processes and not of *creatio ex nihilo*.[36]

We see here a radical distinction between belief and knowledge. Knowledge is not merely a limiting case of believing but a qualitatively different phenomenon. Knowledge claims involve being "objectively certain"; that is, having sufficient evidence which precludes the possibility of deception. Believing, on the other hand, involves being certain (subjectively), even though (objectively) there is the possibility of being wrong in one's judgment. As Climacus defines *Tro* in the *Postscript,* believing is, at its maximum, "an objective uncertainty held fast in an appropriation process of the most passionate inwardness."[37] Belief involves risk; risk incites passion. The intensified passion brings about the movement of the will, the act of believing. "To this end passion is necessary. Every movement of infinity comes about by passion, and no reflection can bring a movement about. This is the continual leap in existence which explains the movement, whereas mediation is a chimera which according to Hegel is supposed to explain everything, and at the same time this is the only thing he has never explained" (*FT,* p. 53; *SV,* III:93).

From this understanding of belief, Climacus shows that belief and doubt are opposite acts—both belonging, however, to the same category of volitional action. They are movements of the will in opposite directions: toward or away from a given proposition. Here the Greek Skeptics are discussed, who did not doubt by virtue of knowledge—that is, simply because they could not help but doubt. This dispositional doubt (or acknowledgment of absence of knowledge) is called by Climacus 'inquiring doubt', the doubt of the person who finds himself unable to believe. However, 'Skeptical doubt' is different; it is not an automatic disposition, but involves methodological *choice*. The Skeptics *chose* to doubt because they did not wish to run the risk of error. They did not deny immediate sensation or cognition, but they refused to give assent where such immediateness was not present. Hence the Skeptics kept their minds neutral about all judgments where deception was possible. This was an act of will, a decision of principle.

Thus, for Climacus, we see that belief and doubt are acts of the same quality. Both are acts of will, not instances of knowledge or passive judgment. The *conclusions* of belief are really *resolutions*.[38] They are decisions which exclude all doubt in assenting to a proposition. When a situation of insufficient reason occurs, it is not reason which decides the matter, because reason is inadequate to bring us to act. It is, finally, the will that overthrows the "equilibrium" between two possible courses of action.

Having said all this, Climacus seems to reverse himself, for in the very next breath he speaks of belief, not at all as an action but as a passion. Belief and doubt are opposite passions. "Belief is the opposite of doubt. Belief and doubt are not two forms of knowledge, determinable in continuity with one another, for neither of them is a cognitive act; they are opposite *passions*" (F, p. 105).

Kierkegaard does not explain this apparent contradiction between calling belief an act of the will, a leap, and calling belief a disposition, a passion. Perhaps the most constructive interpretation would be to say that there is an act of 'assenting' which is volitional, but that having a belief is dispositional, a state of mind. Kierkegaard need not be held as insisting that every one of our beliefs is a product of free choice (assenting), but he seems to think that we are somehow responsible for all our beliefs. We could choose to doubt everything which is not clear and distinct and beyond the possibility of deception.

In the next section we will examine this aspect of willing-to-believe in further detail; at this point we sum up Kierkegaard's understanding of belief in the "Interlude."

1. Belief is an act of the will, a free act. In the act of believing, the mind assents to a proposition and risks error. In this sense, belief is the opposite of doubt, which refuses to assent to a proposition, fearing error.
2. Belief is the opposite of knowledge with regard to objective evidence. Belief involves drawing conclusions from insufficient evidence whereas knowing involves conclusive evidence. Belief involves risk of error; knowledge does not. These are mutually exclusive cognitions.
3. Belief is a sense or faculty for apprehending the past (history). It is the faculty which negates the uncertainty of the past and brings it into immediate contact with the mind as that which is certain.
4. As a faculty of the mind, belief has a passive as well as active aspect. Belief is an opposite passion (as well as opposite action) to doubt. Beliefs are dispositions of the mind toward propositions. However, we are always free to refuse to give our assent to a belief. The faculty of volition rules over the faculty of belief (or is the dominant aspect of that faculty).

At the end of the "Interlude," Climacus ties these ideas about belief with his thoughts on *contemporaneity*. A contemporary witness to an event can take the data he receives as certain, as knowledge.[39] For the person who lives later (even the contemporary at a later time), the event becomes subject to doubt, uncertain. It is not so much that he doubts the 'whatness' of the event, but the 'how' of the event is in question. Which possible is the event an instance of? What is the correct interpretation of the event? What is the meaning of the event?

The problem is the same for the immediate contemporary as for the later individual, but the noncontemporary seems to have an added problem of not having been a witness to the event. How does the noncontemporary come to apprehend the event he never witnessed or does not now witness? He needs a report from a contemporary. "One who is not contemporary with the historical, has instead of the immediacy of sense and cognition, in which the historical is not contained, the testimony of the contemporaries, to which he stands related in the same manner as the contemporaries stand related to the said immediacy" (*F,* p. 105).

The contemporary makes his personal interpretation of an event. The interpretation is not necessary to the event itself, but it is a product of his freedom. He may be constrained by certain circumstances, but essentially the interpretation of the event is left to his judgment (which for Kierkegaard involves the will). From certain evidence, he proceeds to such-and-such conclusion. The later person takes the contemporary's account (including interpretation) and appropriates it for himself by accepting, rejecting, or modifying it in some way. For both the contemporary and the later person, a will to believe must be present if the event is to have an accepted interpretation.[40] Immediacy, whether as sensation or report, is a necessary but not sufficient condition for belief. Will must also be present. Will alone is not a sufficient condition either. One cannot believe in a vacuum—believe anything whatsoever. Together, immediacy and will make up the necessary and sufficient conditions for belief.[41]

We have seen that belief is an 'action passion' which makes the uncertain, the historic, certain. All believing, in this sense, is a sort of contemporaneity with the event. In believing, the event is brought into immediate consciousness as though it were a fact.

Climacus now applies this analysis to Christian believing. Skepticism, on Kierkegaard's terms, shows us that we can only know immediate sense data or *a priori* truths. Everything else must be believed (or doubted). Included in immediate cognition or *a priori* truth are the laws of logic, especially the law of noncontradiction.[42] If something is contradictory, we can know immediately that it cannot be the case. We cannot believe (or will to believe) what we know *not* to be the case.

But this is exactly the position we are in when we are presented with the statement that God has come into existence. The statement implies a contradiction because it implies that that which is unchangeable changes. It is one thing for someone to create a house from materials, plus the idea or plan of that house, but what can it mean to speak of a possible God becoming actual? God cannot *come* into existence because He *is,* He eternally *is.* Coming into existence, becoming temporal, violates God's necessary essence. Hence ordinary belief seems wholly inadequate to apprehend this proposition. The organ for grasping historic statements has to reject this statement as beyond its capacity. "Our historical fact thus stands before us. It has no immediate contemporary, since it is historical in the first degree, corresponding to belief in the ordinary sense; it has no immediate contemporary in the second degree, since it is based upon a contradiction" (*F,* p. 109).

In order to believe this proposition (or "fact") a person must be in possession of a new condition, a different type of faith from that which we have been discussing with regard to historical events. This faith is not a natural faculty or capacity of man. It is *un*natural. It is a gift of God, says Climacus, reminding us of the Pauline concept of faith: "For by grace you have been saved through faith; and this is not your own doing, it is the gift of God—not because of works, lest any man should boast."[43] This faith is not an act of the will.[44] We can do nothing to acquire it. It is a miracle. It is the necessary condition for being able to entertain the proposition that God has come into existence.

Yet, if I understand Kierkegaard rightly, it does not in itself guarantee that a person will make use of the gift, once bestowed. The will must re-enter, become reactivated. As we saw earlier in this section, there is a cooperative effort between God and man in the process of salvation. God gives the capacity to believe and reveals the propositon; man must decide whether he will believe. The will is still free to assent or reject the proposition once faith makes a decision possible. Human freedom is still operative in the midst of grace.[45]

We see, then, that Kierkegaard makes believing in the Christian faith an impossibility for mere mortals. A miracle must enable man to believe the central doctrine of Christian affirmation. In this regard, Climacus echoes Hume's judgment about Christian belief:

We may conclude, that the Christian religion not only was at first attended with miracles, but even at this day cannot be believed by any reasonable person without one. Mere reason is insufficient to convince us of its veracity; and whoever is moved by faith to assent to it, is conscious of a continued miracle in his own person, which subverts all the principles of his understanding, and gives him a determination to believe what is most contrary to custom and experience. [*Enquiry Concerning Human Understanding,* p. 131]

One would like more information about the characteristics of this miracle. Kierkegaard leaves the matter a mystery, but I think we can go far to demystify it. Let us attempt to throw more light on how one might believe in something contrary to "good evidence."

When two mutually exclusive propositions are placed before me, I can say, "Proposition A is much harder to believe than Proposition B," or I can even say, "I cannot believe A. I *do* believe B." But on further reflection it may occur to me that a further proposition must be taken into account, namely C: "My normal judgment in these matters is usually unreliable." That is, what I find easy to believe about a certain class of propositions often turns out to be wrong. Therefore, on the basis of C, I may reverse my judgment about A and B and believe A after all. In this case, I may be said to have good reasons for believing A, although, on a first-level evaluation, I may not be able to say I have any good reasons for believing in it.

Does this sort of analysis help us understand what Kierkegaard says about believing in a 'self-contradiction' in the paradox of the Incarnation? I think it does, for it shows the sort of reasoning—whether justified or not is another matter. We may ask, then, how does Kierkegaard know that his ordinary judgment is usually unreliable or wrong? The answer is that Kierkegaard thinks he is merely stating what must be the case on the assumption that there is a transcendent sphere of being. If there is, it must be so superior to ours that it makes our normal judgment "error" or "ignorance" by comparison, measured by its standards. Our ordinary, common-sense understanding (*Forstand*), like Plato's cave inhabitants, compares only shadows with shadows. However, there is in us one link with the truth—let us call it 'pure reason'—which allows us to make negative inferences from our sphere of existence to a transcendent sphere. That is, from observing the disharmony, injustice, despair, and evil which prevail in this realm, we can infer to the existence of harmony, justice, wholeness, and goodness in that higher realm.

If we suppose such a superior realm (Kierkegaard seems to think this supposition is self-evident truth), which our 'pure reason' shows us, then our ordinary ways of reasoning, our common-sense judgments, must be corrupt (affected by our lower state, environment, and heredity). Hence we can know that we begin our normal reasoning by valuing things incorrectly.

By placing our common-sense understanding in disjunction with transcendent reasoning, we see that our ways of gathering evidence, assessing its value, trusting our senses, and reasoning from probability all tie us to a lower order, from which we need to escape. If we accept the conclusion that, with regard to metaphysical or ultimate truth, this lower form of reasoning is not very helpful (but just the opposite), we may make progress. 'Pure reason', then, can help us by showing the limits of reason (ordinary sense). Kierkegaard trusts 'pure reason', deductive logic—especially in the process of reasoning from negations—but we need some hint of the right content, the proper assumptions to begin reasoning from, some way of guaranteeing that we make a leap into the right metaphysical system. But this we cannot have, at least not in an objective and immediate sense. The next best thing is to have a reliable guide in a subjective sense.

This brings us back to intuition, which we saw as the stuff from which faith develops, as the underlying motif in Kierkegaard's idea of subjectivity (chapter 3). Kierkegaard surely is not altogether wrong in seeing intuitions as basic, but he seems confused in assuming that our intuitions are reliable guides to truth. He does not take into sufficient consideration that our deepest intuitions may be far from the truth even on nonrevelational matters. There is clearly a problem, too, in the relation between faith as an intuitive sense and faith as willing-to-believe. Intuitions happen; they are not acts. Volitions are acts; they are not simply passions. Kierkegaard never gives a satisfactory account of how these two aspects function in a belief situation.

Critique of Kierkegaard's Volitionalism

We have made our way through the labyrinthine discussion of various concepts of faith as they appear in the early work of Kierkegaard, noting that he looked upon his treatment of faith as a significant advancement in philosophical analysis. Although our examination of this treatment is not yet complete, we have much of what is essential to it: the development of the manifestation of faith phenomena from the aesthetic to the Christian religious stage; the distinction between ordinary belief and existential faith; the notion of belief as an organ for apprehending history; belief as an act of the will; and belief as a state of mind (disposition).

Although Kierkegaard is not always as lucid as he could be in these discussions of faith/belief (*Tro*), the context usually makes the concept tolerably clear. Most of what he says I take to be insightful and plausible; however, there is one place where I think Kierkegaard is mistaken, on a doctrine which has had a long history in philosophy—for whose inception Kierkegaard was not responsible but which, perhaps, no one else has done more to propagate. It goes to the very heart of his existentialism and has been accepted uncritically by every successive existentialist. I refer to his doctrine of volitionalism: the thesis that we can attain beliefs by willing to have them, and that we *ought* to attain some beliefs in this manner. Since the issue is of momentous importance to both Kierkegaardian scholarship and modern philosophy, I shall spend some time on this topic (for a fuller treatment, I refer the reader to what I have written elsewhere).[46]

What I call "volitional fallacies" have had a long and, unfortunately, re- spectable history. In the New Testament, we read of Jesus holding men responsible for their beliefs, reprimanding them for doubting, and speaking of an ability to believe. John tells us that people will be saved or damned because of the sort of propositions they assent to. Paul does likewise, and uses the conditional imperative regarding belief (Acts 16:37). Kierkegaard, who seems to have based his volitionalism in part on a misunderstanding of a Pauline passage, wrote: "Faith/belief, surely, implies an act of the will, and moreover not in the same sense as when I say, for instance, that all apprehen- sion implies an act of will: how can I otherwise explain the saying in the New Testament that whatsoever is not of faith is sin" (Romans 14:23).[47] Paul, referring to eating meat that had been offered to idols, used the term 'faith' to signify acting according to a good conscience. Kierkegaard seems to take it to show that a Christian epistemology is based on the will.

Irenaeus, Augustine, and Aquinas all appear to hold one form of this doctrine. Descartes, in the fourth *Meditation,* holds that unless we are respon- sible for our mistaken beliefs, God must be—which is tantamount to blas- phemy, for it makes God into a deceiver. Cardinal Newman adheres to a strong form of volitionalism in his *Grammar of Assent,* asserting, "Assent is an act of the mind, congenial to its nature; and it, as other acts, may be made both when it ought to be made and when it ought not. It is a free act, a personal act for which the doer is responsible." Catholic philosophers and theologians, typified by Pieper and Lonergan, generally espouse such a doc- trine. Pieper is the most explicit: "One can believe only if one wishes to . . . a free assent of will must be performed. Belief rests upon volition."[48]

In a more prescriptive sense, William James speaks of our "right to adopt a believing attitude" wherever the evidence is not overwhelmingly decisive against a certain conclusion and our passional nature has a stake in the matter. Pascal goes so far as to encourage us to "take holy water and say masses" ("pretend you believe") to get ourselves to believe what we don't believe.[49]

Kierkegaard concurs with these ideas. We have already noted (in his state- ments in *Fragments*) that "the conclusion of belief is not so much a conclusion as a resolution" and "belief is not a form of knowledge but a free act, an expression of the will." To these we may add one from the *Postscript:*

> I have . . . carefully enough expounded the thesis that all approximation is useless, since on the contrary it behooves us to get rid of introductory guaran- tees [for religious belief], or proofs from consequences, and the whole mob of public pawnbrokers and guarantors, so as to permit the absurd to stand out in

all its clarity—in order that the individual *may believe if he wills to;* I merely say
that it must be strenuous in the highest degree so to believe. [*CUP,* p. 190; my
italics]

In its fullest form, the volitional theory contains both a descriptive and a
prescriptive feature. The former asserts that believing *is* an act of the will, that
in every belief situation the will is operative. The act is sometimes referred to
as 'assenting'. The prescriptive feature asserts that one *ought* to will to believe
certain propositions; for example, one ought to make oneself believe that
God exists in order to have a better chance at attaining happiness. What I refer
to as "volitional fallacies" must be distinguished from the perfectly natural
relation of the will to believing, that *indirectly* the beliefs I acquire are the
result of previous choices. The volitional schema looks like this:

	Direct	Indirect
Descriptive	1. I will to believe *p* and, by doing so, acquire the belief that-*p* directly.	2. I will certain actions and life policies, and these cause the beliefs I eventually acquire.
Prescriptive	3. I ought to will to acquire a belief that-*p* by directly willing to do so.	4. I set myself a specific course of action in order to acquire a specific belief, *p,* which the evidence alone does not cause.

In this section I will argue that direct descriptive volitionalism, as espoused
by Kierkegaard and others, while not logically impossible, is essentially confused. I shall also argue that prescriptive volitionalism, both in its direct and
indirect forms, is morally suspect. One could be a descriptivist (modified)
without being a prescriptivist; that is, "it is possible to attain beliefs directly
through willing to do so, but we ought not attain them in that way," but it is
not possible to be a direct prescriptivist without being a descriptivist; that is,
it must be possible for one to attain beliefs through willing if one is to have
some duty to do so.

Direct Descriptive Volitionalism

I take a belief to be in its occurrent form an assent (or dissent) to a proposition. I think Frege captures our ordinary intuition when he defines 'belief' as
"judging that so and so is the case," or as "recognition of the truth of a

thought." A more formal definition might be: "Someone, A, believes that-*p* if, and only if, under favorable conditions A would assent to *p*."

Implied in the above characterization of belief is its "truth dimension." Belief is recognition of the truth value of a proposition, and believing involves truth in two ways:

1. Whatever is believed is a proposition, which by its nature is either true or false, and

2. Whatever is believed is believed as true or under the aspect of the true. That is, what one believes concerns states of affairs in the world—past, present, and/or future.

As such, many of these states of affairs exist independently of the believer. Hence believing, in this truth-oriented sense, will have as its goal a reflection of the way the world is. Acquiring a belief will be seen as a process or happening in which the world forces itself upon us.

With this in mind, let us examine the view that we can obtain beliefs directly, simply by willing to do so. Usually the claim is not that we can will to believe just anything at all, but only a large and important number of potential beliefs. Pieper, for example, limits his discussion to propositions that are conveyed through testimony. To believe something is to believe someone. Descartes seems more radical, viewing virtually any nonself-evident proposition as subject to our wills. Actually, few volitionalists argue for their position; they simply state it as introspectively obvious—but I doubt that it is obvious. If we are correct in our analysis regarding a core definition of believing, then believing is not an act but a happening.

Implicit in what I have said is the following argument against direct volitionalism. (I call it the "phenomenological argument against direct volitionalism" because it rests on the phenomenological properties of the experience of believing.)

1. Acquiring a belief is a happening in which the world forces itself upon a rational subject.

2. Happenings in which the world forces itself upon a rational subject are not things one does or chooses; that is, they are not actions.

3. Therefore, acquiring a belief is not something a rational subject does or chooses.

The first premise states that acquiring a belief is like acquiring an intention or emotion or most other propositional attitudes; these are things that happen to us. The second premise merely points out the passive/active distinction: beliefs belong to the class of things which happen to one, regardless of immediate wants, wishes, or choices. Hence a belief is not something I acquire by willing or doing anything, at least not directly. Believing is more like falling than jumping, catching a cold than catching a train, getting drunk than taking a drink, blushing than smiling, getting a headache than giving one to someone else. Indeed, this seems true of most propositional attitudes: anger, envy, liking, wanting, fearing, suspecting, doubting (though not imagining). Propositional attitudes are more aptly described as happening to a person than actions the person does or obtains directly by choosing.

Let us note a few types of belief to see that this seems to be the standard relation—for example, perceptual believing. If I am in a normal physiological condition and open my eyes, I cannot help but see certain things, for example, this white piece of paper in front of me. It seems intuitively obvious that I don't have to choose to have a belief that I see this paper before I see it, nor does it seem to matter whether I choose to see it or not. The perceptual belief comes naturally, of itself, perhaps even against my will (I may have an aversion to white paper). If I am in a normal physiological state and someone turns on some music, I may not want to hear it, but I cannot help but believe that I hear music.

Consider, next, memory beliefs. The typical instances of believing what I remember seem to require no special choosing. I may choose to try to re-member something, but what I finally seem to remember occurs to me whether I like it or not. I may have to struggle to recall an incident, but it would be odd to speak of *choosing* to believe what the memory reports. Granted, too, that there are times (for example, considering events from one's remote past) when we are not sure whether what we seem to remember actually occurred; but even here it seems that it is typically the evidence of the memory which impresses us sufficiently to tip the scales of judgment in one direction or the other. For instance, I may conclude that it is likely that I don't remember my grandfather taking me to the circus at the age of two because it seems reasonable to suppose that whatever impressions I have of that event were formed in my imagination after I had been told many times of the great occasion of my grandfather's taking me to my first circus. What would it mean to say, "I think it would be nicer to believe I actually remembered such an occasion; so let it be the case that I so believe"? Could I acquire such a belief by willing it? Not normally, I take it.

This analysis can be extended to abstract and logical beliefs. I don't choose to believe that the law of noncontradiction has universal application or that $2 + 2 = 4$. If I understand the concepts, I'm compelled to believe; the conclusion is *forced* upon me, as it were. The same holds true of theoretical beliefs, whether scientific, theological, political, or moral. Given a network of background beliefs, some theories "win out" in my noetic structure over others. For a theoretical explanation to force itself upon me as the best expla-nation, or as certainly or probably true, doesn't preclude rejecting it as a plan of action, but it *does* mean that, in some sense, I don't choose to believe what impresses itself upon me. Rather, it means I can't help but incline that way. The evidence can be said to *cause* my belief (it need not be good evidence).

Finally, there is the matter of belief arising through testimony—the type of acquisition emphasized by Pieper. Certainly, this seems a more likely candidate for volitionalism than other types of believing, a more complex type of believing than perceptual believing, but we might still doubt whether (*pace,* Pieper) I am free to believe or disbelieve a speaker at will. If I ask a stranger the way to Texas Stadium and he gives me directions, I come to believe or disbelieve what he says on the basis of a pre-inclination to trust this type of person in this type of situation to give this type of information (to be vetoed only if certain suspicious behavior is present), and the fact that what he says correlates with whatever I know about the way to Texas Stadium. Even if I have to deliberate about the testimony, wondering if the witness is credible, I don't come to a conclusion on the basis of *willing* to believe one way or the other. One of the factors may be that my wants and wishes influence my belief, but once the belief comes, it is held as a product of evidence, not as a product of my choice.

This is not to deny that the will is indirectly present in believing. It may be that we can will to believe almost anything and succeed, if given enough time and resources, but it seems that we cannot bring about these beliefs directly by willing them. For instance, our belief that the world is spherical and not flat wasn't obtained by choosing, nor can we believe the world is flat by willing to do so; but if we had good reason to do so (e.g., someone offered us a million dollars if we could believe the world is flat, to be verified by a lie-detector test), we might go to a hypnotist or use autosuggestion until we attained that belief. This would be a case of indirectly coming to a belief through choosing—the sort of thing that happens in self-deception.

Typically, the self-deceived person holds inconsistent beliefs. On one level, he holds to an original belief (e.g., one he does not want to have) while on another level he holds an induced belief; but he intentionally, or subconsciously, keeps himself from facing up to the inconsistency. Perhaps we need a behavioral criterion to judge which he holds more strongly, but the general tendency of self-deception is to eradicate the original belief in favor of the desired one.

One objection to my thesis that we don't acquire beliefs directly by willing to have them, centers around what William James calls "creative faith," a phenomenon whereby one's *deciding to believe* is crucial to the success of a venture. If, say, you are going to play a game of chess, getting yourself into a state of mind in which you believe you will win the game may actually help you win the game. James's example is a person trapped on a mountain, on the edge of a gorge, who calculates that making such a leap is improbable, but its probability increases as he convinces himself that he will make the leap.

Hence he must get himself to believe what, in the first instance, he didn't believe.

There are two things to be said about this objection. First, it is not a denial of the thesis that we cannot attain beliefs directly by willing them. It seems more likely a *deliberation* process, in which the will indirectly causes belief by refocusing the mind through autosuggestion. Secondly, there is all the difference in the world between getting oneself to believe something about the past or present, which is not in one's control, and getting oneself to believe something about the future, which to some degree *is* in one's control. While there is hope for change, it may be good "to think positively," believing against the odds, but it's simple self-deception to deny or refuse to believe what *is the case*. The situation described by "creative faith" seems to fall legitimately within a normal instance of practical reasoning:

1. I want a state of affairs, A, to come about.
2. If A is to come about, I must do some action, X.
3. I can only do X if I believe I will succeed in X'ing.
4. Therefore, I ought (prudentially) to do whatever is necessary to believe I will succeed in X'ing.

Related to this activity of getting oneself into a state of mind in which beliefs about the future can be changed is the matter of focusing or refocusing the mind. When someone says something at a social event to make me exceedingly angry, the only way I may be able to restrain myself from saying something I would later regret may be either to leave the scene altogether or quickly focus my mind on something else. We may suppress news and views, turn our thoughts from them to something else; and this seems unobjectionable. It may be that such behavior is necessary for social and personal well-being; but there is a point beyond which "turning away" becomes a negative character trait, indicating cowardice or inability to face up to bad news or contrary views. It is probably the case that refocusing the mind affects our believing, is instrumental in producing new beliefs, but the refocusing is not believing. It is more like imagining, a function of the will, something we have control over. We can turn away from a belief and concentrate on other factors until we forget, or even replace, the belief, but this seems to be a process of indirectly acquiring a new belief by *choosing*, not doing so directly.

An illustration of this is the famous duckrabbit picture. I can will what I want to see, then focus my attention on certain features of the picture in order to see the duck or the rabbit, but I cannot *see* the duck or the rabbit by willing to do so. Everyone has tried to see some pattern in this sort of puzzle (e.g., the configuration of clouds) and not been able. Believing is like seeing, in that it allows the mind to focus where it will, but once that is done, the belief comes of its own accord.

My argument has been that, from a phenomenological perspective, it does not seem to make sense to say that we obtain beliefs by directly willing to have them (I have not argued that it is logically impossible). But suppose we *do* obtain some beliefs this way. Suppose, for example, that you obtained the belief that the pope is infallible simply by willing to believe it. Once you obtained this belief, you would (I think) have to believe in some "truth connection" between your believing and the object of your belief. That is, you would believe there is a causal relationship between the belief and what makes the belief true, so that the will played only an accidental role in the process. Willing that it be true that the pope is infallible would not be sufficient or necessary to make him so.

We might put the argument this way:

1. When someone obtains a belief, he believes the belief is true independently of his willing it.
2. Hence, even if he could obtain a belief directly by willing to do so, once he obtained it and consciously considered it, he would believe it to be true on the other grounds than his willing it to be true.

What makes a proposition true is a state of affairs, and because to believe a proposition is to believe it is true, a person, when he believes a proposition and is conscious of what has happened, comes to believe that the propositon is made true by a state of affairs in the world. Now such states of affairs exist independently of him and of his believing the proposition and independently of willing that the proposition be true. Willing that–*p* in general has no effect on *p* itself. Hence if one could come to have a belief through directly willing to have it, the person, once he reflected on the acquisition and saw that the belief was acquired simply by volit, could not continue to believe the proposition. He must see that the purported belief reflects only the content of his will or wishing. It has the same status as a product of the imagination or a dream. It tells us something about the psychology of the person, but nothing about a state of affairs in the real world.

While it is unclear whether we obtain beliefs *directly* by willing to have them (though my analysis makes it unlikely), it is clear that we obtain them *indirectly* by willing. We now turn to this mode of volitionalism.

Believing, Indirect Volitionalism, and Prescriptive Volitionalism

Indirectly believing involves the will. I have argued that we don't normally believe simply by willing to do so, for believing aims at truth and is not an act or direct product of the will. If we could believe whatever we choose to believe, simply by willing to do so, beliefs would not be about reality but about our wants and wishes. Nevertheless, the will plays an important indirect role, and many beliefs we arrive at are results of "policy decisions." Though believing is not an action, actions determine the sort of beliefs we end up with. It is primarily because we judge that our beliefs are to some extent indirect results of our actions that we speak of being *responsible* for them. We cannot be directly responsible for our beliefs, as though they were actions, but we can be said to be indirectly responsible for them. If we had chosen different life plans, been better moral agents, we might have different beliefs.

To be sure, we are not responsible for *all* our beliefs, and responsibility seems to vary in proportion to the evidence available at different times and our ability to attend to that evidence. For example, the person who pays attention to a certain matter often acquires more accurate beliefs than the inattentive person. Attention is generally thought to be within our control (to some degree). As long as we agree that the inattentive person could have acted differently, could have been attentive if he had wanted to, we can conclude that the inattentive person is responsible for not having the true belief which he might have had. In the same way, we can conclude that the attentive person is responsible for the true belief he has.

Being (indirectly) responsible for our beliefs indicates that praise and blame attach to our epistemic states—that, indirectly, beliefs are morally assessable. It may be that I have many beliefs I ought not have. If I had been a different sort of person, had made different decisions earlier in life, I might have many more true beliefs than I now have.

This view, that there is a moral aspect to believing, differs from prudential-ist theories of doxastic responsibility as set forth by philosophers like Mill, James, and Price. For them, no moral significance attaches to our believing, only prudential significance. A person is free to seek whatever goals he desires: happiness, salvation, convenience, pleasure, and so forth. It is simply in one's best interest to seek true beliefs. In most areas of life, experience tells us that true beliefs provide a better chance for reaching our goals than false beliefs; however, if you find yourself inclined to sacrifice truth for some other goal, you have every right to do so. We may call this the 'libertarian view of doxastic freedom,' which affirms that believing is a purely private matter. Each person must be accorded "absolute freedom of opinion on all subjects practical and speculative."

One may readily recognize the virtues of this position. Very few of us want to see a governmental Grand Inquisitor intervening in personal beliefs, or "thought reforms" and brainwashing, to help others acquire "true beliefs." The libertarian position emphasizes human autonomy and the value of a plurality of "belief experiments" in society. Nevertheless, I believe something is seriously deficient in this strategy: it sells the truth short. It is deficient on two counts: it undermines the significance of truth for the individual and it ignores the social dimension of truth seeking. That is, it is both a deontological and a teleological argument against prescriptive volitionalism.

The deontological argument, rooted in the notion of personal freedom or autonomy, runs like this:

1. It is morally wrong to diminish the free will of a person.
2. Acting on less than the best-justified beliefs diminishes the freedom of persons, reducing their autonomy, in that they do not have the best reasons available to them to guide their actions.
3. Volitional belief in what is unwarranted by the evidence causes us to act on less than the best-justified beliefs available.
4. Therefore volitional believing, against sufficient evidence, diminishes the freedom of persons, reducing their autonomy, in that they do not have the best reasons available to them for action guidance.
5. Therefore (by 1 and 4), volitional believing is morally wrong.

At least it is *prima facie* morally wrong. There are other considerations besides our freedom (though freedom is a high value in any moral system), and perhaps this duty to believe on the basis of evidence can be overridden in extreme situations.

The teleological argument for seeking to have true beliefs can be made along the following consequentialist lines:

1. It is very often important for the well-being of the community that we have true beliefs.
2. The best way to assure that we have true beliefs is to have a policy of truth seeking.
3. Therefore, we ought to have a policy of truth seeking, if we have the community's welfare at heart.

I take it that premise 2 is generally acceptable; consider, then, premise 1. In everyday life, wherever people interact, certain information is necessary for the efficient functioning of groups and individuals. An inspector who fails to check the safety devices in a factory that uses lethal chemicals or the safety of the disposal site, but reports that all is well, may report sincerely, but may place an entire community in jeopardy. The doctor who cheated his way through medical school and lacks appropriate beliefs about certain symptoms may endanger a patient's health and life. Even the passerby who gives wrong information to a stranger who asks directions may seriously inconvenience the stranger. Social interaction depends on accurate information. Because beliefs are action guiding and, as such, cause actions, society has a keen interest in our having true beliefs, which is brought about by a policy of truth seeking.

It may be objected, nevertheless, that while it may be important to have true beliefs (or, better, well-justified ones) in areas of our lives that affect the well-being of others, we ought to be allowed a realm of privacy where we can "go doxastic slumming"—as long as we don't harm anyone else in the process. We should be permitted to believe whatever we like about a certain set of beliefs. The trouble with this view is that it ignores the dispositional aspect of truth seeking. If it is to be effective, it must be deeply engrained, so that it's not easy to dispense with. Like all virtues, it must become a habit, and, as such, will manifest itself spontaneously over a wide range of experience.

I suggest that truth seeking in general is a moral duty because social well-being depends on justified beliefs, which function as causes for our actions. However, to say that truth seeking is a moral duty is not to say it is an absolute duty, that it is never overridable. It is a *prima facie* duty, one objective duty among many that may conflict with one another.

In summary, I accept a form of indirect descriptive volitionalism. We are indirectly responsible for many of our beliefs, which depend, to some degree, on the decisions we make and the policies that direct our lives. Furthermore, we can be said to be morally responsible for the beliefs we have (at least many of them). Hence we have a duty to seek well-justified and true beliefs.

I turn now to prescriptive volitionalism and the prescriptivist, who judges it morally right or permissible to acquire beliefs by wanting, willing, or choosing to have certain beliefs without primary concern for truth considerations. Whereas the truth seeker advises: "If you would have true beliefs, the right policy is to pay attention to the evidence, test hypotheses, try to judge impartially, and so forth," the prescriptivist advises: "If you would be happy (or saved, successful, etc.), believe that-*p*." In a sense, truth is the goal of the truth seeker's believing whereas for the prescriptivist, believing is instrumental to other goals. The truth seeker believes, or at least hopes, that truth and happiness (salvation, success, etc.) are causally related in such a way that, in seeking truth, he will have a better chance of reaching these other goals. But there is a sense in which truth has intrinsic value, is desirable for its own sake.

When there is a conflict between our duty to seek truth and our inclination to want to believe what evidence does not seem to warrant, the veracious person is distinguished from the prescriptivist. For example, two mothers' sons are accused of committing a violent crime, and both mothers are deeply distraught and want it to be the case that their sons are innocent, but each has a different attitude toward believing her son is innocent. The veracious mother wants the proposition of her son's innocence to be true, and may do everything in her power to ascertain the facts in order to come to an authoritative judgment. Emphasis is on the *truth* of the belief, not on *wanting* the belief. The mother wants the state of affairs to correspond to her wishes, but she is ready to believe in accord with the state of affairs, not in accord with her wishes.

On the other hand, the prescriptivist mother wants to believe in her son's innocence more than to believe the truth. She wants to believe so strongly that the evidence is never accepted, or is always evaluated in a way that is favorable to what she wants to believe. When, momentarily, she doubts her son's innocence, she purposely (or subconsciously) dismisses the evidence that leads her to doubt, or she uses autosuggestion (or whatever means are available) to overcome the force of the evidence. She cannot live with herself without belief in her son's innocence.

Whereas the second mother can be called "rational" in a pragmatic sense, only the first mother can be called "rational" in the truth-seeking sense. The veracious person tries to believe certain propositions *because* they are true; the prescriptivist wants to believe a proposition *in order that* she might be X (some further goal, such as being happy). In the veracious mother we have a normal state of believing, where the belief is the end in itself, where it makes no sense to speak of achieving anything in believing, of being successful or unsuccessful. In the pragmatic mother, believing is merely a means to another end: happiness or freedom from mental anguish. We might say that in the first case the belief has intrinsic value, becoming the foundation upon which actions are based, whereas in the second case the belief has only instrumental value, being judged by the psychological states it produces.

Application to Kierkegaard

If this analysis of 'belief' and 'will' is correct, there is something wrong with Kierkegaard's understanding of the concepts. He seems to be mistaken on both the descriptivist and prescriptivist theses of volitionalism. He writes as though it were possible to believe directly whatever one wills to believe and that one *ought* to proceed in this manner. Normally, we have seen, believing takes place apart from the will; it is an event rather than an act; and trying to get oneself to believe what the evidence doesn't permit is generally immoral.

Kierkegaard might answer that we have been speaking of ordinary belief ('opinion') whereas he is primarily concerned with existential belief (in spite of his application of volitionalism to historical beliefs in the "Interlude"). In ordinary believing, assent may come automatically as a function of the world's representing itself to us. But existential propositions (and others that have the relevant feature) are equiposed, with equal amounts of evidence on both sides. The evidence is essentially indecisive, insufficient to sway us to either side. In such a situation, one might be allowed to let his desires count in making a choice one way or the other.

If I strongly want p to be the case, but there is no decisive evidence one way or the other, why should I not choose to believe that-p? I can continue to live with a suspended judgment (tailoring my beliefs exactly to the evidence and, hence, believing very little); but if I can give a good reason for wanting p, it seems that there is justification for this action. Why cannot I live with a weaker standard of rationality? This argument is similar to William James's discussion, where the proposition is "lively, momentous, and forced."

The response to the existential argument is to admit that there may be times when one overrides one's duty to seek the truth because of some higher duty. I suppose that if I knew I could do enormous social good (or prevent enormous harm) by believing something there is no evidence for, I might have an obligation to do so. The problem is how do we know when we are in such a situation? Isn't there a presumption toward impartial truth seeking which can only be overcome when an overwhelming case has been made against it? (I trust I have shown that this is the case.)

Has Kierkegaard given us any reason to rescind this presumption and believe the "truth which is true for me," the "truth which edifies"?[50] I think the answer is found in a combination of his skepticism and belief in the passions as the ultimate key to truth. Like Hume (as we noted in chapter 2), Kierkegaard believed that reason functions mainly as a rationalizer of the passions. He believed we have knowledge of very little, and for the rest (beliefs and opinions), the passions are at work. "Reason is and ought to be a slave of the passions."

Concerning any belief, I can find as many reasons for as against; therefore, reflection ends in irrationality of its own, for it prohibits action where an act is forced. "If I really have reflection and am in the situation in which I must act decisively . . . my reflection will put forth as many possibilities pro and contra, exactly as many." This is an absurd situation— "that I, a rational being, must act in the situation where my reason, my reflection says to me, 'You can just as well do the one thing as the other,' that is, where my reason and reflection say to me, 'You can not act,' but where I nevertheless must act" (*Papers*, X^1 A 66).

In the *Postscript*, Climacus speaks of coming to the "fork in the road," as though two roads lie before us, both equally unknown, and we can take only one. How can we choose? Kierkegaard thinks reason is impotent. We must follow the dictates of our feelings, our passions. Reasons come later.

As we saw in the previous chapter, Kierkegaard had enormous faith in the passions as intuitions informing us of the right way. Unfortunately, many people find themselves with conflicting intuitions or with intuitions which are reliably wrong. Nevertheless, we may grant Kierkegaard his point about the insufficiency of reason in certain situations. What is hard to grant is that this is a general truth about our deepest beliefs. Are they as arbitrary as the fork in the road? Even if we admit that our deepest metaphysical beliefs cannot be proved, they are open to rebuttal and falsification, to new evidence and adjustment. At least the person who values objective truth, who wants to have rational beliefs, would strive to qualify even his deepest beliefs.

It is certainly true that the believer in God does not expect his belief to be undermined or disproved by new evidence, but if he is a rational believer, he is always open to argument. Kierkegaard, as we saw in chapter 2, would never admit this. His view of commitment as absolute proscribes impartiality in judgment. Regarding existential beliefs, objectivity is not only useless, it is bad.

I suspect we have reached an impasse, for it may not be possible to refute Kierkegaard. That is, it may not be possible to show that the choice of rational belief is to be preferred to his view of absolute commitment, with its strikingly nonrational component. Kierkegaard would likely reject any justification of rationality as depending on prior acceptance of rationality.

We have seen that Kierkegaard accepted the prescriptive feature of volitionalism: it is good to tailor one's beliefs to one's deepest desires. This prescription fits only his existential beliefs, not his ordinary beliefs, and could be indirect. What remains to be done in this section is to see whether he can be defended vis-à-vis the descriptivist feature of volitionalism: belief is directly a matter of will.

It is probable that Kierkegaard never thought of the relation between ordinary belief and dispositions in relation to the will, for he expressed himself rather loosely on the subject ("the conclusion of belief is not so much a conclusion as a resolution"). It seems to me that he takes it for granted that all believing has a volitional aspect inasmuch as assent is necessary. Here, it seems, he fails to make the distinction between different types of assent. Assenting to an action is quite different from assenting to a belief. I can choose (assent) to tell a lie or assent to a proposal for higher taxes, but I assent to these acts because I have already judged (belief assent) them to be 'good' (in some respect). Assenting in actions is voluntary, but assenting in a belief is not voluntary but automatic, "eventful."

It may be objected, however, that Kierkegaard seems to have in mind, regarding his descriptivist volitionalism, the case of skeptics,[51] who have a strong hatred of being deceived and so refuse to make assertions about contingent affairs. But such refusal tells me nothing about whether the subject (the skeptic) *believes* the state of affairs. There is a difference between believing on evidence (however weak and unstable) and claiming knowledge. The skeptic claims that he does not know what most ordinary persons claim to know. He cannot help (in typical cases) what he believes (except indirectly, by setting himself to disbelieve). So this argument fails to help Kierkegaard.

Kierkegaard's attraction for methodological doubt seems to have obscured the nature of normal belief. Skepticism seems to serve his peculiar purpose. If it is possible to put *every* contingent belief or proposition in suspension (through an indirect process of "mind setting"), it is possible to believe *any* contingent proposition. ("Belief is not a form of knowledge, but a free act, an expression of will.")[52] By reducing all that is not specifically knowledge (undeniable) to the same plane under the sharp eye of skepticism, Kierkegaard makes every belief claim equally legitimate (epistemically). He seeems to agree with Hume, who wrote, "To be a philosophical sceptic, in a man of letters, is the first and most essential step towards being a sound, believing Christian."[53]

If reason is bankrupt, the passions become paramount. In the end, the only justification for faith becomes "I believe it because I want to believe it" or, more existentially, "Only the truth that edifies is truth for you."[54]

6

'FAITH'

in

CONCLUDING

UNSCIENTIFIC

POSTSCRIPT

and

LATER *PAPERS*

'Faith' in *Concluding Unscientific Postscript*

Kierkegaard gives the concept of faith a more strikingly radical analysis in the *Postscript* than anywhere else. He defines 'faith' as "an objective uncertainty held fast in an appropriation process of the most passionate inwardness." This definition in turn is used to characterize the concept 'truth'.[1] This passionate appropriating of objectively uncertain propositions is "the highest truth attainable for an existing individual." It is clear that Kierkegaard is speaking of what we have already analyzed as 'existential faith', rather than ordinary belief.

If we analyze this definition, we see that it has a cognitive, a volitional, and an emotive aspect. The cognitive or epistemological aspect is that the object to which the subject is related is "objectively uncertain." This indicates that faith is not a form of knowledge, and Kierkegaard makes this point over and over again in the Climacus writings.[2] By 'knowledge', I understand Kierkegaard to mean a conviction (subjective certainty) that p is true where the conviction is completely warranted by objective factors, for example, proof, immediate apprehension, etc. 'Ordinary belief', on the other hand, is "a conviction (subjective certainty) that p is true where the conviction is not completely warranted by objective factors." That is, a belief is objectively uncertain. Existential belief resembles ordinary belief in being objectively uncertain, but it differs in that it goes beyond ordinary belief in being "life crucial."

It is this life-crucial or existential aspect that accentuates the 'passion' (emotive) aspect of existential faith over against ordinary belief. Ordinary belief is more or less a taking-for-granted relationship to an object. It seems to fit in with a dispositional account of belief, in being more like a happening than an action, being roughly translatable to "probability calculations." Existential belief, on the other hand, seems to be counterprobabilistic: the less probability, the better!

The above definition also contains a volitional aspect, the 'appropriation process'. Existential faith involves continually holding fast to an objective uncertainty, lest it slip away. The work of faith must be "strenuous in the highest degree." "If I wish to preserve myself in faith I must constantly be intent upon holding fast the objective uncertainty, so as to remain out upon the deep, over seventy thousand fathoms of water, still preserving my faith."[3]

The cognitive, passional, and volitional aspects must be given their rightful place in a faith situation. If any of these aspects is compromised, faith is distorted and becomes something other than existential faith. If the objective uncertainty of the object is not constantly recognized, the temptation is to "confuse knowledge with faith," transforming faith into pseudo knowledge. Hence Kierkegaard's rejection of the proofs for God's existence. Even if they were possible, Kierkegaard would reject them as undesirable (we touched upon this point in chapter 2). Faith is a higher state of being than knowledge. It is the only state appropriate to existing individuals. Kierkegaard quotes Lessing approvingly in this connection: "If God held all truth in His right hand, and in His left hand the passionate, lifelong pursuit of truth, howbeit with the addition that I ever risk error; and if God said to me, 'Choose!', I would touch His left hand and say, 'Give me this, Father, the pure truth is for Thee alone!'" (*CUP*, p. 97; my translation). Knowledge of the truth is for God alone. For an existing individual, it is the pursuit of truth that matters, even with the condition that we are bound to err.

We have noted the importance of the passions in chapter 3. To live without passion regarding one's "existence relationships" is to forget what it is to be human, to cease being part of the human drama, to withdraw from one's divinely given task. Properly to exist is to develop the passions around a suitable object in such a way that the will develops. By exercising one's freedom (will) in the uncertainties of life, the will grows stronger. As the will grows stronger, it seems to follow that it needs more difficult tasks for further development. Kierkegaard believed, as we have seen, that the will is active in believing. It would seem to follow from these premises that the will needs, as objects of belief, candidates which have a low probability. The less probable a proposition, the more will and passion needed to believe it; the more uncertain the proposition, the more "passion volition" needed to believe it. All believing involves risk of being wrong, but as the risk (objectively estimated) increases, so does the potential quality of faith: the more risk, the greater the faith. "For without risk there is no faith, and the greater the risk the greater the faith; the more objective security the less inwardness (for inwardness is precisely subjectivity), and the less objective security the more profound the possible inwardness."[4]

This strikes me as an odd argument; however, I think it is valid, given Kierkegaard's premises, which do not seem substantially different from his contemporaries'. What is wrong with the argument is the inherent volitionalism. Believing is not an act but an event, but Kierkegaard seems to make it analogous to love. By making faith, based on insufficient evidence, a virtuous act, it could be shown to follow—as Kierkegaard does—that it is clearly more virtuous to believe improbable propositions than probable ones. "The probable is therefore so little to the taste of a believer that he fears it most of all, since he well knows that when he clings to probabilities it is because he is beginning to lose faith."[5]

It would be too much to say that Kierkegaard's volitionalism is the only consistent volitionalism, but I think it represents a consistent *reductio ad absurdum* of volitionalism. Kierkegaard's shrewdness lies in the fact that he saw these implications, his weakness in the fact that he accepted them.

Climacus recognizes the paradoxical nature of existential faith: "Faith is precisely the contradiction between the infinite passion of the individual's inwardness and the objective uncertainty."[6] "The eternal essential truth is by no means in itself a paradox; but it becomes paradoxical by virtue of its relationship to an existing individual."[7] That is, the less objectivity, the less objective evidence for the truth of a proposition, and the more entirely it may be a product of subjectivity. "When subjectivity, inwardness, is truth, the truth becomes objectively a paradox; and the fact that the truth is objectively a paradox shows in its turn that subjectivity is the truth."[8] In developing this thought to its ultimate implication, every trace of objectivity must be eliminated in order for subjectivity to reign supreme. "For since the problem in question poses a decision and since all decisiveness, as shown above, inheres in subjectivity, it is essential that every trace of an objective issue should be eliminated. If any such trace remains, it is at once a sign that the subject seeks to shirk something of the pain and crisis of decision" (*CUP*, p. 115).

From the point of view of objectivity, "subjectivity is untruth." From a Christian point of view, where eternal truth and the individual are juxtaposed, subjectivity is also seen as untruth. That is, even the individual's best efforts at willing to believe in the most strenuous sense are inadequate to grasp the eternal. Here Climacus is referring to the infinite qualitative distinction between God and man. Before God we are always in the wrong and our best efforts are sinful. "Let us now call the untruth of the individual *sin*. Viewed eternally he [man] cannot be sin. . . . By coming into existence therefore (for the beginning was that subjectivity is untruth), he becomes a sinner. He is not born as a sinner in the sense that he is presupposed as being a sinner before he is born, but he is born in sin and as a sinner. This we might call *Original Sin*."[9]

If one accepts this concept of original sin, it becomes understandable why and how Kierkegaard can reject probability. All our efforts to attain truth are doomed to failure, the faculties of reason, emotion, and volition all being affected radically by sin. The best we can do is follow our passions in becoming existing individuals. Becoming passionate, becoming a subjective individual, is propaedeutic to receiving grace. Exactly why this should be preferred to following objective evidence—assuming that *both* subjective and objective faculties are depraved—is far from clear.

Climacus seems to presuppose the principle that becoming maximally human (i.e., subjective) is the proper way to prepare oneself for the possibility of revelation. As far as I can see, there is no reason why this should be the case. If subjectivity is sin, there is no reason to suppose it will get one further along the road to salvation than objectivity. However, if we are to allow Kiekegaard's thought experiment to proceed, we must assume that God values inwardness, even in sin, to such a degree that he is more likely to reveal the truth to the subjective than to the objective individual. Climacus seems to imply that being subjective is itself a gift of grace—though in such a way that it does not exclude freedom of will.

In normal existential faith the relationship is paradoxical in that subjectivity increases as objectivity decreases. But the object of faith is not in itself paradoxical (e.g., the existence of God). My relation is "absurd" but truth itself is not absurd. We might call this condition of paradoxical relationship to a nonparadox 'religiousness A' or 'Socratic faith'.[10] It is also what we have been calling 'existential faith'.

Now however, Climacus introduces a further dimension. Suppose we go beyond Socratic faith and posit a relationship in which not only the mode of apprehension (subjectivity) is paradoxical, but the apprehended and appropriated object is also paradoxical. This is a double paradox.

God "reveals the truth" — but then truth is objective after all? It seems to depend
on the subject only . . . indirectly. I must have resolve, will to believe. But finally the truth
comes from outside me.

By virtue of the relationship subsisting between the eternal truth and the existing individual, the paradox came into being [*qua* relationship in subjective truth of existential faith]. Let us now go further, let us suppose that the *eternal essential truth is itself a paradox*. The eternal truth has come into being in time: this is the paradox. . . . Existence can never be more sharply accentuated than by means of these determinations. [*CUP*, p. 187; my italics]

What is the essential paradox? That the eternal truth has entered time, that God has become a man in time. Climacus calls this the "absurd." "Christianity has declared itself to be the eternal essential truth which has come into being in time. It has proclaimed itself as the *Paradox,* and it has required of the individual the inwardness of faith in relation to that which stamps itself as an offense to the Jews and a folly to the Greeks—and an absurdity to the understanding."[11]

If Christianity is to be embraced, it cannot be through the avenue of reason, through probability calculations or scientific investigations. That way is eternally barred. Christianity cannot be understood rationally. We can only understand that it *cannot* be understood. There can be, on this analysis, no such thing as objective faith, "a sum of doctrinal propositions." It is a passionate and paradoxical relationship to a paradox. The paradox cannot be explained; it can only be accepted as the object of faith or rejected as unacceptable. To have "objective knowledge of the truth of Christianity, or of its truths, is precisely untruth."[12]

The only way to apprehend and appropriate Christianity is subjectively. Through developing inwardness to its maximum, the individual is ready for the paradox. At this point in the discussion, Climacus says that if only Pilate had asked *subjectively* what truth is, he would have been prevented from crucifying Christ. "Had he asked subjectively, the passion of his inwardness respecting what in the decision facing him he had *in truth to do,* would have prevented him from doing wrong."[13] (We noted the peculiar implications of the passage in chapter 3.) Subjectivity, as we have seen, is the only way to Christianity. "Subjectivity culminates in passion, Christianity is the paradox, paradox and passion are a mutual fit, and the paradox is altogether suited to one whose situation is to be in the extremity of existence."[14]

The logic of the argument is clear. Subjectivity as existential faith (as truth) demands risk. The greater the risk, the more opportunity for faith to exert itself (as "volition passion"). The less probable a proposition, the more it serves as a candidate for faith. An impossible (or apparently impossible) proposition is beyond the possibility of being grasped by ordinary belief (which responds to probability). It requires the highest degree of faith to believe it. Passionate faith is brought to its most profound depth in appropriating an "absurdity." As Climacus puts it at the end of the *Postscript,* "faith is the objective uncertainty due to the repulsion of the absurd held fast by the passion of inwardness, which in this instance is intensified to the utmost degree."[15] Faith, as passionate appropriation of an objective uncertainty, has become fulfilled by a perfect candidate, the paradox. The paradox intensifies subjective faith to the utmost degree.

It would seem that what Kierkegaard is aiming at or is valuing here is high subjectivity, not the paradox. The paradox is valuable as an instrument to raise subjectivity to its peak, which seems at variance with what he says at other places: it is a relationship to Christ as a person that is important. One could argue that elsewhere Kierkegaard has a different, more normal concept of faith, which is at variance with this strained notion of paradox and subjectivity; and this more normal notion is found in the religious writings. However, it is time to criticize Climacus' reasoning.

I have tried to show the weakness of the volitional theory upon which the argument is based; now I want to criticize it on three other counts: (1) allowing for far more than Christian faith, (2) involving a *reductio ad absurdum*, and (3) as founded on bad psychology.

1. If the goal of Kierkegaard's program is to produce high subjectivity (maximally intensified "passion volition") and a proposition entailing or containing a paradox (contradictory statement) is required for this, it would seem that there is no reason to choose Christianity rather than some other contradiction. Believing that God became a rat or a rotten apple or Adolf Hitler would seem equally contradictory and be even more absurd. If one replies that no one could believe this, it would be all the more reason for passionately believing these propositions. We could, with imaginative effort, construct a whole system of salvation around each of these propositions. Indeed, the problem would be to decide which absurdity is *maximally* absurd. Several— even an indefinite number of propositions—would seem suitable candidates.

The defender of Kierkegaard might reply that Kierkegaard anticipated this objection and has warned us that believing in the paradox is not the same as believing in nonsense. "Nonsense therefore he cannot believe against the understanding, for precisely the understanding will discern that it is nonsense and will prevent him from believing it; but he makes so much use of the understanding that he becomes aware of the incomprehensible, and then he holds to this, believing against the understanding" (*CUP*, p. 504).

But what criteria distinguish the 'absurd' from 'nonsense'? We are not told in the *Postscript*, at least not directly. We could infer from some aspects of the doctrine of subjectivity that it would be psychologically impossible to believe nonsensical propositions whereas it would be possible to believe the paradox of Christianity. But then we want to know wherein the offense of Christianity lies. Furthermore, if we are able to believe (via direct or indirect volitionalism) what seems to be contradictory (sometimes Climacus implies that it *is* contradictory), we should very much like to know why some paradoxes are candidates for maximally subjective faith and others are not. Climacus is silent here. It would seem that as soon as reasons are forthcoming why one paradox is acceptable and another is not, we are beyond the pale of pure subjectivity and back into objectivity, dealing with reasons and rational justification. As soon as we begin to give reasons, we limit the scope of the infinite volitionalism Climacus seems to prescribe, for the weight of reason makes a proposition more probable, so that it is no longer the hardest thing to believe.

Another possible answer to our objection is found in the *Papers*, where Kierkegaard speaks of the transformation of the "absurd" to the "not absurd."

> The absurd is a category, and the most developed thought is required to define the Christian absurd accurately and with conceptual correctness. The absurd is a category, the negative criterion, of the divine or of the relationship to the divine. *When the believer has faith, the absurd is not the absurd*—faith transforms it, but in every weak moment it is again more or less absurd to him. The passion of faith is the only thing which masters the absurd. [*Papers*, X⁶ B 79][16]

If someone comes to believe what he previously believed to be incredible, it would seem to follow that it is no longer incredible to him. It becomes an accepted proposition, in this case a first premise for inferring other things about the world and one's relationship to it. That is, the Incarnation becomes the central proposition (or postulate) around which one builds one's life.

However, this entry still does not tell us what we want to know: how to distinguish nonsense absurdities from nonnonsense absurdities. It only tells us that there is at least one 'absurd' which can be believed and hence, transformed to 'nonabsurd'. Climacus wants to grant special privilege to one and only one 'absurd' proposition, but he has failed to justify that claim.

2. There is a further problem in normalizing the 'absurdity' of Christianity. We have seen that high subjectivity is the *desideratum* and, to reach it, we need to hold passionately to an 'absurd' proposition; to maintain it, we must continue to hold onto an 'absurd' proposition. But once we believe the 'absurd' proposition, it follows that it is transformed to the 'nonabsurd'. How, then, can high or maximal subjectivity be maintained?

It would seem that a new 'absurdity' is needed (possibly denial of the old one, which has now been transformed to a 'nonabsurdity'). Since faith, *sensu eminentiori*, is "objective uncertainty due to the repulsion of the absurd held fast by the passion of inwardness," a new 'absurdity', for example, anti-Christianity, would be needed as the perfect object of faith. As such, subjectivity and anti-Christianity are the "perfect fit." But if anti-Christianity and subjectivity are the perfect fit, anti-Christianity is the 'absurd' which must be believed. But as soon as anti-Christianity is believed, it is transformed to the 'nonabsurd' (except "in every weak moment it is again more or less absurd" to the believer). But once anti-Christianity is normalized in this way, a new 'absurd' is required to keep faith at its pinnacle of passion.

If this analysis is correct, at least one additional undesirable consequence of Kierkegaard's argument is that it leads to a *reductio ad absurdum*. By ingenious dialectic, both Christianity and anti-Christianity can be judged to be the highest truth and untruth, and the 'truth' of each entails the 'truth' of the other.[17]

3. The third criticism of Kierkegaard's argument in the *Postscript*, regarding the need for a paradoxical proposition to bring subjectivity to its maximum, is that it seems bad psychology. People become maximally passionate about all sorts of weird propositions. The sophisticated dialectic of Climacus seems to suppose that only metaphysical paradoxes are sufficient to increase passion to an optimal point, but it is notorious that people become intensely passionate (as passionate as we can imagine) over propositions concerned with the value of their favorite football teams, the rights of their dogs, the destiny of their corporations or nation, or the reputations of their children.

Kierkegaard may not approve of these passions. Indeed, he would reject them as a type of madness, a type of "subjective madness" wherein the passion of inwardness embraces a particular "finite fixed idea."[18] Unfortunately, we are not given any reason for believing that "subjective madness" is less adequate in getting us to maximum subjectivity than believing in Christianity. Kierkegaard wants to insist that the proper way of being subjective is being absolutely passionate about a proposition involving one's absolute relationship or destiny, for example, a proposition involving the immortality of my soul or my relation to God, but this is a prescription rather than part of the meaning of 'maximum subjectivity'.[19]

I have outlined the argument in the *Postscript* regarding existential faith and the paradox of Christianity and have concluded that the argument fails on four counts:

1. It presupposes a volitionalism which is untenable.
2. Its premises seem to allow for any paradox as a suitable candidate for faith.
3. The argument seems to lead to a *reductio ad absurdum* in which Christianity and its denial require each other.

4. It is founded on bad psychology in presupposing that passionate faith is necessarily related to metaphysical paradoxes.

At the beginning of this chapter we noted Kierkegaard's claim that concerning the "whole question of faith," he had "advanced precise dialectical qualifications on particular points which hitherto have not been known." In our examination of Kierkegaard's treatment of faith, we have found some ingenious dialectics, some interesting speculations, and some very dubious doctrines. Kierkegaard's treatment is not as precise as he believed, and not as substantial a contribution as he claimed. There is, however, one more way to view his conception of faith.

'Faith' and 'Hope' in Kierkegaard's Later *Papers*

In this final section of this chapter on faith, we will look at one more notion of faith in Kierkegaard's writings (found primarily in various passages of his latter years in his private *Papers*) that seems to represent a more balanced and plausible thesis: faith is a sort of hoping and not a believing, in the ordinary sense of the term. Of course, this is not the only treatment of faith in the *Papers*. All of the concepts appear, in some form or other, but they are more closely dealt with in the works we have already discussed. However, the relationship to hope is best handled by looking at passages in the *Papers,* not the published works.

"In hope Abraham believed against hope, that he should become the father of many nations."[20] Abraham also hoped to get a son, and to get a son back, when there were no earthly grounds for expecting either; so Abraham's faith is a paradigm of faith for Kierkegaard. Abraham hoped to receive a son when he and Sarah were beyond the age when children could be expected, and he hoped to receive Isaac a second time, after he had sacrificed him to God. "Faith hopes also in this life, but be it observed, not by virtue of human understanding, but by virtue of the absurd. Otherwise, it is only common-sense wisdom, not faith."[21]

In this section, we will examine the concept 'hope', relate it to 'belief', and try to decide how it functions in Kierkegaard's works. We want to find out whether what Kierkegaard calls 'believing' is really 'hoping'.

1. I *hope* that the horse, Happy Dancer, will win the race, but I do not *believe* he will. Yet, because I would like the former to be the case, I bet some money on him. I act on a far-out chance, not on the probability of his winning. I act on hope, not belief—except that I believe, all things considered, that it is reasonable to put a little spare cash on a long shot. The odds are

against Happy Dancer's winning, to such a degree that if, by some miracle, he wins, I will be financially far better off than if I had not bet. We see from this illustration that hoping does not imply believing. I may *hope* that Happy Dancer will win without *believing* he will.

Nor does belief imply hope. I may believe that some horrible event will take place without in the least hoping it will. However, there are some uses of 'believing' where 'hoping' is clearly implied. One may make a tentative distinction here, calling those uses of 'believing' where hope is not implied "belief statements," where what is believed is simply propositional, and calling those statements where 'hope' is implied "faith statements," where a positive attitude toward the proposed state of affairs is included in the concept.

"Belief statements" are purely descriptive whereas "faith statements" are evaluative as well as descriptive. Religious beliefs are typically "faith statements"; they include a pro-attitude toward the object of believing. It would be odd indeed if we heard a believer say, "I have faith in God, but I hope He doesn't exist." Included in the notion 'faith' is the idea of 'hope'. The devils apparently believe without hope (James 2:19).

2. We define 'hope' as a pro-attitudinal anticipation (weak or strong) of a desired state of affairs, S, where one recognizes the contingency of not-S. As such, 'hoping', is near relation to 'desiring'. Both imply a positive attitude toward a state of affairs. The difference is that 'hoping' normally involves an idea of possibility whereas 'desiring' does not. I can *desire* to become a doctor, although I know I cannot, but I cannot *hope* to become a doctor when I know I cannot. In

a) "I desire to live forever, but I know it's impossible," and

b) "I hope to live forever, but I know it's impossible,"

(a) expresses a mere wish. But hoping is stronger than merely wishing; it expresses an expectation (however weak), a possibility. So it is a contradiction to use 'hoping' with 'impossible', as in (b).

3. Often, action is involved in hoping. If you see me standing on a corner and ask me why I am standing there, and I answer that I am hoping that my friend will come in five minutes, you would expect me to remain five minutes more. But if, immediately after stating that I hope my friend will come to meet me in five minutes, I leave the corner, you would be justified in wondering what had happened. Either something had disturbed me, so that I felt it necessary to leave immediately, or I was not hoping but only expressing a weak wish that my friend would come. Hoping implies anticipation, and if my behavior shows that I have not the least expectation that a state of affairs will obtain, it may rightly be questioned whether I really hope.

4. Sometimes our beliefs change our hopes. For example;

a) John hopes that-*p* (where *p* = [e.g.], the moral maxim that it pays to be good).

b) John comes to believe not-p (i.e., it does not pay to be good).

c) John begins to act on his belief (not-p) by not being concerned about the morality of his acts.

d) John comes to hope not-p. He hopes the very opposite of what he hoped in (a); for if morality *does* pay, he will be found to have miscalculated.

The sort of faith or believing that characterizes those committed to an ideology is typically what we labeled 'faith' rather than 'belief' (in the merely descriptive sense). The idea of hope is implied in the concept 'believing' in these religious or ideological contexts. The believer has hopes that the nonbeliever does not or need not have. The believer's hope commits him to a certain type of action. If he hopes for a kingdom where love is the ultimate force, and if he hopes that love will ultimately triumph, it will be a denial of that hope if he constantly commits offenses against what is normally considered loving behavior.

The question that is still before us is whether the person of 'faith', who hopes for realization of what he does not know to be certain, can have 'hope' in his cause without believing (propositionally) in it. Is faith dependent on belief or is faith merely a relation of trust? That is, is it more like my betting on Happy Dancer than propositional belief—with the proviso that I am not betting merely my spare cash but my life?

The question is similar to the one proposed by Pascal in his "wager argument," where he recommends that we place ourselves in the context where belief may be nurtured. We are to sprinkle holy water and say masses because the reasons why faith is better than nonfaith are so enormous. Pascal's dictum puts him in the category of what we called 'nonrational' believing—neither rational nor completely irrational. He recognized that we cannot directly will to believe in something, but we can place ourselves in a context where belief is possible.

I am not sure to what extent this characterizes faith. Usually, we assume that the person who has faith has both the necessary propositional belief plus a positive attitude of trust and hope. However, perhaps the situation of modern believers is more problematic. Some believers are what H. H. Price called "half-believers"; they have hope and trust, but are not sure whether they believe what they want to believe. Their dilemma is whether to take steps to put themselves in the appropriate context where only belief will be nurtured, or to adhere to strict standards of rationality, to attempt an honest evaluation of all the evidence, tailoring belief precisely to the evidence.

For Kierkegaard, the element of hope, of gamble, is very important in 'faith'. "Without risk faith is impossible. To be related to spirit means to undergo a test, to believe, to wish to believe, to change one's life into a trial."[22] The aspect of possibility which is part of the concept of hope, over against belief (where probability is more important), is a defining feature of his concept of faith: "Faith is essentially holding fast to possibility."[23]

One comes to faith only when all other hopes fail: "And now, now that in many ways I have been brought to the last extremity, now . . . a hope has awakened in my soul that God may desire to resolve the fundamental misery of my being. That is, now I am in faith in the profoundest sense. . . . I must never at any moment presume to say that there is no way out for God because I cannot see any" (*Papers*, VIII A 650). It appears that 'hoping' is faith in its "profoundest sense."

There are other places in the *Papers* where faith is described in terms of hoping and acting on the content of the hope. Faith is described as gambling one's life on an "if." Commenting on Socrates' hope for immortality, Kierkegaard writes:

> The question of immortality, Socrates says, concerns me so infinitely, that I stake everything on that 'if'. And so with man's relation to Christ. . . . On this I stake everything. . . . I cannot acquire an immediate certainty as to whether I have faith—for to believe means precisely that dialectical hovering which, although in fear and trembling, never despairs [gives up hope]. Faith is an infinite self-made care as to whether one has faith. [*Papers*, IX A 32][24]

We conclude that, in some passages in Kierkegaard's later *Papers*, hope seems to replace the more radical Climacian faith (faith against reason) as a dominant concept. Having faith is living-as-if-Christianity-were-true, betting one's life on its "truth value." The volitional quality is transferred from belief to life, and one maintains the tension between doubt and belief while planning one's life on the basis of a precious possibility. This attitude seems more favorable to the demands of reason, recognizing its rightful function in life. It is almost as if Kierkegaard has changed his mind on the subject, or perhaps what he wrote earlier is to be taken as a stage in his development. Whatever the reasons, his later understanding seems a more plausible and mature understanding of faith, which has not been noticed in the literature.

Ending this chapter (and the last two) on the concept of faith, we sum up the results—seven different concepts under the name 'faith' (*Tro*):
1. Aesthetic faith: an immediate, animal intuition. This is primordial faith, the stuff out of which faith proper must grow. It is the passional, imaginative, subjective element in man.
2. Ethical faith: commitment to ideals and, in particular, the rational order which is part of natural law. Faith is a reasoned allegiance to the ideals which reason discovers.

3. Religious or existential faith: a second immediacy, an attitude of passionately holding onto an object (proposition) in spite of the apparent evidence. This type of faith is immediate, like aesthetic faith—that is, spontaneous—but it appears after a certain sophistication in the ethical realm; so it is called a "second immediacy." It is the type of faith which is characterized as a leap into the unknown or swimming over 70,000 fathoms of water.

4. Ordinary belief (*Mening*): common sense, propositional belief. Kierkegaard says little about this kind of believing and seems uninterested in it. It is the kind of faith which philosophers call "belief," in the sense of automatic judgment or assessment of evidence. It differs from aesthetic faith in having evidence or being empirically based, but it is part of our animal heritage.

5. Faith as an organ for apprehending the past (history): the function or process of making the past present ("contemporary"). The believer, through a resolution of the will, appropriates the testimony of others for his own purposes. He decides to believe. This is the volitional type of belief, which we criticized in the last chapter.

6. Salvific faith (faith in 'religiousness B'): that form of faith or belief which is a combination of miraculous grace and the effort of the will (this is discussed mainly in *Fragments*). Grace must be present as the condition that enables the subject to believe, but the will must be present to decide whether the individual *will* believe. This is the faith necessary to believe the 'Paradox', which is against all reason. Here, faith is both above and against all reason. This is Climacus' idea of Christian faith.

7. Faith as hope: a modified form of religious faith (found in Kierkegaard's later papers) which suggests an attitude of living *as if* an important proposition were true—of risking one's life on behalf of an idea, even though one's mind has not been made up regarding the truth value of the proposition.

These are the ways in which the concept 'faith' is used in Kierkegaard's writings, whose uses we have examined and criticized. We have seen passionate concern with the idea, manifested in several theories. Sometimes the logic seems strained, but the insights are there. If we take what he has written as experiments for examination, we have fascinating material for a philosophy of religious faith.

7

A

JUSTIFICATION

of

CHRISTIAN

FAITH

We may conclude, that the Christian religion not only was at first attended with miracles, but even at this day cannot be believed by any reasonable person without one. Mere reason is insufficient to convince us of its veracity; and whoever is moved by faith to assent to it, is conscious of a continuous miracle in his own person, which subverts all the principles of his understanding, and gives him a determination to believe what is most contrary to custom and experience. [David Hume, *Enquiry Concerning Human Understanding*, p. 131]

Although this was written by Hume, Kierkegaard thought it was written by Hamann, a Christian humorist who quoted this passage without identifying its source. Kierkegaard was unaware of its Humean ironic twist, written (as it was) to undermine Christian faith. On the surface, it would appear that Hume and Kierkegaard could agree on one thing: it is irrational to be a Christian; it subverts all the principles of understanding. This has been the traditional interpretation of Kierkegaard's position, especially in the *Concluding Unscientific Postscript*.

From Brandes and Schrempf to Barrett and Blanshard, friend and foe alike have united in labeling Kierkegaard an irrationalist, his position an "intellectualistic anti-intellectualism."[1] A few interpreters (viz. Fabro and Søe) have denied this, as an exaggerated reading of Kierkegaard, and have made a case for a *supra rationem* position, but these interpretations tend to neglect important contrary evidence. They are heavily dependent on Kierkegaard's later journal entries.[2]

Herbert Garelick, on the other hand, has shown that the antirationalist and the transrationalist positions are consistent with each other.[3] Something which is contrary to our ordinary ways of thinking may also be *beyond* our ordinary ways of thinking, and he criticizes the *supra rationem* position for failing to take the antirational aspects in Kierkegaard's thought seriously enough. To this extent, I agree with Garelick, and I wish to show that the irrationalist and suprarational aspects are rationally combined by Kierkegaard into a consistent argument that results in a rational justification for Christian belief. I will bring together the conclusions of the earlier chapters to show the nature of the underlying argument for a rational defense of the leap into Christian faith. The argument centers on the Climacus writings; hence it may be more appropriate to call the argument Climacus', though I find no good reason to deny that the premises are also Kierkegaard's.

My thesis is that an ingenious argument is embedded in the Climacus writings, which, if sound, would make it not merely rationally permissible to accept Christianity but rationally incumbent to do so. My thesis (which I have already set forth elsewhere)[4] has received a protracted critique in Gregory Schufreider's "Kierkegaard on Belief without Justification"[5] in which he agrees that there is a serious argument in Kierkegaard's writings, but he disagrees sharply on the matter of subjectivity resulting in objective truth. In this chapter, I will make use of Schufreider's critique to reconstruct the argument.

My point, I must emphasize, is not to be faithful to Kierkegaard's intentions (it may be that he missed the implications), but to work out the implications of the premises he held and set forth in the *Postscript* and supporting works. At the end, I shall point out the logical consequences of the argument. First, however, I shall state, then discuss, the argument.

1. It is possible to have an appropriate relationship to the highest truth. Call this the truth-relation (TR).
2. One can attain TR either subjectively or objectively; there is no other alternative.
3. Objectivity, the way of disinterested reflection, is wholly inappropriate, because
   a) It fails on its own terms;
   b) It leaves out the self, which is essential to the relationship to truth.
4. Therefore (by 1, 2, and 3), TR must be attained subjectively (by interested reflection).
5. Not every type of subjectivity but only a subclass brings one to TR (there are inadequate forms of subjectivity). Only a state of faith is adequate for TR; it is both a necessary and sufficient condition for TR.

(Faith may be defined as subjective certainty over a proposition involving one's eternal telos, which is objectively uncertain.)

6. Faith increases in quality, in passion, in proportion to the objective uncertainty or improbability of the proposition believed. Faith involves risk, and the more risk the more faith there may be.

7. Therefore (by 6), the less objective evidence a proposition has in its favor or the more evidence it has against it, the greater the faith necessary to believe it.

8. Christianity (the proposition that God became man to save man) is the uniquely absurd proposition that has the most objective evidence against it. It is the Paradox and, as contradictory, is objectively impossible.

9. Therefore (by 7 and 8), if one has faith in Christianity, one will be in a maximal state of faith. No greater faith is possible.

10. Therefore (by 5 and 9), faith in Christianity constitutes being in TR.

11. To be in TR is to transcend temporality in such a way as to cause the individual to *know* the eternal (highest) truth. That is, if one is in TR over a proposition p, then p must be true. TR is a necessary and sufficient condition for possessing highest truth.

12. One can know when one is in TR; it is self-authenticating via introspection.

13. Therefore (by 11 and 12), one can know when one's faith has a true proposition as its object. But this is to know the highest truth.

14. Therefore (by 10, 11, and 13), one can know that Christianity is true. It is the highest truth, and through subjective reflection via faith, one can know it.

15. Hence (by 11 and 14), if one wants to enjoy TR and have knowledge of the highest truth, it is incumbent on one to become a Christian: to make a leap of faith into the absurd, believing the Paradox of the Incarnation. It would be positively irrational not to do so, given the desire for eternal truth and eternal happiness.

This argument, as I see it, is implicit in the *Postscript*. Whether a better or different, but equally valid, reconstruction is possible, I shall not decide here. The first ten premises are relatively uncontroversial. (Schufreider, for one, seems to concur with most of this part of the argument.) At issue are premises 11 to 15. Hence I will go through the argument, up to 11, more quickly than adequate analysis calls for, then spend more time on the eleventh premise.

1. *It is possible to have an appropriate relationship (TR) to the highest truth.*

Kierkegaard never doubts that there is a highest truth, an "eternal essential truth," and that somehow eternal happiness (the individual's telos) is in a relationship with it. He "assumes that there awaits [him] a highest good, an eternal happiness," predicated on a relationship to some proposition or doctrine (p. 19). The rest of the *Postscript* is elucidation of the nature of that relationship and the doctrine espoused.

Climacus professes to leave the question of the truth of Christianity unexamined, but he does not doubt that there is metaphysical truth. "Reality itself is a system—for God" (p. 107). Whether we need to assume the existence of God at this point is an open question, but I think the argument can work without it. (It will come in soon enough by other means.) What is vital is the assumption that there is metaphysical truth and that, somehow, we can be related to it. Whether we can *know* it in some sense is another matter.

2. *One can attain TR either subjectively or objectively; there is no other alternative.*
3. *Objectivity, the way of disinterested reflection, is wholly inappropriate because*
   a) *It fails on its own terms;*
   b) *It leaves out the self, which is essential to the relationship to truth.*

Objectivity signifies disinterested reflection; subjectivity signifies interested reflection; thus they are mutually exclusive. Objective reflection demands impartial use of deductive or inductive reasoning that disallows the self from inferring more than what is in the premises. Subjective reflection demands that the self's deepest instincts be allowed to reign in spite of the evidence. All commitment, trust, faith, as well as propositional belief (contrasted with knowledge), take place within subjectivity, where the passions and decision of the will are necessary factors.

Climacus tries to show the double deficiency of objectivity. It can never reach the certainty demanded by the need for eternal happiness and it leaves out the self, whose happiness is precisely in question. Deductive reason can never reason successfully to metaphysical conclusions without assuming the conclusions in the premises; hence all proofs of this sort are question begging. "In beginning my proof I presuppose the ideal interpretation, and also that I will be successful in carrying it through; but what else is this but to presuppose that God exists, so that I really begin by confidence in Him" (*F*, p. 52).

Inductive reasoning has a similar defect. Instead of placing the conclusion within the premises, however, one makes a leap from the premises to the conclusion. "As soon as I form a law from experience, I place something in which is more than there is in the experience itself."[6] All the observation in the world will never get one from empirical statements to metaphysical truth.

However, even if it were possible to know the highest truth objectively, it would be undesirable because of the nature of man. Objective knowledge, if possible, would be inimical to development of the self, which is essentially a passional entity that needs to develop its emotional and volitional aspects through striving in situations of risk and objective uncertainty. Kierkegaard sometimes refers to this as the "self's freedom." It is this eternal aspect in man which calls forth the idea of an eternal telos in the first place. Objective truth, imposed on the self by objective means, would be an impersonal operation, for objective truth is impersonal and using objective means stifles the spiritual development of the self.

Climacus admits that if there is eternal life, in the sense of an afterlife, we may someday have objective knowledge of metaphysical truth—in heaven—but here, in temporality, our task is to develop our self through striving and exercise of the will in overcoming difficulties. So it is clear that objectivity fails on Climacus' view of the matter.

> 4. *Therefore (by 1, 2, and 3), TR must be attained subjectively (by interested reflection).*

By denying the disjunct, we obtain 4. Subjectivity is the only way to obtain a proper relationship to the highest truth, whatever it is. We cannot, and ought not, use objective reflection to attain the highest truth. We need to use a means appropriate to our station as existing, finite individuals. Eternal happines is an existential problem, and as such it demands passionate reflection. "All existential problems are passionate problems, for when existence is interpenetrated with reflection it generates passion. To think about existential problems in such a way as to leave out the passion, is tantamount to not thinking about them at all, since it is to forget the point, which is that the thinker is himself an existing individual" (*CUP*, p. 313).

> 5. *Not every type of subjectivity but only a subclass brings one to TR (there are inadequate forms of subjectivity). Only a state of faith is adequate for TR; it is both a necessary and sufficient condition for TR. (Faith may be defined as subjective certainty over a proposition involving one's eternal telos, which is objectively uncertain.)*

Climacus strives to differentiate various forms of subjectivity. He speaks of "subjective madness," being passionately concerned with a finite, fixed idea (p. 175) as a form of aberrant inwardness. He contends that the understanding will discover the difference between nonsense and a valid candidate for subjective espousal, though the exact criteria are not given (p. 504). True subjectivity must have an object which involves the self fundamentally and must make sense within a wider anthropological framework. The framework Climacus supposes is one wherein the self develops spiritually by ascending a hierarchy of life forms until one reaches an eternal telos, and ascent takes place largely through subjective introspection and decision.

Faith, the highest form of subjectivity, may be defined as holding to an objectively uncertain proposition on which is predicated one's eternal happiness with passionate certainty. Faith is a decision-making apparatus; it decides to believe and commit oneself to propositions. It is in this overcoming of uncertainty of evidence that it develops itself, raises the level of its passion, bringing it to a high state. Only in this passion of faith, the "happy passion," is the self purified. In this way, anyone who has a sufficient degree of faith may be said to be "in truth"—"subjectivity is truth." More precisely, faith at a certain level guarantees a proper relationship to TR. It is the appropriate response to the eternal telos.

> 6. *Faith increases in quality, in passion, in proportion to the objective uncertainty or improbability of the proposition believed. Faith involves risk, and the more risk the more faith there may be.*

Climacus makes a radical distinction between belief and knowledge. In knowledge I have objective certainty, the assurance which comes from using the standard methods of reasoning, of science, in order to achieve certain results. Believing, on the other hand, implies the possibility of erring objectively. It is a state of being objectively uncertain about the truth value of a proposition, yet assenting to the proposition. As such, belief involves risk, which is a correlate of uncertainty. As soon as certainty is present, risk is no longer present.

The less objective evidence I have for p, the greater the risk in believing p, the greater the chance of being wrong. The greater the chance of being wrong in espousing a belief that p, the more difficult it is to believe that p; the more effort required of the will. "Without risk there is no faith, and the greater the risk, the greater the faith; the more objective security, the more profound the possible inwardness (for inwardness is precisely subjectivity), and the less objective security, the more profound the possible inwardness" (p. 188).

> 7. *Therefore (by 6), the less objective evidence a proposition has in its favor or the more evidence it has against it, the greater the faith necessary to believe it.*
>
> 8. *Christianity (the proposition that God became man to save man) is the uniquely absurd proposition that has the most objective evidence against it. It is the Paradox and, as such, is objectively impossible.*

The greater the unlikelihood of p obtaining, the greater the effort of the will to hold fast to p. The improbability of p repulses the rational aspect of man and forces the passion into extreme intensity. If a person is to believe p, he must believe it against his reason, against probability. "Faith is the objective uncertainty due to the repulsion of the absurd held fast by the passion of inwardness" (p. 540). It follows that not only is probability not possible for faith, *sensu eminenti*, it is not even desirable.

Usually, we regard high probability as necessary to justify belief in a proposition, but, viewing faith as intense passionate believing, we come to the opposite conclusion. Probability is the enemy of faith because it diminishes the challenge of the will, the enormity of the risk. "Probability is therefore far from precious to the believer. He fears it most of all, since he knows well that when it is present, he has begun to lose faith" (p. 209). In effect, faith's proper correlate is the Paradox, a uniquely absurd proposition.

So there is a type of faith which goes beyond even ordinary faith. Ordinary faith is believing *in spite* of weak evidence or no positive evidence; extraordinary faith is believing *against* all the evidence. In ordinary faith, which is a determinant of religiousness A, the object of faith is objectively uncertain. In extraordinary faith, which is a determinant of religiousness B, the object of faith is, objectively, certainly absurd.

> When Socrates believed that there was a God, he held fast to the objective uncertainty with the whole passion of his inwardness, and it is precisely in this contradiction and in this risk, that faith is rooted. Now it is otherwise. Instead of the objective uncertainty, there is here a certainty; namely, that objectively it is absurd; and this absurdity, held fast in the passion of inwardness, is faith. Socratic ignorance is as a witty jest in comparison with the grave strenuousity of faith. [*CUP*, p. 188]

The candidate that passes all the tests for a suitable object of faith at its peak is an Absolute Paradox, the proposition embodied within the doctrine of the Incarnation. Presumably, it will be the only candidate to pass all relevant tests. It is not nonsense, nor a finite idea, but contains a contradiction having to do with the eternal in relation to temporality. It follows from the argument:
   a) God is infinite, eternal, beyond becoming (beyond temporality), all knowing, etc.
   b) Man is finite, noneternal, becoming (temporal), not all knowing, etc.
   c) Therefore, God and man are mutually exclusive genuses. In Kierkegaard's words, there is an "infinite qualitative distinction between God and man."[7]
   d) Hence to say that God became man in Jesus of Nazareth is to state an apparent contradiction: there is someone who is finite and not-finite in

the same respect, eternal and not–eternal in the same respect, all knowing and not–all knowing in the same respect.

> 9. *Therefore (by 7 and 8), if one has faith in Christianity, one will be in*
> *a maximal state of faith. No greater faith is possible.*

The Paradox, the central affirmation of Christian faith, corresponds perfectly to the requirements of faith. By being highly improbable and seem-
ingly impossible, it requires the most strenuous and passionate effort, the
greatest risk and sacrifice of finite understanding to believe. "If I wish to
preserve myself in faith I must constantly be intent upon holding fast the
objective uncertainty, so as to remain out upon the deep, over seventy thousand fathoms of water, still preserving my faith. . . . Subjectivity culminates
in passion, Christianity is the paradox, paradox and passion are a mutual fit"
(*CUP*, pp. 182, 206).

> 10. *Therefore (by 5 and 9), faith in Christianity constitutes being in TR.*

If our argument is correct to this point, then, according to Climacus,
Christianity turns out to be the proper way of relating to the eternal truth.
One must believe the Paradox. One cannot *understand* the Paradox—only
that faith demands such as its proper object. One must believe against one's
understanding, even against one's higher understanding. From an objective
point of view, the matter must be judged absurd, but from the point of view
of faith, it is the only thing that would ever qualify as a suitable object.

Up to this point, most Kierkegaard scholars seem to be in substantial
agreement. Except for some possible difference on the nature of the first two
propositions, Schufreider also seems to agree with this analysis (I think he has
simply overlooked the assumptions that form the background of the
Postscript). However, it is at this point that significant differences appear.

> 11. *To be in TR is to transcend temporality in such a way as to cause the*
>   *individual to* know *the eternal truth (highest truth). That is, if one is*
>   *in TR over a proposition* p, *then* p *must be true. TR is a necessary*
>   *and sufficient condition for possessing highest truth.*
> 12. *One can know when one is in TR; it is self-authenticating via*
>   *introspection.*
> 13. *Therefore (by 11 and 12), one can know when one's faith has a true*
>   *proposition as its object. But this is to know the highest truth.*

Kierkegaard's anthropology holds the view that man is a composite being,
made up of both the finite and the infinite, the temporal and the eternal.
Hence he can have an eternal telos. Somehow, this aspect is qualitatively

different from God's eternity (Kierkegaard doesn't throw a great deal of light on this distinction). As both infinite and finite, eternal and temporal, the individual may be cured of essential alienation by uniting the two factors in a higher unity, grounded in the power which posited them in the first place. The reason, according to Climacus, why we cannot have metaphysical knowledge normally is that we are locked into temporality and finitude (from a Christian point of view, we are cut off from the truth by sin); but in faith or maximal passion (which results from faith) we may overcome that temporality and, hence, have access to truth. Precisely in passion, Climacus says, this occurs "momentarily."

> If an existing individual were really able to transcend himself, the *truth* would be for him something final and complete; but where is the point outside himself? . . . It is only momentarily that the particular individual is able to realize existentially a unity of the infinite and the finite which transcends existence. The unity is realized in the moment of passion . . . In passion the existing individual is rendered infinite in the eternity of the imaginative representation, and yet he is at the same time most definitely himself. [*CUP*, p. 176]

The failure of objectivity, it seems, is that it uses the wrong means to get to the right goal. The way to the highest truth, according to this anthropology, is through subjectivity, through the stages of various forms of life to the highest peak of passionate faith. In the passion of ecstasy (which I am tempted to call 'mystical') the eternal truth is guaranteed.

As support for these conclusions, note the strong emphasis Kierkegaard placed on the doctrine of recollection throughout the Climacus works, including his comments on these works in the private *Papers*. It has been insufficiently noticed that Kierkegaard embraced the Platonic doctrine of recollection as a way of knowing immanent metaphysical truth (though not the Paradox). To take but the most conspicuous example, he says that we can know through recollection that God exists and that we are immortal (have an eternal telos). We cannot know these things through objective reason, but we can have objective knowledge through passionate introspection.

> Both [proving and being convinced by an argument for the existence of God] are equally fantastic, for just as no one has ever proved the existence of God, so no one has ever been an atheist, although many have never willed to allow their knowledge of God's existence to get power over their mind. It is the same with immortality . . . with regard to God's existence, immortality, and all problems of immanence, recollection is valid; it is present in every man, only he may not be aware of it; however, this doesn't mean that his concept is adequate. [*Papers*, V B 40; my translation. The passage is a comment on chapter 3 of *Fragments*.]

In another place Kierkegaard says, "I do not believe God exists, I know it, but I believe that God existed [the historical]."[8] Numerous passages, neglected by most scholars, point to epistemological results of subjectivity via introspection. Every man knows the moral law which is based in God. Through subjectivity, one will be led to do and believe the truth. If Pilate had been subjective, he would not have condemned Christ to be crucified.[9] God will lead the truly subjective person to the truth (p. 543).

> But verily, as little as God lets a species of fish remain in a particular sea unless the plant also grows there which is its nutriment, just so little shall God leave in ignorance of what he must believe the man who was truly concerned. That is to say, the need brings the nutriment, the thing sought is in the seeking which seeks it; faith is the concern at not having faith . . . by virtue of God's ordinance. [*CD*, p. 248f.]

This certainly seems at odds with Climacus' earlier asseverations that objectivity is inimical to spirituality. He must have meant that objective reflection is the wrong way to objective truth, but at the height of subjectivity one gets what objective reflection couldn't give. What is bad about objectivity is the way it holds objective truth—as impersonal. Subjectivity seems to become a mere appropriation process which is the true guarantee of the truth. Live within your light and you will get more. "Truth manifests itself to the lover of truth."[10] When the proper 'how' is present, "the 'what' is also present."[11] The process seems self-authenticating: you'll know it when you see it!

14. *Therefore (by 10, 11, and 13), one can know that Christianity is true. It is the highest truth, and through subjective reflection via faith, one can know it.*

If the above is accurate, it seems that Climacus is committed to say that we can not merely believe the Paradox is true, but we can know it. If maximal passion guarantees believing in a true proposition and if Christianity is the proposition necessary to raise the passions to their peak, one cannot be wrong when he believes in Christianity. If this is so, we can know that Christianity is objectively true. In spite of what Kierkegaard says, he seems committed to saying that faith, at its pinnacle, is a "kind of knowledge": "When the believer has faith, the absurd is not the absurd—faith transforms it, but in every weak moment it is more or less absurd to him. The passion of faith is the only thing which masters the absurd—if not, then faith is not faith in the strictest sense, but a kind of knowledge" (*Papers*, X[6] B 79).

The absurd, so to speak, is "naturalized" in the moment of faith; but, *contra* Kierkegaard, it seems that it *does* become a "kind of knowledge." It is a true belief, there is inward certainty, and if the argument is correct and you see the logic of it, then you can *know* that it is true. It doesn't mean that you can understand *how* it can be true. Presumably, God's omnipotence overrides even the laws of logic, so that the Paradox can be believed on a higher authority.

> 15. Hence (by 11 and 14), if one wants to enjoy TR and have knowledge of the highest truth, it is incumbent on one to become a Christian: to make a leap of faith into the absurd, believing the Paradox of the Incarnation. It would be positively irrational not to do so, given the desire for eternal truth and eternal happiness.

It would seem that we have here an argument for the imperative of becoming a Christian. Christianity is not irrational, nor merely a rational option, but the *only* way to knowledge of the highest truth and enjoyment of eternal happiness. Anyone who wants these *desiderata* must necessarily want to become a Christian. However, we need to add a few more premises to our argument, premises that are implicit in what we have already noted.

> 16. But if one can know that Christianity is the highest truth, there is no longer any risk in believing it, and hence it is not a suitable object for either faith or TR (by 6 and 14).
> 17. Therefore (by 5), if one wishes to be in TR, one must believe in a new absurdity, something which is contrary to Christianity.
> 18. But each new candidate for TR will be handicapped with the same consequences as Christianity (in 16): to know it is true is to disqualify it as a suitable proposition for faith's epistemic and passionate risk. This will lead to an infinite regress of absurdities which, unfortunately, are self-refuting.
> 19. Therefore (by 1 and 18), there can never be a suitable candidate for TR. So proposition 1 must be false (or at least a paradox). We can never have an appropriate relationship to the highest truth.

That is, once faith takes you to the point of maximal passion, it ceases to function as faith. What results is a state (an achievement) of maximal passion which must be differentiated from the activity (faith) that brought one there. But the state transforms the "absurd to the not-absurd." Indeed, it seems to guarantee knowledge. Hence a new absurdity is needed to take the place of Christianity, something like anti–Christianity. But an infinite amount of contraries is possible, all of which refute themselves. Hence, either we cannot have a relation to the highest truth or Kierkegaard's way of getting there is wrong.

If Kierkegaard's epistemological psychology is true (which I argued against in the last chapter), the "absurd conclusion" seems exactly what follows. Only a paradox about the Absolute is sufficient to raise the passions to their highest pitch, because it requires the most intense effort of passion to believe such a paradox. If this is true, we are in a state of maximal subjectivity (M) only at the moment of overcoming our rational inhibitions, in which we believe a contradiction (the *sacrificium intellectus* which is necessary for the occasion). If we believe that the Paradox is true (for whatever reason or by whatever cause), it is no longer, as Kierkegaard states, absurd; for we believe it is somehow true. But if we believe it is true and no longer absurd, faith has lost its *fitting* object, that which was necessary to bring passion to its height. So if faith has lost its suitable object, the Absurd *qua* absurd, it is no longer in M. But M is the real goal (as Schufreider says, "the sole significance of Christianity resides in its possibility for inciting subjectivity").[12] Hence the subject must either lose his faith, in order to regain the moment M, or find a new absurdity which is adequate to raise subjectivity to M. The argument goes like this:

1. If one believes (occurrent) a contradiction about the deity, one must be in a state M.
2. Once one believes (dispositional) a contradiction about the deity, one is no longer in M because the contradiction is no longer seen as impossible (absurd).
3. But M is the *desideratum*.
4. Hence the subject must seek to believe a fresh absurdity about the deity in order to attain M.

It is very important to make a distinction between belief in its occurrent sense and belief in its dispositional sense. Kierkegaard fails to notice this difference, treating faith entirely as an occurrence, as an act, but failing to realize sufficiently that when one comes to believe, one is in a state of settlement where doubt and uneasiness over the proposition vanish (as Peirce points out). Faith as an occurrence may be a necessary condition to M, but, on Kierkegaard's premises, it can only be operative so long as it doesn't attain a belief. As soon as the subject attains its object in belief, he must lose it (being in M), because the tension and excitement are in the striving, not the attainment.

Of course, the "absurd conclusion" of the last four premises (16–19) depends on premise 11 being true. ("To be in TR is to transcend temporality in such a way as to cause the individual to *know* the eternal truth [highest truth]. That is, if one is in TR over a proposition *p*, then *p* must be true. TR is a necessary and sufficient condition for possessing highest truth.") This, the reader will recall, is what we identified as the Platonic version of the subjectivity thesis in chapter 3. I have tried to show that there is evidence that Kierkegaard sometimes wrote as though this were his position, but at other times he seems to have had other positions in mind.

If one believes that the typical thesis regarding subjectivity is either the Socratic (reduplication) thesis or the necessary-condition thesis, then the more preposterous implications of the argument are removed. However, the argument still suffers from the fact that it is impossible to believe consciously in a contradiction, believing—as Kierkegaard would prescribe—that the proposition about the Incarnation is both absurd (which implies that it is false) and true. One must modify the notion of absurdity to "seems absurd to ordinary human reason," but, as we have shown, there may be good reason to suspend "ordinary human reason," at least some of the time, in favor of *un*ordinary reasoning.

Perhaps more fundamental still is the fact that the first segment of the argument (premises 1 to 4) seems misleading. As I showed in chapter 2, discussing Kierkegaard's view of faith and history, the subjectivity/objectivity dichotomy may be a false opposition. It presumes an impossibility of being impartial and passionate at the same time, and it assumes that objectivity and neutrality are somehow closely related or even near-synonyms. I have argued that they are not, and that reason can be very passionate. One can seek the best objective evidence by passionate inquiry.

8

CONCLUSION

I have tried to show that Kierkegaard can be examined as a philosopher who sets forth theses and defends them, who uses reason to establish his theses. I have examined their content as well as his arguments, especially those in the published Climacus writings. I have distinguished his first-order uses of reason (i.e., using reason directly to establish a conclusion) from his second-order uses (i.e., giving reasons for the limits of reason). He approves the latter with regard to religious truth, but not the former. I have distinguished various forms of the theory of subjectivity, showing that the matter is ambiguous in Kierkegaard's works, but that it aims at the highest objective truth (eternal truth).

If I am correct, Kierkegaard is not essentially a deconstructivist, an anti-philosopher, as Mackey would have it. He has a message: that Christianity is objectively true, though he doesn't claim to understand how it is true or how one can reconcile apparently incompatible assertions within it.

His stages of existence are not merely optional life styles, equally valid, as Thompson and others have claimed. They presuppose a teleological view of man that Kierkegaard believes must culminate in Christian faith.

Essentially, Kierkegaard is not even an existentialist, if this means that existence precedes essence, for, on his view, existence is the means of reaching eternal essences, only asymptotically in this life but more substantially in the next. Subjectivity, in a dialectical sense, is both truth and untruth, but no substitute for objective, eternal truth. That he did not emphasize this ontological commitment is explained by his mission to awaken "Christians" in Christendom to the inappropriateness of their relation to faith.

I have tried to show that Kierkegaard's philosophy is an outworking of orthodox Christianity. Perhaps it can be seen more precisely as an explication of Lutheranism, with its emphasis on faith and grace. It is true that Kierkegaard does not "go along" with the Lutheran doctrine of election; he holds a synergist position (as I have shown in chapter 5), embracing the notion of free will. However, important as free will is for him, he does not value it as highly as the positive notion of freedom as liberation to divine service. True freedom is in submission to God's will. "The most tremendous thing conceded to man is—choice, freedom. If you want to rescue and keep it, there is but one way—in the very same instant unconditionally in full possession to give it back to God and yourself along with it."[1]

In his theory of subjectivity we see the most revealing similarity with Luther. Compare Kierkegaard's discussion in the *Postscript* with the following passage in Luther's *Greater Catechism:*

What means it to have a God? Or what is God?

Answer: God is one from whom we can expect all good and in whom we can take refuge for all our needs, so that to have God is nothing else than to trust him with all our hearts; as I have often said, that trust and faith of the heart alone make both God and Idol. If thy faith and thy trust are right, then thy God is also the right God, and again if thy trust is false and wrong, then thou hast not the right God. For the two, faith and God, hold close together. Whatever then thy heart clings to (I say) and relies upon, that is properly thy God. [*Luther's Primary Works*, p. 34][2]

Kierkegaard attempted something great: a comprehensive Christian philosophy based on human developmental psychology. He offered a dialectical mapping of life's terrain as a guide to serious pilgrims. The center of his philosophy is a view of man that emphasizes an eternal telos yet acknowledges a depth of alienation and self-deception in an ever-rationalizing egoism. Reason is useless and inappropriate in overcoming ultimate despair because sin and deception distort the nature of things. However, reason can play a role of servant, pointing to the place where the leap of faith must be made. The place where it must be made, to which reason properly and finally points, is Christian faith.

Kierkegaard, as I say, attempted something great but failed to attain it, partly because subjectivity is both too narrow and too broad for the task. It is too narrow in its neglect of the objective factors of existence. Probability is, after all, the guide of life and, incomplete though it is, must be brought into the debate, even if it may cause us to have a less tenacious faith than Climacus would like. Subjectivity is also too broad, for it seems to allow almost any object at all. In the end, in spite of Climacus' concern to delimit the notion, the criteria fail to distinguish between sense and nonsense.

Nevertheless, the concept serves as an antidote, as a corrective to an overly rigid and smug objectivity. Kierkegaard realized that he had sometimes exaggerated the claims of subjectivity, and in his later journals he seems to modify his earlier absolutist and fideist position. Gradually, the concept of hope replaced the strenuous and strained notion of believing against all evidence.

Isaiah Berlin has reminded us of a difference between a hedgehog and a fox. Quoting the Greek poet Archilochus, he writes, "The fox knows many things, but the hedgehog knows one big thing."[3] Yet with regard to Kierkegaard, both metaphors apply. On the one hand, he is an *arch*hedgehog, having but one truth for which he will live and die: one must be subjectively a Christian if one is to be a Christian at all. On the other hand, he is a dialectician and sees two sides (at least) of every issue. With all the cunning of the fox, he weaves the dialectical threads together, sometimes apparently contradicting himself while offering brilliant observations on the human condition, the pretensions of reason, and the various possibilities for human existence. In the end, however, the hedgehog dominates.

Or if Kierkegaard is a fox, he (like Tolstoy), found himself pulled apart by disparate tendencies and heterogeneous insights while longing for one great synthesizing idea which would make sense of the whole: the notion of subjectivity as truth. He was never finished with the idea. Indeed, if my analysis is correct, he didn't give us one idea but a family of ideas related to inwardness. In the last analysis, we must regard him as opening our eyes to the logic of inwardness in a way that few philosophers have done. We can learn more from some of his errors than from many a thinker's truths.

I do not claim that my study is the last word on any of these important matters. I have given a fairly thorough analysis of the material in the published Climacus writings and claim to have shown their fundamental arguments. My reading of the *Papers* has been a serious undertaking, and I believe I have unearthed some passages which have brought new light to the subject and, at the same time, supported my theses.

However, I have not dealt with all of Kierkegaard's works, nor all the intricacies of his thought. It may be that his treatment of the will and the nature of man in *Sickness unto Death* needs greater emphasis and that this would alter some of my conclusions about subjectivity and volitionalism. There are other interpretations of what Climacus is up to in his works and, more importantly, of Kierkegaard's purposes in using Climacus the way he does. After all, it might be claimed (as Allison does), Climacus is a humorist (as we shouldn't need to be reminded); so shouldn't the whole of the *Postscript* be viewed as a pedagogical joke (note the title alone: *un*scientific postscript)?

I have given considerations (especially in chapter 5) to negate this claim, but I haven't ended the debate. On this and many other issues (interpretations of subjectivity, the concept of volitionalism and its application to Kierkegaard, the relation to Hegel and other philosophers) there is a great deal more to be said.

I offer my research on the logic of subjectivity as data for a richer debate. Kierkegaard is not the sort of thinker who can easily be captured for all time in a series of syllogisms. That is what drives the scholar away from him in despair and, at the same time, entices him to try to unravel his enigmatic thought.

APPENDIX

KIERKEGAARD ON INDIRECT COMMUNICATION

One of the most misunderstood concepts in Kierkegaard's works is his notion and use of indirect communication. It is often stated that Kierkegaard used this mode of discourse simply to draw people inward, where "subjectivity is truth, the only truth there is." In this section I shall set forth the assumptions and purposes which underlie and motivated Kierkegaard's use of indirect discourse, showing that it plays a specific and theoretical role in his work. I shall use Kierkegaard's notes on that topic, written in his journals (*Papers*, vol. VIII B 81–89) in 1847, shortly after he finished his pseudonymous works. My focus is not on the modes of indirect communication—parable, metaphor, irony, humor, and poetic style—but on Kierkegaard's intentions and beliefs in using them.

Every observant reader of Kierkegaard's pseudonymous works must be struck by his indirect methods of communicating. His Chinese-box characters in *Either/Or* (I), who depict in various ways the essence of the aesthetic way of life; the judge in *Either/Or* (II), who preaches pedantically against aestheticism and for the ethical; Johannes de Silentio, who marvels at the faith of Abraham in *Fear and Trembling*; and Johannes Climacus, who portrays Christianity as the "Absolute Paradox" in the *Fragments* and *Postscript*—all use an indirect means of communication, so that the apparent meaning is not necessarily the real meaning. Even the acknowledged writings of the corpus, *Edifying Discourses* and *Christian Discourses*, use poetic style to create a mood in the reader. It might even be said that no single work of Kierkegaard's literary corpus, with the possible exception of *Point of View for My Work as an Author* (published posthumously), escapes the classification of indirect communication.

Perhaps the most thoroughly indirect of Kierkegaard's works is *Fear and Trembling*, an exercise in dialectical lyricism which lends itself to about as many levels of interpretation as a medieval allegorical reading of the Scriptures. On one level, the book is a panegyric to Abraham, who is contrasted with mere "knights of infinite resignation." On a more personal level, it seems to be a veiled letter to Regina (with whom he had recently broken an engagement)—an attempt to convey to her his pent-up passion and the religious motivation behind his outrageous behavior. On a metaphysical level, it is a tract about faith and reason, locating an area in life which is not subject to rational justification, which may be approached only with fear and trembling. On a specifically religious level, it is an address to comfortable bourgeois "Christians" who have ceased to see anything scandalous and absurd in the Christian gospel.

The fact that all Kierkegaard's attempts at indirect discourse seem to have failed to convey their inner message or to effect the change in attitude he hoped for caused him to wonder about the effectiveness of such a medium and to modify it greatly in his later, more explicitly Christian writings. *Either/Or* was read for its description of a seduction rather than as a warning of the bankruptcy and demonism inherent in the aesthetic way of life. Regina never understood *Fear and Trembling*, and very few copies of the Climacus works were bought or read. Judged on the basis of what Kierkegaard hoped to effect in his lifetime, the enterprise of indirect communication seemed a great failure. Kierkegaard later came to believe the method, as he employed it in the pseudonymous works, involved a type of deception which is unacceptable to the spirit of the Christian message. Nonetheless, he never abandoned it entirely, nor did he believe that all deception is wrong. Although his style changes greatly in the religious writings, vestiges from the earlier period can be seen.

In 1847, at the age of thirty-four, a year after publishing his last pseudonymous work, *Concluding Unscientific Postscript* (at the end of which he disclaimed responsibility for the views set forth by the pseudonyms), Kierkegaard set about to write lectures on the use and significance of indirect discourse.[1] He tells us that his motivation was to force people inward, where, he hoped, they would gain self-understanding and make better choices pertaining to ethical and religious matters. He identified this exercise with the Socratic maieutic method, which brings out latent knowledge through a process of suggestion and mental stimulation. However, whereas Socrates used the method to produce objective knowledge (cf. *Meno*), Kierkegaard used it to produce character and action.

The premises which led to Kierkegaard's conclusion on the appropriateness of indirect communication seem to be the following:

1. There is a hierarchy of values in human existence in which the ethical-religious modalities rank higher than the scientific or the cultural, which presupposes that there are ethical facts and that values are facts. It is, broadly, a classical view of the nature of man as having a telos, becoming a certain kind of being wherein fulfillment and happiness reside. The true man is a good man, who has realized his innate potential in a specific way. That is, he has special or peculiar abilities which must be realized if he is to be fulfilled, but he must realize these abilities in such an ethical-religious way as to realize the "universal human." The good carpenter must become not only a skilled craftsman but, more importantly, a good person.

2. One can know the ethical-religious truth. "The ethical presupposes that every person knows what the ethical is. Why? Because the ethical requires that each person realize it in every instant, but if this is the case, he must know it. The ethical does not begin with ignorance which is to be transformed to knowledge, but it begins with a knowledge and requires a realization."[2]

Kierkegaard often used 'ethical' to refer to the whole ethical-religious domain, that which has to do with man's essential being or telos. Hence, in the above quotation, he seems to refer not only to our moral duty but to knowledge of religious and metaphysical truth as well. He believes we can know that God exists, that we are immortal, and that we are free beings.[3] This may seem odd, in light of what he says in the *Postscript* and *Fear and Trembling* about the virtue of uncertainty in these matters.

The only way I can reconcile these texts is to suppose that the knowledge is had only in subjectivity. That is, the knowledge that comes from looking within can sustain us only while we are deeply subjective; ordinarily we use normal (objective) modes of justification, which leave the matter in doubt. We see here, again, the Socratic-Platonic doctrine of recollection; indeed, Kierkegaard's epistemology seems to contain a strong Platonic strain. We can know metaphysical truth only through introspection. If people will only look earnestly within themselves, they will find all the truth they need "to get on with" this life and the next.

3. We have the ability to do our duty in the ethical-religious domain. We have free will and can choose the good, if we will. Kierkegaard here—with his version of original sin, which states that it affects the totality of our lives, our reason as well as our ability to choose the good—simply follows Luther. The main effect of original sin, however, is to prevent or hinder us from *wanting* to do what we know is our duty. Presumably, if we weren't sinful, we could do our duty more easily and would have more immediate access to God's will.

To reconcile all statements in the Kierkegaardian corpus about sin, and especially original sin, would be to undertake a large work indeed. He struggled, especially in *Concept of Anxiety*, to make sense of the apparent discrepancies in holding to both the doctrine of original sin and the idea of free will. In *Concept of Anxiety* his view is that the increment of sin in the world has made it very difficult to fight against the power of sin; however, it is not impossible. We could resist being contaminated by original sin if we had chosen correctly originally. An increasingly sinful culture is imposed on every man in coming into the world; yet choice is always free.[4] Even in sin, one never entirely loses the ability to choose the good.

While Kierkegaard's philosophy is essentially practical (rather than theoretical) in intention, the focus is not on specific rules, acts, or consequences of acts, but on character. What is important for him is becoming a good person, who wills the good with all one's heart and expresses the good in virtuous living. The notion of 'the good' here seems Platonic. It is a unique, undefinable, nonnatural property which the intuition can perceive. To aim at the good is already to be on one's way toward the religious stage of existence.

If these three propositions are true, it is of the utmost importance to do everything possible to enable people to choose the good, to become ethical and religious beings who fulfill their telos. But how does one get others to choose the good? What sort of communication is appropriate to the task?

Let us answer the first question first. Something negative must happen before a person can be in a position to make the choice. The individual must be stripped of the outer encumbrances and anti-ethical "protective devices" which keep us from the important choices in life. There must be a dying to worldly concerns: sophistications which lead us away from our primitive humanity—concern with objective knowledge (scholarship, science, mathematics, and so forth) and concern for public opinion, whose noise drowns out the still small voice within.[5] We must become honest with ourselves, get back to a certain childlike simplicity (minus the childishness). Kierkegaard refers to this process as "becoming an individual" and as regaining our essential "primitivity."

> What is the importance of primitive genius? It is not so much to produce something completely new, for there really is nothing new under the sun, as it is to reexamine the universally human, the fundamental questions. This is honesty in its deepest sense. Complete lack of primitivity and the resulting reexamination, the acceptance of every-

thing automatically as common practice . . . and consequently to evade responsibility for doing what everyone else does—this is dishonest. [*Papers*, VIII B 89]

Much of Kierkegaard's authorship is dedicated to this negative task of getting people away from the din of the crowd so that they can hear their inner voice speak again. The voice speaks the truth about the meaning of life and one's moral duty. In turning inward and in advising us to do so Kierkegaard sometimes appears solipsistic, an extreme individualist, but his intentions are otherwise. He hopes to enable the individual to reach the sort of fundamental decisions that will make him a better and, in the long run, happier person.

How can all this be accomplished? What sort of communication is appropriate if our aim is to draw the individual away from his false loves and to the place where he can hear his conscience speaking with eternal authority? How do you communicate the truth of the ethical-religious domain? If you want to tell someone his house is on fire, you can tell him as much and be reasonably certain that he will understand you and take appropriate action. But how do you communicate to someone that he is living an unworthy life, has inappropriate values, is missing his telos?

Kierkegaard begins to answer this question by describing direct communication. Normal communication has three elements: the speaker (teacher), the listener (pupil), and the object (that which would be communicated).[6] Someone communicates something to someone who, on understanding the object, attains knowledge. This is the paradigm for objective knowledge. What happens with subjective knowledge, ethical-religious knowledge? Kierkegaard says the situation is altogether different.

1. The object is canceled out. Since we all know the object (viz., the ethical), we need not communicate it. Moreover, there is something inappropriate even in attempting to communicate it. "To desire to attempt to communicate the ethical in this manner is precisely the unethical."[7] Something like a category mistake is made when we try to communicate the ethical directly.

First of all, like Plato's 'Good', it is ineffable. It cannot be said, but only seen with the mind's eye. Second, and more relevant to what Kierkegaard says in the eight volumes of his private papers, the ethical is a capacity, a 'knowing how' more than a 'knowing that'. Kierkegaard refers ony to this latter reason in the text before us, but I think a good case can be made that he believed in a certain ineffable knowledge of the ethical (as suggested above).[8] That is, we have not only innate capacity to be certain kinds of people, but innate knowledge of what sort of people we ought to become.

2. The communicator is canceled out. If everyone knows what is to be communicated, it is impossible to communicate it. You cannot teach me what I already know.

3. The receiver is canceled out. It makes no sense to speak of a receiver of a communication if there is no communicator or communicated message. The conclusion is that there is "only one communicator, God."

Knowledge of the ethical is not like objective, empirical knowledge. It cannot be communicated directly. You may be able to *in*culcate science and objective information, but you can only *ex*punge the ethical. To show this, Kierkegaard likens our innate knowledge of the ethical to a farm boy's innate ability to be a soldier. The potential must be brought out by drill and practice, until the recruit becomes a soldier.

> The military assumes that every country boy who joins the army possesses the necessary capacities to develop into a soldier. . . . Now the communication begins. The corporal doesn't explain to the soldier what it is to drill, etc.; he communicates it to him as an art. He teaches him to use the abilities and potential so that they are actualized. And this is the way the ethical is communicated. . . . The object of communication is consequently not an objective knowledge but a realization. [*Papers*, VIII B 81, #5, #13]

Changing the metaphor, Kierkegaard says that, in the realm of the ethical, God is the master-teacher and we are the apprentices. Hence we must learn by doing, by obeying the teacher, which consists in knowing-how rather than knowing-that. Hence it must be communicated as an art, not a science. The error of modern philosophy, according to Kierkegaard, is to presume that ethics is a science which can be taught as any other science. He believes that adequate self-reflection will make this point self-evident. If we have a libertarian view of freedom of the will, I think it follows that external conditions (including teaching) are insufficient to make us moral. Something internal must be decisive.

How, then, does God the Teacher communicate with us? He uses "midwives" of the spirit to induce labor until we give birth to a new person—until we are forced inward and, if we choose rightly, become new creations (know how to do the good by doing it). We become virtuous beings.

What is our role in teaching or enabling others, in turn, to learn the ethical? It is clear that we cannot help anyone directly, for three reasons:

1. We are not teachers; God is.
2. The receiver already knows the objective content of the thought; so there is nothing to teach.
3. "Ethically every man must stand alone in his God-relationship."

We throw out hints, symbols, signs, and suggestions; tell parables and stories which will turn the auditor within. This is where irony serves as an appropriate speech act, which, if unraveled, points to something hidden. Likewise for Kierkegaard, humor has its essence in paradox, in the juxtaposition of opposites, and so points to what cannot be spoken. Humor is the mode of discourse, through this use of the paradox, which uniquely points to the irreducible duality between temporality and eternity. Life itself, in its contradictoriness, reflects this essential duality.[9]

Kierkegaard admits that there is something deceptive about this use of indirect communication. The helper says one thing to the auditor but means another: uses oblique language, and even falsehood, in the service of the truth. The question is, Does anyone have a right to be such a "midwife"? There is enormous risk, not only because, once people have their "consciousness raised," they may destroy themselves or choose wrongly, but because they may misinterpret the clue or symbol, in which case the "midwife" is somewhat responsible for any untoward consequences. All this is recognized by Kierkegaard, who cautions care on the part of the "midwife." Nevertheless, there is no way getting around indirect communication, for all its risks. To attempt to communicate the ethical directly would be unethical, and *not* to try to communicate it would be at least as reprehensible.

Although indirect communication of the ethical is an art, not a science, it differs from communication of the other arts, which use the medium of the imagination or fantasy. Communication of the ethical goes one step further and involves communication through the medium of actuality in a two-step process. First there is inciting of the imagination, which in turn incites the will to choose, but then there is, in addition, communication of the ethical (its content) through the life of the communicator, who exemplifies the message.

> All communication of knowledge is in the medium of imagination, the communication of an art less so, inasmuch as it is an execution. But communication of the ethical can only be given in actuality, in such a way that the communicator or teacher himself exists in it and in the situation of actuality which he teaches. When someone teaches stoic indifference—from a lectern—what he teaches is not true ethically. No, the situation must be such that while he teaches about stoic indifference, he manifests the same in his life. For example, if someone is teaching stoical indifference while surrounded by a mob of insulters and in the situation manifests stoical indifference, this is a situation of actuality. [*Papers*, VIII B 81, #28]

The individual must become what he (ethically) knows, for only to the extent that he becomes what he knows can he be said to know it. The communicator must become what he would communicate; otherwise the communication will be incomplete. The communicator must *incarnate* the message. The medium is the message.

Nevertheless, the point needs to be modified. Kierkegaard admits that God can use the strangest vessels to do his bidding in bringing people to the truth and, furthermore, that no human being can perfectly exemplify the truth—still, we can be messengers in good faith. In Christian communication, where the paradox of the Incarnation is communicated, the aspect of direct communication re-enters the picture—with a difference. Unless an appropriation of indirect communication has prepared the individual in the ethical-religious, the direct message of the Gospel will not be appreciated, let alone appropriated. Only the person who has delved deep within, striving to become ethical, to obey the voice from within, will get to the place where the Gospel can be appreciated and received. Christianity, without the process of inwardness through the stages of existence to the ethical-religious, is a caricature of the original product. Within Christian communication is an alternating indirect/direct process, so that the learner appropriates and becomes conformed to the Gospel through suffering and faith.[10]

Once grace enables us to receive the paradox of the Gospel (a message that must be communicated directly because it is not immanent in man, as the knowledge of God's existence is), indirect communication reappears in helping us develop into genuine Christians. Once the believer knows the transcendent reality of the Gospel, in all its scandal and paradoxicality, indirect communication is needed to help him realize the implications of this truth.

While one can appreciate Kierkegaard's use of indirect communication without accepting his interpretation of its place in life, it is by understanding the role of this mode of discourse in his writings that one begins to appreciate the difficulty of the task, as well as the genius of the writer. Every sentence is written with the goal of awakening the sleeping spirit within the reader. As Kierkegaard himself realized, the task is impossible. We cannot manipulate an awakening in rational beings; we can only make it possible. We have a prior duty to bear witness to the truth as best we see it. Hence in the later years of his life, when he wrote explicitly religious works, he gave up the attempt to lead his audience unwittingly into the religious domain. He became disillusioned with the failure of his pseudonymous works to do what they were supposed to, and turned to a more direct form of discourse.

Although we must take the matter of indirect discourse seriously when we study Kierkegaard, it does not mean that we should disregard the propositions set forth in the pseudonymous works, as some have suggested. Most of the ideas are Kierkegaard's own, as the *Papers* and *Point of View for My Authorship* witness.

Finally, his care and precision in working out a theory of communication make us aware of the rational side to Kierkegaard's work. For all his suspicion of the pretensions of reason, he used reason on a highly abstract level to work out the beginnings of a theory of indirect communication. The theory rests on an Idealist and Platonic epistemology, married to a Lutheran interpretation of Christianity, and so is vulnerable to attack from all other quarters; but it reveals a sensitivity to the problem of communicating in the domain of the ethical-religious that is rarely seen in philosophy. What's more, Kierkegaard *lived* this theory. For him, philosophy and autobiography are inseparable.

NOTES

Preface

1. Mackey, *Kierkegaard: A Kind of Poet* (1971), p. xi and, esp., ch. 6 (henceforth I refer to this work as "Mackey"). See also "Subjectivity Is Something or Other," a response to my paper "Kierkegaard on Subjectivity," both given at Western Division Meeting of American Philosophical Association (APA), Detroit, April 27, 1980.

2. "Kierkegaard's Phenomenology of the Stages of Existence" (forthcoming in *Philosophy Today*).

3. This is especially true of the pseudonymous writings. Elrod's recent, important work, *Kierkegaard and Christendom* (1981), makes a good case for a shift of emphasis and even a certain difference in the "second literature," those works published after *CUP* (1846).

Chapter 1: Introduction and Orientation

1. See Jaspers, *Reason and Existence* (1955); Jean Wahl, *Philosophies of Existence* (London, 1962); Barrett, *Irrational Man* (1962).

2. See Thompson, "The Master of Irony," and Mackey, "The Poetry of Inwardness," both in *Kierkegaard, A Collection of Critical Essays* (1972) (henceforth, *CE*).

3. See Elrod, *Being and Existence in Kierkegaard's Pseudonymous Works* (1975).

4. See Walter Kaufmann, ed. and tr., *Hegel, a Reinterpretation* and *Hegel, Texts and Commentary* (Garden City, N.Y.: Doubleday, 1976).

5. *The Point of View for My Work as an Author*, pp. 5–6 (henceforth *PV* in footnotes and *Point of View* in text).

6. *Concluding Unscientific Postscript*, unnumbered pages at back of the book (henceforth *Postscript* in text and *CUP* in notes and excerpts).

7. "No, illusion can never be destroyed directly, and only by indirect means can it be radically removed. If it is an illusion that all are Christians—and if there is anything to be done about it, it must be done indirectly, not by one who vociferously proclaims himself an extraordinary Christian, but by one who, better instructed, is ready to declare that he is not a Christian at all" (*PV*, p. 24). We can also say that this mode of communication is a function of Kierkegaard's idea of irony: asserting something in such a mood that the auditor will see the possibility of its opposite. Kierkegaard's pseudonymous works are cases of "mastered irony," irony in the service of a message.

8. "The productivity is essentially not my own but that of a higher power." *Papers*, X¹ A 250.

9. Cf. *PV*, p. 76f. Fourteen years later he wrote concerning his early relation to Christianity: "As a child I was sternly and seriously brought up in Christianity. Humanly speaking, it was a crazy upbringing. Already in my earliest childhood I broke down under the grave impression which the melancholy old man who laid it upon me himself sank under. What wonder then that there were times when Christianity appeared to me the most inhuman cruelty—although never, even when I was farthest from it, did I cease to revere it, with a firm determination that (especially if I did not myself make the choice of becoming a Christian) I would never initiate anyone into the difficulties which I knew. . . . But I have never definitely broken with Christianity nor renounced it."

10. *Papers*, I A 95, October 19, 1835.

11. *Papers*, I A 89, October 9, 1835.

12. *Papers*, II A 440, May 22, 1839. Cf. II A 190.

13. *Papers*, I A 111, January 7, 1836, "The decisive thing in speculating is the talent to see the individual entities in the whole. As such the majority of men never really enjoy a tragedy because for them it falls to pieces in sheer monologue. The same may be said of their appreciation of operas falling into arias, etc. The same process is active in the physical world when I, for example, walked along the road on which there lay interspersing parcels of land between two other parallel roads. Most people can only see the roads, the piece of land, and then again the road; but they would not be able to see the whole as being like a piece of cloth with different stripes in it." Cf. II A 249.

14. *Papers*, I A 75.

15. *Papers*, I A 273 (Dru's tr., #78).

16. *Papers*, II A 752, 1838.

17. *Papers*, I A 182, 1836; I A 75, August 1, 1835.

18. *Papers*, II C 324.

19. Robert Perkins has challenged this statement in light of Climacus' words in *Fragments*, which state that the teacher must give the condition for an individual to be saved (p. 77f.). This is true. The teacher must give the condition, but it is often overlooked that the condition can be idle. The condition only enables the prospective disciple to *choose* the teacher, and he can refuse him. "Faith is not an act of will; for all human volition has its capacity within an underlying condition. Thus if I have courage to will the understanding, I am able to understand the Socratic principle, i.e. to understand myself, because from the Socratic point of view I have the condition, and so have the power to will this understanding. But if I do not have the condition . . . all my willing is of no avail; although *as soon as the condition is given, the Socratic principle will again apply.*" *Philosophical Fragments*, p. 77f.; my italics. Cf. ch. 5, "The Climacus Writings."

20. Cf. Mark Taylor, *Journeys to Selfhood: Hegel and Kierkegaard*, pp. 181–262, for a helpful comparison of Hegel's *Phenomenology of Mind* with Kierkegaard's notion of the stages and, in particular, of the passage just quoted in the text. Cf. my article "Kierkegaard's Phenomenology of the Stages of Existence," forthcoming in *Philosophy Today*.

21. See Elrod, *Kierkegaard and Christendom*, p. 36f. The first chapter provides one of the best introductions to Kierkegaard's historical context that I am aware of.

22. Descartes, *Meditation*, III.

23. *Sickness unto Death*, p. 147.

24. Thompson, "The Master of Irony," in *CE*.

25. Cf. *CUP*, p. 473n., where Kierkegaard mentions seven spheres: "immediacy; finite common sense; irony; ethics with irony as incognito; humor; religiousness with humor as incognito; and then finally the Christian religiousness, recognizable by the paradoxical accentuation of existence." Cf. *E/O* II:172, where he speaks of "neutral men" who don't fit neatly into any sphere.

26. *Papers*, VII A 127.

27. *Papers*, IX A 448.

28. *Papers*, IX 413.

29. Cf. my article, "Kierkegaard's Phenomenology of the Stages of Existence," mentioned above.

30. *Purity of Heart Is to Will One Thing*, p. 53f. For an interesting interpretation of this work and the ideas mentioned in the text, see Jeremy Walker's *To Will One Thing*.

31. E/O, II:271f.

32. Ibid., p. 356.

33. *Sickness unto Death*, p. 162.

34. Cf. Elrod, *Kierkegaard and Christendom*, p. 86f.

35. Elrod, *Being and Existence in Kierkegaard's Pseudonymous Works*, p. 65. For Taylor's view, see his *Journeys to Selfhood*, pp. 130ff.

36. Elrod seems to have modified his position somewhat, or at least believes that there is a more teleological strain in the authorship. See *Kierkegaard and Christendom*, p. 140f.

37. *Papers*, VIII B 89; cf. *Christian Discourses* and *Attack on Christendom* (by Kierkegaard) on this point.

Chapter 2: Attack on Objectivity

1. Thompson, "The Master of Irony," in *CE,* pp. 113, 163.

2. One can find Hegelian influence in Kierkegaard's development of Socratic irony, the stages of existence, the existential modalities, the notion of the self, and his use of dialectics. However, in every case significant changes have been made and Kierkegaard's originality has transformed Hegel's ideas so that his position is usually defined against Hegel's. Nevertheless, something of the original remains. For useful works dealing with these relations, see Malantschuk, *Kierkegaard's Thought;* Stack, *On Kierkegaard: Philosophical Fragments*; and Taylor, *Journeys to Selfhood: Hegel and Kierkegaard.* See also my doctoral thesis, *The Dialectic of Freedom in the Thought of Søren Kierkegaard,* as well as ch. 3 of this work ("The Domain of Subjectivity"), where I show the resemblance between Hegel and Kierkegaard on certain epistemological aspects.

3. Thompson, "The Master of Irony," and Mackey, "The Poetry of Inwardness," both in *CE*.

4. *PV,* p. 73.

5. "I am a poet, but a peculiar kind of poet; for dialectic is the essential qualification of my nature, and usually poets are not dialectical" (*Papers,* IX A 213). Cf. *Papers,* X 4 A 663. Note also that the full title is *Fear and Trembling: A Dialectical Lyric.* He refers to his Climacian writings as "dialectical analysis." *CUP,* p. 15.

6. "Philosophy and Christianity will never allow themselves to be united, for if I hold to the most essential element in Christianity; namely, the redemption, so this element must, if it really is to be something, be extended over the whole person. Or must I consider his moral ability as impaired while viewing his cognition as unimpaired? I certainly could consider the possibility of a philosophy according to Christianity or a philosophy after one becomes a Christian, but it would be a *Christian philosophy.* The relation would not be a philosophy's relation to Christianity, but Christianity's relation to Christian epistemology" (*Papers,* I A 94). In the *Postscript,* Kierkegaard calls his work a speculative activity (pp. 46f., 54).

7. *Fragments,* p. 137. For references to Hegel, see *Encyclopedia of the Philosophical Sciences, the Logic of Hegel,* tr. William Wallace, sec. 32 Z and 48 (henceforth *Enc.*).

8. *Papers,* II A 454.

9. *Papers,* V A 68.

10. *Papers,* X² A 354. One may compare Kierkegaard's use of 'negativity' with Hegel's, who no doubt influenced his use of the concept. For both men the 'negative' is an instrument for reaching the truth; however, the ways are quite different. Kierkegaard's fundamental orientation is Aristotelian whereas for Hegel the 'negative' has a stronger dialectical role vis-à-vis 'being' (cf. *Enc.,* sec. 91f.). For helpful discussions, see Stack, *On Kierkegaard: Philosophical Fragments,* esp. ch. 2, and Mark Taylor, *Journeys to Selfhood: Hegel and Kierkegaard,* ch. 5.

11. Cf. ch. 1, "Kierkegaard's Conception of Human Existence." Note also the argument in *Fragments* which illustrates this argument form: (1) Either the Socratic or the Christian way, but not both, leads to the truth. (2) There is no other way (*F,* pp. 16, 18, 24, 30, 70). (3) The Socratic way involves its own internal defeat (reason collapses in paradox). (4) Therefore, the Christian way must be the only way. Or, again in *Fragments,* there is the argument: (1) Either some man invented Christianity or God must have done so. (2) No man could have invented something so entirely against ordinary understanding. (3) Therefore God must have invented it (p. 27).

12. *Enc.,* preface to 2d ed., p. 10.

13. *Enc.,* sec. 28 Z, 62.

14. *Enc.,* sec. 32.

15. *Enc.,* sec. 87.

16. *Logic,* I:31.

17. *Papers,* VI A 73.

18. *CUP,* p. 270.

19. Cf. Mackey, *Kierkegaard: A Kind of Poet,* ch. 6.

20. *Fragments,* p. 20f.

21. Op. cit., p. 137.

22. *Papers,* X¹ A 66. One may recall Epictetus' remark in this regard: "Reflection is endless, action is lost."

23. *Papers,* IV C 75.

24. *CUP,* p. 310.

25. Hume, *Treatise on Human Understanding,* II, 3.3.

26. *Papers,* X¹ A 481.

27. *Book One: The Objective Problem Concerning the Truth of Christianity* has thirty pages and is divided into two parts: "Chapter 1. The Historical Point of View," and "Chapter 2. The Speculative Point of View."

28. But apparently it is allowable to be subjective and, from the subjective point of view, show objectively that the objective way is misguided, which is what Kierkegaard is doing here. For an early formulation, see *JC,* p. 151f.

29. *CUP,* p. 179n.

30. *CUP,* p. 206.

31. *Fragments,* p. 104.

32. I owe this point to Adams's "Kierkegaard's Arguments against Objective Reasoning."

33. *CUP,* p. 28.

34. *CUP,* p. 26.

35. Ibid.

36. *CUP,* p. 30.

37. Alvin Plantinga, "Is Belief in God Rational?" in *Rationality and Religious Belief,* ed. C. F. Delaney (Notre Dame, Ind.: Notre Dame University Press, 1979).

38. *CUP,* p. 278. My teacher, Dr. Gregor Malantschuk, used to insist that in many places Kierkegaard recognizes this weakness and affirmed that there is no objectivity without some subjectivity, and vice versa, but the affirmation is usually offset by Kierkegaard's actual treatment. Cf. *Kierkegaard's Thought,* pp. 140–142.

39. *CUP,* p. 42.

40. *CUP,* p. 46.

41. *CUP,* p. 51.

42. *CUP,* p. 55.

Chapter 3: Subjectivity and Epistemology

1. Many of these uses can be found in the second book of the *Postscript;* some can be found in Kierkegaard's *Papers,* e.g., VI B 19, VIII A 8, VIII A 535, X¹ A 438, X³ 251 and 101.

2. Roberts, "Thinking Subjectively," *IJPR,* vol. 11, no. 2 (1980).

3. Earl McLane, "Kierkegaard on Subjectivity," *IJPR,* vol. 8, no. 2 (1977).

4. *Papers,* VI B 19.

5. *Papers,* IV C 75.

6. Louis Mackey, "Subjectivity Is Something or Other," paper delivered at Western Division of APA, Detroit, April 27, 1980.

7. *CUP,* pp. 171ff.

8. Stephen Evans, "The Concept of Subjective Understanding Which Underlies Kierkegaard's Theory of Indirect Communication," paper delivered at Western Division of APA, April 1979.

9. *CUP,* pp. 107, 183, 186f.

10. *Fragments,* p. 104.

11. *Papers,* V B 40.

12. *CUP,* p. 51.

13. *Papers,* VI B 19.

14. *CUP,* p. 51.

15. *CUP,* p. 174f.

16. Roberts, "Thinking Subjectively." In fairness to Roberts, he concedes that he is not sure whether his analysis applies directly to Kierkegaard.

17. Cf. Pojman, *Faith and Reason in the Thought of Kierkegaard* (1977). Also see Pojman, "Kierkegaard on Subjectivity: Two Concepts," *Southwestern Journal of Philosophy,* vol. 12, no. 2 (1981).

18. Cf. Gregory Schufreider, "Kierkegaard on Belief without Justification," *IJPR* (1981); Roberts, "Thinking Subjectively"; Benjamin Daise's comments were in a response he gave at Western Division meeting of the APA in April 1979; Mackey, *Kierkegaard: A Kind of Poet* (1971).

19. Gregor Malantschuk in lectures on Kierkegaard's thought at the University of Copenhagen, 1970, and in private conversations.

20. Evans, "Kierkegaard on Subjective Truth: Is God an Ethical Fiction?" Pojman, *Faith and Reason in the Thought of Kierkegaard* and "Kierkegaard on Subjectivity: Two Concepts."

21. *CUP,* p. 184.

22. *CUP,* p. 107.

23. *CUP,* p. 178.

24. *CUP,* p. 180.

25. *Papers,* VI B 19.

26. *CUP,* p. 302.

27. *Papers,* VIII B 81f.

28. *Fragments,* p. 108.

29. *Papers,* VI B 45 (my tr.).

30. *Fear and Trembling,* p. 38.

31. *Papers,* X³ A 438.

32. *CD,* p. 248.

33. *Fragments,* ch. 3, where Climacus argues that the highest object of reason is the Paradox.

34. *Fragments,* p. 22; *CUP,* p. 180.

35. *CUP,* p. 185f.

36. *Fragments,* p. 22.

37. *Papers,* I A 94.

38. Sponheim, *Kierkegaard on Christ and Christian Coherence* (London: SCM Press, 1968), p. 7f.

Chapter 4: Faith and the Stages of Existence

1. *WL,* p. 199f.

2. Hegel, *Enzyklopädie*, I:50–51 (my tr.).

3. Hegel, *Philosophy of Religion* (London: Kegan Paul, Trench, Trubner, 1895), III:317.

4. *FT*, pp. 57–59; *SLW*, pp. 271, 364; *Papers*, VIII A 649–50.

5. *Papers*, I A 273.

6. *FT*, p. 58.

7. *Either/Or*, II:172f.

8. *FT*, p. 52.

9. *Either/Or*, II:260.

10. *FT*, p. 64.

11. *FT*, p. 59f.

12. *FT*, pp. 32f., 46f.; *SuD*, p. 171.

13. *Papers*, IV A 108, 109.

14. *FT*, p. 31.

15. *FT*, p. 65.

Chapter 5: 'Faith' in *Philosophical Fragments*

1. *Papers*, II A 335.

2. *CUP*, p. 545. "The undersigned, Johannes Climacus, who has written this book, does not give himself out to be a Christian; he is completely taken up with the thought how difficult it must be to be a Christian; but still less is he one who, having been a Christian, has ceased to be such by going further. He is a humorist." Cf. *CUP*, pp. 400ff., 447ff.

3. *CUP*, p. 496.

4. *CUP*, pp. 400ff., 451ff. Sometimes Kierkegaard uses "contradiction" to characterize these opposites. It is well known that there is a sort of "contradictoriness" in humor. Note, for example, Charlie Chaplin's comment on his costume: "On the way to the wardrobe I thought I would dress in baggy pants, big shoes, a cane and a derby hat. I wanted everything a *contradiction*: the pants baggy, the coat tight, the hat small, and the shoes large. I was undecided whether to look old or young, but remembering [Mack] Sennett had expected a much older man, I added a small moustache." *The Times*, February 28, 1976.

5. *CUP*, p. 473.

6. Cf. Thompson, "The Master of Irony," in *CE*, pp. 112f., 143f., and Allison, p. 127, in the same collection. Allison thinks Kierkegaard regarded these writings as an ironical jest, but I find his arguments unconvincing.

7. *Papers*, X⁶ B 79. Cf. X⁶ B 82, where Kierkegaard says, "Anti-Climacus repeats what is said in the pseudonymous writings." Passages such as these should go a long way toward infirming the position that Kierkegaard did not endorse the substance of what he said in the pseudonymous works.

8. The best discussion I know of the authorship and unity problems in Kierkegaard's work is in Sponheim, *Kierkegaard on Christ and Christian Coherence*.

Sponheim's distinctions, 'diastasis' and 'synthesis', while a bit artificial and contrived, are useful for an understanding of various motifs in Kierkegaard's writings.

9. *Fragments,* p. 77f.

10. *Papers,* X² A 301.

11. *Fragments,* p. 17f.

12. Ibid., pp. 17, 22, 139.

13. Ibid., p. 80.

14. Ibid., p. 80f.

15. Ibid., pp. 82–88.

16. Ibid., pp. 100ff., 108f.

17. Ibid., p. 73f.

18. Ibid., p. 76.

19. Ibid., pp. 103ff.

20. Ibid., p. 77f.

21. Ibid., p. 118f.

22. I have heard commentators use the sections on opinion in *Fragments* and *CUP,* where Climacus disavows having an opinion on the matters discussed, as proving that Kierkegaard himself had no opinion or belief about these matters. This seems an unwarranted conclusion. First of all, it is Climacus, not Kierkegaard, who says he (the humorist, non-Christian) has no opinion or belief. Secondly, these commentators miss the significance of "opinion" in Kierkegaard's meaning. He may not have a "mere opinion," but he certainly seems to have what approximates existential faith. Cf. Mackey, "The Poetry of Inwardness" (in *CE,* p. 61f.): "Above all it is necessary to take [Kierkegaard] at his word when he says he has no opinion and proposes no doctrine." This is a misunderstanding. Kierkegaard is *filled* with doctrines. What is his theory of subjectivity or his view of the Incarnation *but* a doctrine?

23. *TC,* p. 140 (my tr.).

24. *Fragments,* p. 89.

25. Cf. Aristotle's *Physics,* II:200F. Kierkegaard was influenced in his use of Aristotle by Tennemann's *Geschichte der Philosophie.* The clearest exposition of this aspect of Kierkegaard's ontology is A. Hügli, *Die Erkenntinis der Subjectivität und die Objectivität der Erkenners bei Søren Kierkegaard,* pp. 62ff. I am greatly indebted to this book.

26. We may note that Kierkegaard sometimes treats physical necessity and logical necessity as one and the same thing. This error is probably due to his dependence on Hegel at this point. "The spheres with which philosophy properly deals, which properly are the spheres for thought are logic, nature, and history. Here necessity reigns." *E/O,* II:178.

27. Hegel, *Wissenschaft der Logik,* II:207: "Das Notwendige *ist,* und dies Seiende ist *selbst das Notwendige.* . . . So ist die Wirklichkeit in ihrem Unterschiedenen, der Möglichkeit, identisch mit sich selbst. Als diese Identität ist sie Notwendigkeit."

28. Actually, Climacus is a bit unclear in his use of 'necessity' in the "Interlude." Sometimes the term seems to mean 'logical identity', at other times 'essence'.

29. *Fragments,* p. 51n. Climacus quotes Spinoza as the proponent of the doctrine of degrees of being: "The more perfect a thing is by virtue of its nature, the more being it has and the more necessary is the being which it has; and conversely, the more

necessary the being included in a thing by virtue of its nature, the more perfect it is."
This is the view that he is rejecting.

30. *Fragments*, p. 93; *Papers*, X² A 439.

31. *Fragments*, p. 94.

32. Ibid., p. 93.

33. Ibid., p. 98. Cf. Bertrand Russell's remark, "We all regard the past as determined simply by the fact that it has happened; but for the accident that memory works backward and not forward, we should regard the future as equally determined by the fact that it will happen." *Mysticism and Logic* (Garden City, N.Y.: Doubleday, 1957), p. 201f.

34. *Fragments*, p. 100.

35. Ibid., p. 101.

36. Ibid.

37. *CUP*, p. 182.

38. "Belief is not a form of knowledge but a free act, an expression of the will. . . .The conclusion of belief is not so much a conclusion as a resolution." *Fragments*, p. 103f.

39. We have already drawn attention to the fact that Climacus seems to conflate sensation with perception (chapter 4, above). Climacus seems to take historical accuracy (e.g., that Caesar crossed the Rubicon) for granted, sometimes as knowledge. At other times he seems to acknowledge that this, too, comes under the Skeptics' neutrality. There seems confusion here.

40. We must add a note about the role of contemporaneity within Christian believing. The idea of contemporaneity is related to the idea of the 'moment' (*Øjeblikket*), which is the expression for two different but related phenomena. The 'moment' (1) is the expression for God's entrance into human affairs in the person of Jesus Christ; the 'moment' also (2) signifies the individual's conversion, the time when he believes that God entered time. In this moment (2) of faith, the moment (1) of the Incarnation becomes a present moment. The two moments coincide. Christ becomes contemporaneous with the believer.

"For in relation to the absolute there is only one tense: the present. For him who is not contemporary with the absolute—for him it has no existence." *TC*, p. 67.

41. This interpretation is based on Kierkegaard's interpretation of freedom, which involves preconditions. The will never decides arbitrarily but always in a context where the passions are incited toward an object. Cf. *CD*, p. 44f., and *Papers*, X⁴ A 175.

42. *Fragments*, p. 137. Here Climacus speaks of the law of noncontradiction as a self-evident truth.

43. Ephesians 2:8–9 (RSV).

44. *Fragments*, p. 77.

45. Ibid., p. 81. I think this is what Climacus means when he says, "Faith is itself a miracle, and all that holds true of the Paradox also holds true of faith. But within the framework of this miracle everything is again Socratic." Cf. *Papers*, IV A 109, where Kierkegaard speaks of faith as a divine madness. Also cf. *Papers*, X² A 301.

46. Cf. "Belief and Will" in *Religious Studies* (London, 1978), vol. 14; "Volitionalism and the Acquisition of Belief," in *Philosophical Topics*, vol. 12 (1983); "Believing and Willing," in *Canadian Journal of Philosophy*, vol. 14 (1983).

47. *Papers,* I A 36.

48. Cf. Matthew 17:20f., 21:21; Mark 9:23; Hebrews 11:6; Newman, *Grammar of Assent* (London, 1870); Lonergan, *Insight, a Study of Human Understanding* (New York, 1968), p. 709f.; Pieper, *Belief and Faith* (New York, 1947), pp. 25ff.

49. William James, *The Will to Believe* (New York, 1956), p. 11; *Pascal's Pensees,* tr. H. Stewart (New York, 1954), p. 125.

50. *E/O,* II:356.

51. *Fragments,* p. 102f. "The Greek skeptic did not doubt by virtue of knowledge, but by an act of will (refusal to give assent. . .). From this, it follows that doubt can be overcome only by a free act of the will."

52. Ibid., p. 103.

53. Hume, *Dialogues Concerning Natural Religion* (Indianapolis, 1980), p. 89. Cf. Popkin, "Kierkegaard and Scepticism," in *CE.*

54. *E/O,* II:356.

Chapter 6: 'Faith' in *Concluding Unscientific Postscript* and Later *Papers*

1. Actually, Climacus first defines subjective truth as "an objective uncertainty held fast in an appropriation-process of the most passionate inwardness." It is "the highest truth attainable for an existing individual." Then he identifies this definition with faith. "But the above definition is an equivalent expression for faith. Without risk there is no faith. Faith is precisely the contradiction between the infinite passion of the individual's inwardness and the objective uncertainty." *CUP,* p. 182.

2. "Belief is not a form of knowledge, but a free act" (*Fragments,* p. 103). In *CUP* (p. 30), Climacus speaks of the "temptation to confuse knowledge with faith."

3. *CUP,* p. 51.

4. *CUP,* p. 182.

5. *CUP,* p. 188. Kierkegaard's view is the exact opposite of Bishop Butler, who said that probability is the very guide of life.

6. *CUP,* p. 208.

7. *CUP,* p. 183.

8. Ibid.

9. *CUP,* p. 186.

10. *CUP,* p. 191.

11. Schmitt has shown that this relationship is not really paradoxical, in "The Paradox in Kierkegaard's Religiousness A."

12. *CUP,* p. 201. I think Kierkegaard means to say "*merely* objective knowledge."

13. *CUP,* p. 206.

14. Ibid.

15. *CUP,* p. 540.

16. But contrast this with what is said in the *Postscript:* "When he stakes his life upon this absurd, he makes the motion in virtue of the absurd, and he is *essentially*

deceived in case *the absurd* he has chosen can be proved to be *not the absurd.*" *CUP,* p. 296; my italics.

17. By 'truth' I mean, in the first place, subjective truth, but if we are to take Kierkegaard literally, it would seem to imply objective truth as well. We pointed out in chapter 4 that he at one place says that where subjectivity reaches its maximum, it turns into objectivity. Hence it would seem that Christianity and anti-Christianity are both objectively true when they are held in high or maximal subjectivity. Cf. *Papers,* X² A 299, quoted in ch. 3.

18. *CUP,* pp. 173–175.

19. *CUP,* pp. 347ff., where Climacus speaks of absolute respect for the absolute telos.

20. Romans 4:18 (RSV).

21. *Papers,* IV A 108.

22. Ibid., X² A 408.

23. Ibid., IX A 311.

24. Ibid., X² A 406: "I choose. That historical fact means so much to me that I decide to stake my whole life upon that 'if'."

Chapter 7: A Justification of Christian Faith

1. Cf. T. Bohlin, *Kierkegaard Tro och andra Kierkegaardstudier*; Barrett, *Irrational Man* (1962); Jerry Gill, *Essays on Kierkegaard* (1969), contains three articles supporting the irrationalist viewpoint; Murphy, "On Kierkegaard's Claim that 'Truth Is Subjectivity'"; Blanshard, "Kierkegaard on Faith"; and Allison, "Christianity and Nonsense."

2. Fabro, "Faith and Reason in Kierkegaard's Dialectic," and N. H. Søe, "Kierkegaard's Doctrine of the Paradox," both of which are in *A Kierkegaard Critique,* ed. H. A. Johnson and N. Thulstrup.

3. Garelick, *The Anti-Christianity of Kierkegaard.* My article has benefited from his work.

4. "Kierkegaard on Justification of Belief," *IJPR,* vol. 8, no. 2 (1977).

5. *IJPR,* vol. 12, no. 3 (1981).

6. *Papers,* IV C 75 (my tr.).

7. *SuD,* p. 258.

8. *Papers,* VI B 45.

9. *CUP,* p. 206.

10. *Papers,* X A 438; cf. also VIII B 81 and *E/O,* II:171.

11. *Papers,* X A 299.

12. Gregory Schufreider, "Kierkegaard on Belief without Justification," *IJPR,* vol. 12, no. 3 (1981).

Chapter 8: Conclusion

1. *Papers,* X² A 428.

2. I am indebted to Heywood Thomas for this insight; see his *Subjectivity and Paradox*, p. 49.

3. Isaiah Berlin, *The Hedgehog and the Fox* (New York: Clarion, 1970), pp. 1ff.

Appendix: Kierkegaard on Indirect Communication

1. Although the translations in this section are my own, I have consulted the relevant sections in *Søren Kierkegaard's Journals and Papers*, translated by Howard and Edna Hong (pp. 254–319). Kierkegaard's most important comments on indirect communication are in his *Papers*, VIII B 81–89.

2. *Papers*, VIII B 81, #10.

3. "With regard to God's existence, immortality, and so forth, in short with regard to all problems of immanence, recollection is valid; it is present in every man, only he is not aware of it; but it still doesn't follow that his concept is adequate." *Papers*, V B 40. Cf. also VI B 45.

4. For the relevant passages, see *The Concept of Anxiety*, pp. 60ff.; *Fragments*, pp. 77–78. Cf. my doctoral dissertation, *The Dialectic of Freedom in the Thought of Søren Kierkegaard* (1972).

5. *Papers*, VIII B 81. Cf. also *Fear and Trembling*, pp. 39ff., 78ff.; *CUP*, pp. 386ff.

6. *Papers*, VIII B 81.

7. Ibid.

8. *Papers*, I A 327; cf. *CUP*, p. 176.

9. *E/O*, p. 175f.; *Fear and Trembling*, p. 65f.; *CUP*, p. 315f.; *SuD*, p. 146.

10. *Papers*, VIII B 89; cf. also Kierkegaard's *Christian Discourses*.

SELECTED BIBLIOGRAPHY

Primary Sources: Works of Kierkegaard

In Danish

Søren Kierkegaards Papirer, ed. P. A. Heiberg, Victor Kuhr, and Einer Torsting. 20 vols. Copenhagen: Gyldendalske Boghandel Nordisk Forlag, 1909.
Søren Kierkegaards Samlede Vaerker, ed. A. B. Drachman, J. L. Heiberg, and H. O. Lange. 14 vols. Copenhagen: Gyldendalske Boghandel Forlag, 1901.

Translations in English

Either/Or, I, tr. David Swenson and Lillian Marvin Swenson; II, tr. Walter Lowrie; 2d ed. rev., Howard A. Johnson. Garden City, N.Y.: Doubleday, 1959.
Johannes Climacus, or De omnibus dubitandum est, and A Sermon, tr. T. H. Croxall. London: Adam and Charles Black, 1958.
Edifying Discourses, I–IV, tr. David F. Swenson and Lillian Swenson. Minneapolis: Augsburg Publishing House, 1943–46.
Fear and Trembling, tr. Walter Lowrie. Garden City, N.Y.: Doubleday, 1954.
Repetition, tr. Walter Lowrie. Princeton: Princeton University Press, 1941.
Philosophical Fragments, tr. David Swenson. 2d ed. Princeton: Princeton University Press, 1962.
The Concept of Anxiety, tr. Reider Thomte. Princeton: Princeton University Press, 1981.
Stages of Life's Way, tr. Walter Lowrie. Princeton: Princeton University Press, 1940.
Concluding Unscientific Postscript, tr. David F. Swenson and Walter Lowrie. Princeton: Princeton University Press for American Scandinavian Foundation, 1941.
On Authority and Revelation: The Book of Adler, tr. Walter Lowrie. Princeton: Princeton University Press, 1955.
Purity of Heart, tr. Douglas Steere, 2d ed. New York: Harper & Row, 1948.
Christian Discourses, including *The Lilies of the Field and the Birds of the Air* and *Three Discourses at the Communion on Fridays,* tr. Walter Lowrie. London and New York: Oxford University Press, 1949.
The Sickness unto Death, tr. Howard and Edna Hong. Princeton: Princeton University Press, 1980.
Training in Christianity, tr. Walter Lowrie. Princeton: Princeton University Press, 1957.

The Point of View for My Work as an Author and My Activity as an Author, tr. Walter
    Lowrie. New York: Harper & Row, 1962.
Attack upon "Christendom," 1854–55, tr. Walter Lowrie. Boston: Beacon Press, 1956.
The Journals of Søren Kierkegaard, a Selection, tr. Alexander Dru. London and New
    York: Oxford University Press, 1938.
Søren Kierkegaard's Journals and Papers, tr. Howard and Edna Hong. Bloomington and
    London: Indiana University Press, 1967, 1970 (vols. I and II) (III–V in preparation).

Secondary Sources: Works on Kierkegaard

Adams, Robert. "Kierkegaard's Arguments against Objective Reasoning in Re-
    ligion," *Monist* (April 1977).
Allison, Henry E. "Christianity and Nonsense," in *Essays on Kierkegaard,* ed. J. H.
    Gill. Minneapolis: Burgess Publishing Co., 1969.
Barrett, William. *Irrational Man.* Garden City, N.Y.: Doubleday, 1962.
Blanshard, Brand. "Kierkegaard on Faith," in *Essays on Kierkegaard,* ed. J. H. Gill.
    Minneapolis: Burgess, 1969.
Brookfield, C. M. "What Was Kierkegaard's Task? A Frontier to Be Explored,"
    Union Seminary Quarterly Review, vol. 18.
Brown, James. *Kierkegaard, Heidegger, Buber and Barth: Subject and Object in Modern
    Theology.* New York: Collier Books, 1962.
Burgess, Andrew. *Passion, 'Knowing How' and Understanding: An Essay on the Concept
    of Faith.* Missoula, Mont.: Scholars Press, 1975.
Collins, James. "Faith and Reflection in Kierkegaard," in *A Kierkegaard Critique,* ed.
    H. A. Johnson and N. Thulstrup. New York: Harper, 1962.
Dietrichson, Paul. "Kierkegaard's Concept of the Self," *Inquiry,* vol. 8, no. 1 (1965).
Dupre, L. K. *Kierkegaard as Theologian.* London: Sheed and Ward, 1963.
Edwards, Paul. "Kierkegaard and the 'Truth of Christianity,'" *Philosophy,* vol. 46, no.
    176 (April 1971).
Elrod, John. *Kierkegaard and Christendom.* Princeton: Princeton University Press,
    1981.
──────. *Being and Existence in Kierkegaard's Pseudonymous Works.* Princeton: Princeton
    University Press, 1975.
Evans, Stephen. "Kierkegaard on Subjective Truth: Is God an Ethical Fiction?" *Inter-
    national Journal for Philosophy of Religion [IJPR],* vol. 7, no. 3 (1976).
──────. *Subjectivity and Religious Belief.* Grand Rapids, Mich.: Eerdmans, 1978.
Fabro, Cornelio. "Faith and Reason in Kierkegaard's Dialectic," in *A Kierkegaard
    Critique,* ed. H. A. Johnson and N. Thulstrup. New York: Harper, 1962.
Garelick, H. M. *The Anti-Christianity of Kierkegaard.* The Hague: Martinus Nijhoff,
    1965.
Geismar, Edward. *Søren Kierkegaard, Hans Livudvikling og Forfattervirksomhed.*
    Copenhagen: Gads, 1928.
Gill, J. H., ed. *Essays on Kierkegaard.* Minneapolis: Burgess, 1969.
Hirsch, Emmanuel. *Kierkegaard Studien.* 3 vols. Gutersloh: C. Bertelmann, 1930–33.

Holmer, Paul L. "On Understanding Kierkegaard," in *A Kierkegaard Critique,* ed. H. A. Johnson and N. Thulstrup. New York: Harper, 1962.

Hügli, Anton. *Die Erkenntinis der Subjectivität und die Objectivität der Erkenners bei Soren Kierkegaard.* Zurich: Editio Acedemica, 1973.

Jaspers, Karl. *Reason and Existence.* New York: Noonday Press, 1955.

Johnson, H. A., and Thulstrup, N., eds. *A Kierkegaard Critique.* New York: Harper, 1962.

Kuhr, V. *Modsigelsens Grundsaetning.* Copenhagen: Gyldendalske Boghandel, 1910.

Lønning, Per. *Samtidighedens Situation.* Oslo: Forlaget Land og Kirke, 1954.

Mackey, Louis. "Loss of the World in Kierkegaard's Ethics," in *Kierkegaard,* ed. J. Thompson. Garden City, N.Y.: Doubleday, 1972.

———. "The Poetry of Inwardness," in *Kierkegaard,* ed. J. Thompson. Garden City, N.Y.: Doubleday, 1972.

———. *Kierkegaard: A Kind of Poet.* Philadelphia: University of Pennsylvania Press, 1971.

Macquarrie, John. *Existentialism.* Harmondsworth (Eng.): Penguin, 1973.

Malantschuk, G. *Kierkegaard's Thought,* ed. and tr. H. V. and E. Hong. Princeton: Princeton University Press, 1971.

McKinnon, A. "Kierkegaard, Paradox and Irrationalism," in *Essays on Kierkegaard,* ed. J. H. Gill. Minneapolis: Burgess, 1969.

McLane, Earl. "Kierkegaard and Subjectivity," *IJPR,* vol. 3, no. 3 (1977).

Murphy, A. E. "On Kierkegaard's Claim that 'Truth Is Subjectivity,'" in *Essays on Kierkegaard,* ed. J. H. Gill. Minneapolis: Burgess, 1969.

Perkins, Robert L., ed., *Kierkegaard's* Fear and Trembling: *Critical Appraisals.* University: The University of Alabama Press, 1981.

Pojman, Louis. *The Dialectic of Freedom in the Thought of Søren Kierkegaard.* Ph.D. thesis (1972), on deposit in Union Theological Seminary, New York.

———. "Kierkegaard on Justification of Belief," *IJPR,* vol. 7, no. 2 (1976).

———. *Faith and Reason in the Thought of Kierkegaard.* Ph.D. dissertation (1977), on deposit in Bodleian Library, Oxford University.

———. "The Logic of Subjectivity," *Southern Journal of Philosophy,* vol. 19, no. 2 (April 1981).

———. "Kierkegaard on Subjectivity: Two Concepts," *Proceedings of the Southwestern Philosophical Society, October 1982.*

Popkin, R. H. "Kierkegaard and Scepticism," in *Kierkegaard,* ed. J. Thompson. Garden City, N.Y.: Doubleday, 1972.

Roberts, Robert. "Thinking Subjectively," *IJPR,* vol. 11, no. 2 (Summer 1980).

Schacht, Richard. "Kierkegaard's Phenomenology of Spiritual Development," in *Hegel and After.* Pittsburgh: University of Pittsburgh Press, 1975.

Schmitt, R. "The Paradox in Kierkegaard's Religiousness A," *Inquiry,* vol. 8 (Spring 1965).

Schrader, G. A. "Kant and Kierkegaard on Duty and Inclination," in *Kierkegaard,* ed. J. Thompson. Garden City, N.Y.: Doubleday, 1972.

Schufreider, Gregory. "The Logic of the Absurd," *Philosophy/Research Archives* (Bowling Green, Ohio, 1979).

Sløk, Johannes. *Die Anthropologie Kierkegaards*. Copenhagen: Rosenkilde und Bagger, 1954.

Søe, N. H. "Kierkegaard's Doctrine of the Paradox," in *A Kierkegaard Critique,* ed. H. A. Johnson and N. Thulstrup. New York: Harper, 1962.

Solomon, Robert. "Kierkegaard and Subjective Truth," *Philosophy Today,* vol. 21, no. 3 (Fall 1977).

Sponheim, Paul. *Kierkegaard on Christ and Christian Coherence*. New York: Harper & Row, 1967.

Stack, George J. *On Kierkegaard: Philosophical Fragments*. Atlantic Highlands, N.J.: Humanities Press, 1976.

Swenson, D. *Something about Kierkegaard*. Minneapolis: Augsburg, 1945.

Taylor, Mark. *Kierkegaard's Pseudonymous Authorship*. Princeton: Princeton University Press, 1975.

————. *Journeys to Selfhood: Hegel and Kierkegaard*. Berkeley: University of California Press, 1980.

Thomas, Heywood J. *Subjectivity and Paradox*. Oxford: Blackwell, 1957.

Thompson, Josiah, ed. *Kierkegaard: A Collection of Critical Essays*. Garden City, N.Y.: Doubleday, 1972.

————. "The Master of Irony," in *Kierkegaard: A Collection of Critical Essays,* ed. J. Thompson. Garden City, N.Y.: Doubleday, 1972.

Wyschogrod, Michael. *Kierkegaard and Heidegger: The Ontology of Existence*. New York: Humanities Press, 1954.

INDEX

171